Tempo Rubato

Tempo Rubato

Published by WWL Publications

ISBN 978-1-0685719-0-9

Typesetting by The Book Typesetters
thebooktypesetters.com

TEMPO RUBATO:

MEMOIRS of a RANK-and-FILE MUSICIAN

Warwick Lister

WWL Publications

To Susan

Tempo rubato ('robbed' or 'stolen' time): in music, a term denoting the slight alteration of the tempo or rhythm, 'robbing' time in some places and (sometimes) adding in others, for the sake of expression. Sometimes it is indicated in the score, more often not.

CONTENTS

PREFACE

What's this? An unknown musician publishing his memoirs? A violinist whose name is recognized only by a few friends and a few very small audiences? A musician looking back on a career in which disappointments and, yes, failures, loom as large as successes? An upstart from the lower orders of the musical world—orchestral player, sometime chamber music player, sometime musicologist, a musical sansculotte who doesn't know his place, with a bad case of *cacoethes scribendi*? Yes, because perhaps the life and career of a rank-and-filer, though not glimmering with high achievement or reflected glamour (rubbing shoulders with the great), may be of interest, may even strike a sympathetic chord with musicians, for example, who have had similar experiences.

Apart from musicians, this book is intended for classical music lovers and those who might be curious about a musician's life. Here they will have a more representative glimpse into a 'normal' musician's life than in the autobiography of a celebrity. There are a number of music examples included, though these are not essential for an understanding of my words.

As my title suggests, if there is an overarching theme in the pages that follow, it is that often, perhaps too often, I have spent ('robbed') time on pursuits that might have been more constructively spent on my musical career.

I have kept my marriages, all three of them, in the background. Here, I venture only to say that the first two came to an end in some measure because the strain of living apart on two different continents could not be sustained.

I do not propose, as some men have done in their autobiographies, to sing a catalogue aria of sexual exploits, not only because I have fallen far short of *mille e tre* but also because I find such recitals tedious.

I include many excerpts, perhaps too many, from my correspondence with my mother. Some readers will be tempted to see this as an attempt to exorcise, or at least come to terms with, the powerful influence she had on me. But they will have to reach their own conclusions—I make no attempt to psychoanalyse myself.

I condemn, among other things, the autobiography of the great pianist Arthur Rubenstein as 'self-indulgent and far too long'. Uncharitable readers may have the same opinion of this book. I quote prodigally from my writings, letters, emails, even my marginalia. I wander in the forests of digression, founder in the marshlands of self-absorption, sink into the bog of regrets and self-recriminations, walk on the hot coals of unrestrained condemnation of what others have written. I slyly draw attention to my accomplishments behind a façade of modesty. I have committed most of the sins possible in a memoir. Perhaps worst of all, I have skated over or omitted a number of things (though by no means all of them) that reflect badly on me.

In sum, I have told the truth, nothing but the truth, but not the whole truth.

CHAPTER 1

Family matters: Parrsboro, Moncton

I am a frightened little boy in a row-boat in the deep water just off Cape Blomidon, its craggy cliffs looming behind me. The tide, the highest in the world, has turned. It is that narrowest and most dangerous passage, the Minas Channel, through which, every twelve hours, millions of gallons are pulled back with unimaginable power from Minas Basin into the Bay of Fundy. My mother is standing on the shore a few yards away, holding a line tied to the stern of the boat, where I am sitting. Her face is a mask of fear; she can do nothing. The rope has somehow become entangled around me. If I am pulled overboard, I will be swept into the cold vastness of the Bay of Fundy, thence into the Atlantic Ocean.

We had come on the flood tide, a party of twelve or fifteen, in someone's modest cabin cruiser, which was anchored offshore, and had rowed to the beach. It was a pleasant excursion, looking for amethysts, which, in those days, could still be found there. When it was time to leave, the row-boat, with three or four passengers at a time, was pulled to the cruiser with a line, while, to keep it steady, another line was held by someone (my mother) from the shore. I have played this scene many times over in my mind since it happened, more than seventy years ago (someone disentangled me, of course), but I was well into adulthood before its umbilical implications dawned on me. The beckoning watery embrace, my mother, and the cord between us—as if that old ringmaster, Dr Freud himself, had arranged it.

The majestic tides of Minas Basin, in the northern part of Nova Scotia, near the town of Parrsboro, were the all-pervading backdrop to my childhood summers and my brother Harold's. It dominated the rhythm of our days. We liked it best when high tide was at mid-afternoon. We walked out to meet the tide, while it was slightly less cold coming in over the seemingly endless flats, and swam for hours; we had got used to the coldness of the water—visitors complained of it—as we had got used to running in our bare feet on the pebbles of the beach. We had a flat-bottomed row-boat and we built a crude raft that we could use as a diving platform. For two full months of the year, we amused ourselves together, almost always on or near the beach, which most of the time we had entirely to ourselves. We made little hollowed-out spaces—'camps'—in the woods, where we felt remote from civilization. When we saw Keith, a local man, rowing in after a day of fishing, we ran to his special place up the beach to watch him gutting the flounder on a wooden table he had made. We were inseparable, my brother and I; we shared this idyllic, privileged childhood until, as adolescents, our interests began to differ. When, at the end of August or early in September, we came back to our house in Moncton, New Brunswick, the bathroom basin always seemed lower than it had been before the summer.

Low tide, Minas Basin, Nova Scotia, viewed from Parrsboro Beach. Photo by Erick Greene.

High tide, Minas Basin, Nova Scotia, viewed from Parrsboro Beach. Photo by Erick Greene.

Warwick, (l.) and Harold, (r.) Parrsboro Beach, about 1951. I have always been vain about my looks. In this slightly prissy pose, I am pulling in my stomach muscles. Harold, who loved the water more than I, is in his element.

At night in bed in the cottage, I loved the sound of rain on the roof, lulling me to sleep; the muffled roar of low tide, a mile away; and the gentle lapping at high tide, a few feet from my bedroom window. The mournful two notes of the Parrsboro Harbour lighthouse foghorn, which some visitors found annoying, were for me

Family at the cottage, August 1946.

deeply comforting. The interval between the two notes was a descending diminished fifth, the *diabolus in musica*, a great hoarse, lugubrious sigh.

Our maternal grandmother, Emma Berry, was born in a farmhouse in a settlement, Two Islands, about ten miles up the shore from Parrsboro. Her great great-grandfather had come to Nova Scotia from Ireland in about 1765; his son was given a Crown grant at Two Islands, where for four generations they lived by subsistence farming and fishing. Among my earliest memories are Grammy's grim accounts, told matter-of-factly, of the deaths of her forebears. Her great-grandfather drowned in 1815; her grandfather was injured by falling from a loaded hay wagon in 1850 and was an invalid for fourteen years before dying. The accident occurred very near the Berry farm in a place we called The Dugway, where the road precipitously descended into a deep ravine, crossed the river bed and climbed up again on the other side. As a boy, whenever we drove through, the thought of this violent, calamitous event a century earlier troubled me. Now, the space has been filled in and paved over; not a trace remains of its menacing presence.

Grammy's father died in 1887, aged forty-one, of blood poisoning from a thistle in his hand while haying. He lay on a couch for several days, Grammy told us, his face turned to the wall, and died. The nearest doctor, if there was one, would have been in Parrsboro. In any case, he could have done nothing. Joseph Berry was survived by his wife, aged about thirty-five, and four children, the youngest, my grandmother, Emma, aged three. I try to imagine how his widow coped with a farm and four children. Emma's two older sisters, aged twelve and nine, could have helped; her brother, Albert, aged six, would have had a man's burden thrust upon him very soon. None of them would have had much more than five or six years of schooling.

The farmhouse in which they lived, now long gone, was still occupied by Albert when I was growing up. It had no indoor water, no electricity. It commanded a superb sloping view over fields and a high bank to the water and the two islands a few hundred yards offshore. At low tide, you can walk across to the islands. Albert kept a horse, one or two cows and some sheep, and tended a weir on the flats, where he caught flounders and an occasional salmon. Our family often had picnics with friends on the beach, having clambered down the steep path from the road. Grammy loved these excursions, so near to the scene of her exiguous, not to say impoverished, childhood.

Almost certainly, it is she whose name appears on the passenger list of the SS *Yarmouth* from Yarmouth, Nova Scotia, to Boston, 15 October 1899: 'S. Berry [she was called Susannah in her youth], female, age 14; nationality and last place of residence: Nova Scotia; destination: Cambridge.' She had been sent to Cambridge, a suburb of Boston, perhaps to stay with a family acquaintance and to work, though this is pure conjecture on my part. It was not uncommon for young Nova Scotians from poor families to go to the 'Boston states' to take menial jobs. She went to work, aged about fifteen or sixteen, in a tailor's shop in Parrsboro. At some point she met an up-and-coming railway express agent in Truro, Nova Scotia, and married him in 1905.

Before she became too old, she baked delicious muffins—'Here we are, boys, piping hot'—that Harold and I were especially fond of as our mother never baked. She taught us to play a card game known as Forty-Fives[1]—we would shock her by making outrageously high bids. In her old age, Grammy's childhood caught up with her; she would hoard food, and her butter was sometimes rancid. Harold and I, with the thoughtlessness of youth, would joke about this, though not in her presence. She lived to read about Alan Shepard's space trip in May

---

[1] I have only recently learned that the game has Irish origins and that it is played almost exclusively in Atlantic Canada.

1961; her much-loved doctor was named Shepard, a coincidence that delighted her.

She and her daughter, my mother, were very close; their love for each other shines out from their letters. They occasionally quarrelled and didn't speak to each other for days or weeks, but they always eventually forgave and forgot.

My mother's paternal grandfather died in 1931, aged eighty-one. On the death certificate, the officiating doctor gave the cause of death as 'Softening of the Brain'. Her father, Percy Linton, in turn, was increasingly senile for the last ten or so years of his life. He was a severe, somewhat humourless man, utterly unlike his wife, Emma, who liked nothing more than having a good laugh. Though not university-educated, he had had a well-stocked mind; when, as a twelve-year-old, I told him that I was learning about the War of 1812, he regaled me with the story of the HMS *Shannon*–USS *Chesapeake* naval battle. He was used to hard work. More than once, he shovelled the foot-deep snow from our fifty-yard-long drive, a job that took most of the day. But his mind began slipping away. Towards the end, before he was put into a home, he urinated into the heating registers in his house, and would get into bed fully dressed in a suit and tie, with his shoes on. On his last few visits to us in Moncton, with Emma, he would wander away from the house and get lost. On one occasion, he got into a taxi and asked to be taken to his home address: Park Street—he thought he was in Truro, Nova Scotia, some hundred miles away. On another, he kept insisting that he would go home and became obstreperous, driving my mother, alone in the house with him, to the breaking point; in desperation she grabbed a golf club and struck him with it, which apparently calmed him. All of this Harold and I and our father heard from her later. But as testimony, I have a photograph of my grandfather with Grammy and my mother, taken not long afterwards. There is a curious duality about the image: mother and daughter in their best dresses, smiling and relaxed, my grandfather in a black serge suit, sitting bolt upright as always, his left eye luridly black and blue.

In the last year or so of her life, my mother, too, with grim predictability, began to show signs of short-term memory loss. But she was snatched away by cancer, aged seventy-four, before dementia could take hold. Harold and I now exchange macabre jokes about which will claim us first, cancer or softening of the brain. For the past few years, I have become increasingly aware of my wife Susan's creeping dementia.

My mother, her mother and father, about 1957.

My first musical memories are of my mother's piano practising. (Still, when I am walking in an unfamiliar neighbourhood, the sound of someone practising the piano on an upper floor pulls at me. I must stop and listen.) She had an invariable warming-up routine, beginning with a chordal finger exercise, very repetitive and deliberate, moving by semitone up the keyboard, followed by a playthrough of the first movement of Bach's *Italian Concerto*. She had studied at the Mount Allison Ladies College in Sackville, New Brunswick with James Noel Brunton, a pupil of Godowsky, according to the Mount Allison website, but I am certain my mother told me that it had been Leschetizky (perhaps it was both). It is clear to me now that, as a young woman, she was ambitious of a career as a pianist. She married, however, in 1932; afterwards, she managed to give a few recitals until I was born in 1940 and Harold two years later. She gave piano lessons in our house and accompanied various soloists and groups. One of her greatest joys was playing piano duets with a bosom friend, Gwendolyn Black, who lived forty miles away.

Ruth Lister (l.) and Gwen Black (r.), piano duet partners.

For as long as I can remember, she kept on her dresser (painted pale blue, glass knobs) in the cottage at Parrsboro, a frayed, yellowed programme of a piano recital given by Rachmaninov. It would be there, leaning against the mirror, summer after summer, when we opened the cottage and swept up the hundreds of winter-killed flies. It never occurred to me to ask her about it. A few years ago (so slow, so late!) I found, on the Ancestry website, her name on the passenger list of an overnight ferry trip she took alone on 27–28 October 1934, from Saint John, New Brunswick, to Boston. Rachmaninov's recital was on the afternoon of the 28th in Symphony Hall. She must have spent that night in Boston—but where? And when did she return? She was four months pregnant with her first child.

Harold and I were aware that our mother had given birth, before us, to a stillborn baby boy. It was she who told us, and there was a photograph of the baby in a casket, which understandably impressed itself on our imaginations. We both vaguely remember, as children, our

6

SYMPHONY HALL   .   .   .   .   BOSTON
Sunday Afternoon, October 28, 1934, at 3.30

SERGEI
RACHMANINOFF

Direction: CHARLES FOLEY

Programme

1. Toccata and Fugue, D minor .... Bach-Tausig

2. Sonata, Op. 10, No. 3 .... Beethoven
   Presto
   Largo e mesto
   Minuetto
   Rondo

3. Ballade in G minor .... Brahms

4. (a) Tarentelle
   (b) Mazurka .... Chopin
   (c) Scherzo

INTERMISSION

5. (a) Prelude
   (b) Moment Musical .... Rachmaninoff
   (c) Oriental Sketch

6. (a) Funerailles
   (b) Dance of the Gnomes .... Liszt
   (c) Rhapsody No. 11

STEINWAY PIANO

Management: NBC Artists Service

FRITZ KREISLER will give his second recital of the season in Symphony Hall, Sunday Afternoon, December 2

Recital programme, with my mother's note of the encores: 'Bizet Minuet, [Chopin] C♯ minor Prelude and 4 others'.

parents visiting the grave in Sackville, New Brunswick, where they had lived before coming to Moncton. But, with the passing of time and long after the deaths of both of them, having no idea when our older brother had died and no recollection of where the grave was, we decided to find it. Finally, one summer day in 2015 (so slow, so late!), we found the small, flat gravestone in a corner of Sackville's York Street Cemetery:

Infant son of Ralph & Ruth Lister

30 Mar. 1935

Minnie Linton, née Warwick; her son, Percy Linton; his daughter, Ruth Lister; her son Warwick Lister, July 1941.

We scraped away the earth and grass. Harold, who is not the emoting type, said, 'It's very emotional.' 'Yes,' I said, 'it is.' We had found our brother. I am certain that he would have been named Warwick, the maiden name of Mum's paternal grandmother.

Our mother might have intended another name for Harold, but the loss of her much-loved older brother, torpedoed aboard an oil tanker in the North Atlantic in September 1942, made the decision for her. The *Esso Williamsburg*, bound for Reykjavik from Aruba, took several hours to sink; a few survivors, some of them grievously wounded, got into a lifeboat and radioed for help using a hand-cranked transmitter. A Canadian destroyer, the *Skeena*, heard the distress call, separated from her convoy and went to the rescue, keeping fragile, sporadic radio contact with the survivors. A transcript of the conversation, unbearably poignant, has been preserved. The *Skeena* came within a few miles of finding them; it had apparently been seen by the men in the lifeboat, but encroaching darkness, fuel problems and the danger of enemy attack forced the rescuers to turn away. Our mother was not aware of these details until my brother recounted them to her—he had read the story in *The Crowsnest*,[2] the official magazine of the Canadian Navy. She seemed not to want to hear about it. Perhaps it would have been better had he kept it to himself. Of course, we do not know if our uncle, Harold Cedric Linton, First Assistant Engineer, aged thirty-eight, was in that lifeboat. It was not until months later that his parents received the letter informing them that all hands were presumed lost. My brother was born in January 1943.

Uncle Harold had always been drawn to the sea. As a boy during WWI he had kept a scrapbook, using one of his father's bulky old railway express ledgers, in which he pasted newspaper photos, mostly of ships in the war news, as well as of prominent British royal and political figures. Tucked into the ledger (Canadian Express Company, fifteen columns on each page, all filled in with Percy's copperplate hand, page after page) is Harold's linen-covered booklet, McDougall's *Songs from Far and Near*. On the inside of the back cover, Harold has drawn

---

[2] Vol. 9, No. 4 (February 1957).

Uncle Harold, somewhere at sea, about 1940.

in pencil, with precision and careful detail, a two-funnelled freighter sinking by the stern, lines for survivors hanging over the side; a submarine has surfaced in the foreground, its deck gun manned by three figures … . In October 1922, aged eighteen, he took ship from Halifax to New York and began the life of a seaman.

My brother and I always thought that our mother was born in 1908. It was only some thirty years after her death that I came upon her birth certificate and discovered that it was 1907. Why had she lied all those years about her age? I can only think that it was because she didn't want to be seen as older than her husband, who was born in 1908. Did he know?

It was our mother who brought us up, disciplined us, instructed us, sang to us ('Row, row, row your boat, gently down the stream' was a favourite), taught us how to swim, how to skate, how to fold our shirts. She cooked our meals; in July she made strawberry jam, stored in glass jars sealed with hot liquid wax. These lasted through the winter, until about April or May when we were down to the last jar and then felt deprived. She got us off to school, arranged our music lessons, took us to the doctor. In the winter, when we came back from playing (we would lie on our backs and swing our arms to make 'angels' in the snow; we would dig tunnels in the hard-packed snow ploughed up higher than our heads on the edges of the sidewalks), she would have us stand on the veranda while she swept the snow and icicles off us with a kitchen broom.

Warwick and Harold, in front of our house, Moncton, New Brunswick, 1945.

When we asked her how babies were made, she told us that the father puts his peepy into the mother's and then the baby grows inside her. She ran the house. When the furnace wouldn't work, it was she who called about it. At the cottage, when the breakwater needed to be repaired, she found the men to do it. She did the gardening in the vegetable plot and flower beds in Moncton, at least in the early years, though there are one or two photos of Dad mowing the lawn and raking leaves. Dad ran the shoe store, but Mum at the very least advised him on buying the women's shoes, if not actually deciding on the styles. She often worked in the store, selling shoes to customers on the busy days— Friday evenings, when the store stayed open until 9 p.m. and often was very busy, and Saturday mornings, for as far back as I can remember. She continued to do this until well into her sixties. Here is her diary entry for Friday, 29 April 1960:

Went at 9.30 to Notre Dame d'Acadie & adjudicated [a competitive music festival] until 5.30 p.m. with an hour for dinner [lunch]—then worked at store—then back to accompany in voice class. Quite an experience. I'm glad it fell my way.

The next day: 'Worked in store in morning, then to art class in afternoon.'

It is true that these are perhaps unusually busy entries, but they give an idea of the sort of life she led.

When Harold and I were growing up, she often complained of being tired. In her diary, 13 July 1945, when she was thirty-eight years old, she wrote: 'I am reading *How Not to Be Tired* with the hope of getting the work done without wilting by nightfall.' She often suffered from back pain and would ask Harold and me, when we were about three and five years old, literally to walk on her back as she lay on her bed. We took turns doing this, holding onto the headboard for support. I remember the difficulty, but also the pleasurable sensation of her skin on my bare feet, going up the slope from her lower back to her shoulder blades.

I wrote hundreds of letters to my mother after I left home, around once every two or three weeks, the first in 1957, the last in the year of her death, 1981. She kept most of them, as I have in turn, though there are gaps—several years' worth—lost probably when the house was sold after her death. She wrote to me more often; I was less constant in keeping her letters. This is her first, a postcard from Parrsboro to me in Moncton, postmarked 14 September 1948:

Tuesday.

Dear Warwick: …

Harold and I walked to the pier last night and saw a big freight boat come in from St. John. The moon made a big path over the water as we walked home. Harold chewed ten sticks of gum yesterday and still sniffed.

Much love, Mummy

I was seven years old, in Moncton with Dad because school (Grade 3) had started. Harold was not yet of school age; the weather probably still warm enough, Mum would have decided to stay on in Parrsboro with him. I have forgotten what the gum and sniffing were about—possibly he was suffering from sinus problems and had been told to chew gum to keep his respiratory tubes open? Or chewing gum was a distraction from a sniffing tic.

My first kiss

When I was young, in Moncton, it was a sign that a boy had earned the affection of a girl when she allowed him to walk her home from the ice rink, carrying her skates. I was extremely shy and inept with girls.

But once, Destiny smiled: Annie Tucker offered (yes, offered!) me the privilege of carrying her skates. We were six years old. She had blonde, curly hair. I had admired her for weeks because she knew how to write longhand well before the rest of us in first grade. It mystified and annoyed me. I was one of the clever ones at school; what gave her the right to be so much cleverer? One late afternoon, after an hour circling the rink to the sounds of swinging organ waltzes (did we skate arm in arm? No, I think not—that was for older kids. Perhaps holding hands), I walked Annie home in the gathering dusk, carrying her skates. She was mine at last. But there was no kiss.

A few months later, I was taken ill with one of those spring ailments that all of us often came down with. My mother put me to bed, and she it must have been, in collusion with the Grade 1 teacher, who arranged for Annie to bring my homework lesson to me. My mother escorted her into my bedroom. Then, daringly (she was quite capable of choreographing such a *mise en scène*), she left us alone in the room. Annie sat at the foot of the bed. I cannot recall what she wore— perfidious memory, to deny me this! She showed me the homework. We talked. Two birds were singing outside the window. At length, she approached me, her skate-bearer, she bent over me and, dear Reader, tremulously, with infinite tenderness, she kissed me. Was it on the lips?

Perhaps not, nor do I remember what tremors, if any, coursed through my loins. Then she left. I immediately fell on my knees and kissed the bedcovers where she had been sitting. So there were two kisses.

Still, in my mind's ear is the sound of distant church bells on blustery Sundays in Moncton, ebbing and flowing in the swirling gusts of the wind. And still, I occasionally feel a kind of wild exhilaration at the sound of the bells of the parish church around the corner from our house in Florence, clanging, jangling on a windy day. Different altogether is the deep, majestic knell of the Duomo, a kilometre away. I try to plan my excursions to the nearby Piazza Santo Spirito to the time when the bells ring at twelve noon. From the piazza you can look up to the top of Baccio d'Agnolo's superb campanile and see the two bells swinging with untrammelled exuberance, their different tones in ever-changing rhythmic counterpoint, then gradually slowing down until the last weak knell, almost inaudible.

One Sunday morning, walking along our street, my mother and I came upon Mr Selick, who ran a dry-goods store in Moncton. He was a quiet, slow-moving man; his two daughters took piano lessons from my mother. He was standing on the paved path from his house to the street, casting his eyes downward, as if bemused. Someone had chalked on the cement, 'Jews are shits'. I was eight or ten years old. My mother said 'Good morning, Mr Selick'; we pretended not to notice. Afterwards, my mother said nothing, which seems strange to me now. Perhaps she thought that there was nothing to explain, or rather that it could not be explained. It was my first encounter with the idea of human cruelty. Like most boys my age, I myself experienced minor episodes of bullying— the most memorable was having my head held down in deep snow until I thought I would suffocate. I swore revenge against my tormentor but was unable to carry it out because I didn't know who he was. A few years later, I read of the torture in Room 101 in Orwell's *1984*, but the final loss of my childhood innocence of evil occurred in the autumn of 1956 when I saw in *Life* magazine the horrific photograph of Russian army officers facing their executioners, crossing their arms in front of their bodies against the bullets, the knowledge of imminent death in their eyes, on the steps of a public building in Budapest during the Uprising.

When I was nine years old, my mother took me to New York City, and a couple of years later, she did the same for Harold. We stayed with an old friend of my mother's, Mary King. Mary, a baseball fan, took us to Yankee Stadium where we saw Joe DiMaggio play. I don't think he distinguished himself at bat that day (he retired the next year), but he loped easily a few yards to his right from centre field to catch a fly ball—sheer grace! We took the boat tour around Manhattan—thrilling! I was captivated by the Automat—the height of glamorous, big-city sophistication! But there was one bad moment. On a busy Manhattan street, I caught sight of a boy of about my age staring at me. It was my breeches—hopelessly provincial, hopelessly old-fashioned. I was mortified and begged my mother to let me wear real trousers.

One day, Mary's mother gave me a nicely bound diary, suggesting I write up each day of my visit, which now strikes me as a thoughtful gift for a boy my age. I was distinctly unenthusiastic. I took it home without writing a word. And it never occurred to me to thank my mother for taking me on this trip. Did other nine-year-olds thank their mothers for such things? Do they now? Dear Mum, dear Mrs King, thank you, and I'm sorry. Another thing: surely I was taken to a museum or two. But I have no recollection of it. Was I that incurious, that unreceptive? I'm afraid so.

In the autumn of 1951, Princess Elizabeth and Prince Phillip came to Moncton on a Canadian tour. They were driven through the city in an open convertible. Our mother took Harold and me to watch on a street corner not far from our house. They were sublimely glamorous, elegant, regal, waving smilingly to left and right, the radiant princess already in that inimitable Windsor manner. My mother said that Phillip, blonde and godlike in his naval uniform, looked straight at her as they passed. Of course, we believed her.

The next summer, Harold and I went to a YMCA camp for two weeks. On the first day, the cabin councillor organized an informal 'election' by secret ballot, to choose the head boy of our cabin. I took one of the other boys aside and said, 'If you vote for me, I'll vote for you.' I had no intention of voting for him—I voted for myself. Since, when the results were announced there were no votes for the other boy, he knew that I had tricked him. His cry of outraged protest still gnaws at my conscience. Was I embarrassed and ashamed because of my deceit or because of my stupidity at not foreseeing this outcome? And why had I been willing to go to such lengths? Over the years I have become acutely aware, as a result of other failed attempts, as I wasn't then, of my inability to deceive, to lie successfully, not because of a highly developed conscience, not because I lack the desire to lie or deceive, but because I lack the necessary foresight and cunning to see a lie through to the end. My other strongest memory of those two weeks is of a long hike through woods and fields on a hot morning. Finally, famished, we stopped under the shade of a tree. Our leader built a fire and heated a few cans of 'Irish Stew', which we fell upon. It was the most delicious, the most memorable meal of my life.

There was always a cat when I was growing up. My mother loved them and so did my brother and I; our father didn't so much dislike them as considered them 'useless'. I loved one cat in particular, black and white, very affectionate, but adventurous. I have a half-dozen photos of me cradling him in my arms. It was, I felt, a love that would last forever. One autumn afternoon, I saw him run out onto the street in front of our house where he was hit by a passing car. I picked him up, rushed to my mother who took him in her arms. With his eyes staring at me, I watched as his head collapsed sideways grotesquely, his neck broken, a sight that haunts me still. Our mother wrapped him in a piece of silk, waited until nightfall, lit a candelabra, and took Harold and me out into the garden behind the house, where we dug a grave and, in solemn silence, buried him, the candles casting flickering shadows. Nothing was said. I remember the expression on Mum's face. It was serious, but she shed no tears, at least not in our presence. She performed this ceremony for my brother and me, to lead us into the remote, as yet unexperienced realm of ritual, the sublimation of grief, the acceptance of mortality. The silken shroud, the candelabra were necessary props for this rite of passage. I was about twelve at the time; I was never able to feel the same affection for subsequent cats, though my mother did. When I left home, she would send me photos of whatever cat she loved at the time.

Warwick with beloved cat, summer 1952.

I reached the peak of my academic career in Grade 8, aged twelve-to-thirteen. Our teacher was Mr Eagles. I remember as if it were yesterday his vigorous demonstration of World War I bayonet drills, using a blackboard pointer, in his classroom in the King George School (I had gone to the Aberdeen School until Grade 8, then we were moved to the King George, an older building in a less salubrious part of town—we always felt that it somehow was a kind of demotion—a dark conspiracy on the part of the French-speaking elements of the city). Mr Eagles had his own personal way of adding up large figures—slightly unorthodox, which he taught us; he advocated the decimal and metric systems years before they were even considered in North America; he knew from memory the names of all the kings of England, along with their nicknames: 'Richard Crookback', 'Edward Longshanks', and so forth. I made good grades in Grade 8 and was accepted into the accelerated three-year high school programme. From then on it was steadily downhill—I graduated from high school by the skin of my teeth. My parents, I'm sure, were disappointed. My worst results were in English—the subject I liked most. I had a tendency to take too long on the first questions of examinations, thereby running out of time—a pattern that I was never able to shake off.

     Once, in high school, between classes, I was playing chess with a classmate. A boy looked over my shoulder and asked an elementary question about one of the moves. I said, 'Oh that's so ignorant. If there's anything I can't stand it's ignorance.' I was fifteen or sixteen years old; I cringe with shame at the memory. My mother was aware of this unpleasant side of my character. At around the same time, after I had been arrogant or rude to her, I found pinned to my desk a slip of paper with a quotation from La Rochefoucauld: 'There is no room in the universe for the least pride or arrogance, but only for a kind and gentle heart.' A few years later, after I had left home, she remonstrated with me—no, that's too strong a word—for my never having sent her a birthday card. I do not recall our ever celebrating her birthday, though she always gave me a birthday gift. I felt chastised by her words but not enough to change my ways to any great extent. I scarcely knew the date of her birthday, and I don't believe I ever sent her a birthday card, let alone a gift. Occasionally I felt pangs of guilt. In May 1962, away at the Eastman School of Music, I did send her a Mother's Day card:

> It struck me that I had forgotten your birthday, and a great, terrible wave of remorse flooded over me, and I went upstairs and sat on my bed and thought about you and cried and cried. A great bunch of memories came over me of all the things you have done for me and how ungrateful I've been, I thought of the millions of times you rubbed my back for me, and made orange juice for me, and comforted me in the middle of the night, and put up with my tantrums when we played Mozart sonatas etc., and when we played golf, and I just sat there like a big boob and felt miserable.

> Anyway, the reason I forgot your birthday is because I am a self-centred, egotistic, selfish slob, as you already know, and <u>not</u> because I don't love you, because I do love you very, very, very much. Violin exam next week some time, other exams week after. I may be home last week of May, depending on when the last exam is.

And again, in April or May of 1965: 'Is your birthday May 1?' [It was 6 May]. I always forget but love you just the same.'

My mother went through various studious phases. The first I remember was her interest in the Old Testament. She was not particularly religious but was obviously moved by certain passages and would read them aloud to Harold and me in a highly emotional manner, which to my young ears sounded out of proportion to the text: 'For everything there is a season ... a time to be born and a time to die; a time to plant and a time to pluck up that which is planted ...'—here her voice almost broke with quiet, suppressed sadness. Could she have been relating these words to something going on in her life? The next, I think, was an intense period of learning German. She bought textbooks, dictionaries and records which she spent hours listening to, and tried to interest me in, with little success. Then came French. She and a friend attended a course; she would come home with stories of how charming and witty the instructor was. Next was Greek mythology. I still have her well-thumbed copy of Edith Hamilton's *Mythology*. Harold and I encouraged her in this; we told her that she should compete in one of those American quiz shows.

She painted for most of her adult life, albeit sporadically. Two of her oils are now on the walls of my wife's and my apartment in Florence. For years, she attended painting classes taught by French-Canadian nuns at the Notre-Dame d'Acadie College for Girls in Moncton.

She became very fond of two or three of the nuns, especially one, Sister Léonide, an art teacher. This now seems to me extraordinary, because her attitude towards French-Canadians was ambivalent. Moncton has always had a high percentage of French-Canadians, about a third of the population. She professed not to like them in general, she was against their efforts to gain equal recognition of the French language, and she was incensed by the separatist movement in Quebec. I remember reminding her that the Acadians had settled in New Brunswick and Nova Scotia more than a century before the English-Scottish-Irish, to which she replied that the English won the war against the French in the eighteenth century, and that should have settled it. Her prejudice extended to English-speaking Catholics. She never was able to reconcile herself to her younger brother Bill's marriage to a Catholic. And yet, she worked hard attempting to learn French, and her friendship with Sister Léonide was close and enduring. On Friday, 6 May 1960, she wrote in her diary, 'My birthday, worked in store …', the day after, 'Worked in store. Art class in afternoon. Sister Léonide gave me [a] beautiful piece of ceramics.' It is a small, very pretty plate with a glazed floral design; on the back the name 'Ruth' is incised. I have it on my desk.

My father, Ralph W. Lister, like my mother, was the first generation of his family to go to college—Mount Allison University, in Sackville, New Brunswick, where they met. His great-grandfather had come to New Brunswick in 1843 from Dumfriesshire in the southwest corner of Scotland. They, too, were farmers until Dad's father opened a general store near the village of Harvey, where my father was born. While researching my parents' forebears I came to admire these early settlers, who braved a harsh climate and a reluctant soil, gradually improving their lot through the generations. My father's chief interest in life was sport. As a young man he excelled in baseball and basketball; in middle age he curled in the winter and golfed in the summer. He became the athletic coach at Mount Allison in 1932, in which position he compiled an enviably successful record. In those days there was only one head coach for all the sports, with an assistant. During the Depression, he and other faculty members were obliged to take a salary cut; my father decided that there was not a bright enough future as things stood, so he took over a shoe store in Moncton in 1937.

With our father at breakfast, about 1952. Kitchen sink realism in Moncton. On the table, among other things: an ashtray (Dad quit smoking only several years later) and a jar of maple syrup. On the shelf, among other things: a box of Shreddies.

In a way, my parents were an unlikely couple since their interests were so different. Dad was not in the least interested in classical music. But he never discouraged me from becoming a musician, though he must have had his doubts and probably would have preferred for me to join him in the shoe business. He was a gentle and fair-minded man. I was spared the classic adolescent agony of the rebellious son challenging his father. But there was an underlying feeling of alienation that occasionally rose to the surface, exacerbated by my closeness to my mother—a relationship nurtured by music, from which my father was excluded.

Mum and I on the Spencer's Island wharf, about twenty-five miles downshore from Parrsboro, about 1953. She had complained of a headache.

Harold joined Dad in the shoe store for several years and ran the business, before it was decided to sell it in 1974. I worked in the store occasionally from the age of about sixteen onwards, especially on Friday nights and Saturday mornings. One of my jobs was to take parcels of shoes to a tiny local post office to be mailed to customers. It was run by two elderly (so they seemed to me) French-Canadian men, who were friendly and full of jokes as they weighed the parcels that I had carefully wrapped and tied with string. I looked forward to my visits there. When I was old enough to have a bicycle and ride it on the streets, I often delivered shoes to houses in various parts of the city. In the winter, bicycling through snow and slush in cold weather, I felt heroic. Occasionally, I took shoes to be repaired by Mr Hanusiak, a Polish immigrant. There was a strong smell of leather in his cluttered shop; he would examine a shoe critically when I handed it to him.

One summer, when I was seventeen or eighteen, it was decided that I would stay for several weeks in Moncton and work in the store, instead of going to the cottage. I cannot now remember why this course of action was taken, nor how much say I had in the matter, though I do not recall feeling put upon. I had a daily routine: a pleasant fifteen-minute walk to the store, opened it at 9 a.m. and swept the sidewalk in front. Business was slow in the summers—only an occasional customer; besides, I worked in the men's side of the store, which always was less busy, so there was not much to do except chat with the two women clerks who worked in the women's side, with one of whom, a pretty French-Canadian girl about my age, I flirted desultorily. At about noon, I walked home, and I must have made my own lunch, though I have no recollection of what I ate for any of my meals. Perhaps I had a sandwich at a soda fountain near our house. Then I would practise the violin for about an hour and a half, then exercise for a half-hour with dumb-bells, then at about 3 p.m. walked back to the store, which I then closed at 5.30 p.m., walked home, made my supper and went to bed. It was a solitary, strangely monastic existence for someone my age, but I felt independent, not at all lonely, and not at all overworked. I missed being at the cottage, however.

My mother, before marrying Dad, had apparently come very close to marrying another man. Harold Henderson was the bursar at Mount Allison University at the time my parents lived in Sackville. Mum told me about him just once, and how much she had admired (loved?) him. I have two of his letters to her that appear to be postmarked May and June of 1931, in which it is clear how strongly he felt about her. Dad must surely have known about him. As late as 7 June 1932, less than three months before her marriage, a college friend wrote to her, 'Do write to me about the Lister–Henderson combat—I'm absolutely on the fence and am willing to cheer for either side because they are both great tho' entirely different.' I find this entry in Mum's diary, 28 June 1933 (about ten months after her marriage): 'Went for a short car drive with Mr Henderson & enjoyed him too well.' It seems odd that she refers to him as 'Mr Henderson'. In his letters to her he wrote 'Ruth Darling' and 'Ruth Dearest' and 'I'm missing you so much, Ruth. Sometimes it seems as though the past year were just a dream and that I will wake up and find myself alone again. I console myself with writing notes to you in the evening and tearing them up again the next day. Goodnight, Dearest.' He died of heart failure in 1942, aged forty-two. On 24 July 1945, Mum wrote in her diary:

> Tomorrow is Harold Henderson's birthday—July 25th—one of the finest men this world can ever have known and the best friend I shall have on this earth. Why must such men die so young, and the dregs of society hang on for no good purpose. I keep thinking that I may [not?] know another so good and fine, and so above pettiness, but they must be so few that to have known one such in a lifetime is a privilege.

So, Mum placed him on a higher plane than her husband, or at least a different plane; had her feelings for him always been on such a platonic level?

For most of her adult life, she chaffed against the position of women in the world, a feminist *avant la lettre*. I find it first in her diary, 8 May 1945 (Victory in Europe Day):

> We [she and Dad] have spent [the last three months or so] quibbling about washing dishes and keeping children, etc. It seems that man, for the simple reason that he is born male, retains the inalienable right to loaf ... while woman must adapt herself to any and every task which presents itself, be it scrubbing floors, wiping babies' bottoms, and cleaning porridge pots.

I remember one occasion when she confronted Dad in my and Harold's presence. It was about his spending so much time playing golf or cards with his friends and so little helping around the house. At the climax of the argument, she ran sobbing out of the kitchen and upstairs. I ran crying after her, 'Don't leave us, Mummy!' I still feel anguish at the memory. But such outbursts were rare. For most of the time, she kept her resentment to herself, at least in the presence of me and Harold.

On another occasion, however, when Dad and I were leaving the house to play golf together, she said through clenched teeth, 'Just because you have a pecker between your legs you think you can go off whenever you please.' This time her animosity was directed at both of us. I was shocked by her language and deeply hurt. It was the only time in my life that I can remember her speaking to me with such venom.

My brother and I both remember her disapproval of, or even hostility towards, the girls and women in our lives. She never approved of any of Harold's girl-friends (he never married). She may well have (subconsciously?) resented my first wife, Barbara, because she was forging ahead with a career as a professional pianist.

She was, I now believe, quite highly sexed—more than her husband. Once, in the kitchen, Dad, in a playful mood, fondled her breasts. He was playing, teasing, but she was clearly aroused and looked at him provocatively. I was about twelve, old enough to recognize the sexuality in her eyes. I think that brief incident stood for their entire physical relationship. They slept in separate bedrooms, and I do not recall ever seeing a sign of real physical intimacy between them.

It was inevitable that she would seek it elsewhere. In her forties she began an affair with her first cousin, whom she had known since she was a girl. He was an 'alpha male', barrel-chested, a yachtsman and outdoorsman, a close friend of the family. He had a cottage at the beach, not far from ours. Since I was no longer living at home, the news came as a surprise to me, but Harold had seen it developing for several years, when he was at a vulnerable age, and he still feels the acute discomfort, even humiliation, it caused him. It was horrible to see my father's pain. When I was home on vacation, I came upon him sobbing as he leafed through some of the love letters that he had found, stuffed away in a cupboard. She stopped seeing her cousin; the wounds healed slowly. By the 1970s, as old age encroached, she and Dad rediscovered their love for each other and slept in the same bed.

Mum and Dad at the cottage, about 1978.

CHAPTER 2

Musical beginnings: Moncton, Acadia

At some point, my mother began to teach me the piano and the rudiments of music, but I see in her diary that she had me begin piano lessons with another teacher in January of 1947. This lasted for two or three years. I can still hear the sound of Miss Murray's fingernails clicking gently on the keys. I was not a good pupil, practised very little.

When I was a few days short of my seventh birthday, my mother took me to a Community Concert recital given by Adolf Busch and Rudolf Serkin. She typed on the programme 'December 9th, 1947, with Ralph and Warwick'. I have no recollection whatsoever of this concert. It was the first time, surely, that I had heard any serious music-making other than my mother's. I am annoyed that it made so little impression on me. No doubt I was bored and fidgety. I had not yet had my Don Messer epiphany. Now, I would give my eye teeth to hear these two play this programme. As it happens, their Brahms and their Schubert are both available on YouTube in live performances at the Library of Congress in Washington, the Brahms in 1939 and the Schubert in 1946, a matter of months before I heard it. Both performances are masterly, both surely similar to what reached my uncomprehending ears.

I

Sonata in D minor, Op. 108   *Johannes Brahms*
(for piano and violin)

Mr Busch and Mr Serkin

II

Variations on the Name of   *Robert Schumann*
'Abegg' Op. 1

Rondo Capriccioso, Op. 14   *Felix Mendelssohn*

Mr Serkin
Intermission
III

Aria, Op. 108   *Max Reger*

Scherzo (The Elf)   *Robert Kahn*

Two Hungarian Dances   *Johannes Brahms*

Mr Busch
Mr Serkin at the piano
IV

Fantasy in C major,   *Franz Schubert*
Op. 159 (for violin and
piano)

Mr Busch and Mr Serkin

Was it the two performers who were responsible for the careful but
misleading distinction between the Brahms sonata 'for piano and violin'
and the Schubert Fantasy 'for violin and piano'? At any rate, it is a
serious and thoughtful programme, despite being confined almost
entirely to the nineteenth century. 'Aria, Op. 108' appears to be a
mistake, as Reger's Op. 108 is a symphonic piece. Busch and Serkin had
long championed Reger's music. They took the first, third and last

movements of the Brahms sonata quite fast in comparison with more recent interpretations, the Adagio very slow. In the *pizzicato* variation of the *Fantasy*, Busch plays all of the sixteenth-note arpeggios *arco*, not just the last, and, in the Allegro vivace, plays the simplified *ossia* versions of awkward arpeggios (appearing in the posthumous first edition), demonstrating in a small way that his espousal of *werktreue*, for which he is remembered, was not ironclad. I wonder how my father managed to get through the evening.

When I was nine years old, I asked my mother if I could take violin lessons. What had inspired me were the recordings and radio broadcasts of Don Messer and His Islanders from Prince Edward Island. Messer performed Irish reels and popular songs with a pianist, a clarinettist and a soprano. I was enamoured with the sound of his violin. My mother saw an advertisement in the Halifax *Chronicle Herald* for a violin on sale and bought it. It was sent on the bus to Parrsboro from its owner, a lady in Lockeport, Nova Scotia (NS), in the summer of 1950. Her letter to my mother:

> I received your letter and I have decided to sell my violin to you for twenty-five dollars … I will probably send it by express next week. I will have to get my sister to wrap it as I have been unfortunate and am in bed sick. You can send the checque [*sic*] after you receive it.

It turned out to be a Rigat Rubus violin, 'St Petersburg, 1850', with rounded edges, that is, no plate overhang on the edges, typical of this mysterious maker. I began lessons that autumn with a local teacher in Moncton, along with my younger brother, whom my mother dragooned into taking lessons, though he had not expressed the least desire to do so—not a good idea, in my opinion—one of the few errors that I consider my mother to have made bringing us up. Our violin teacher was James Davis, who had a full-time non-musical position with a local company and taught in the evenings. Harold and I went together to our lessons—a dollar for each of us. He was a kindly, soft-spoken man, not at all demanding. He rarely played during lessons; when he did, the sound he produced was, like him, unassertive. He talked about an unspecified future time when I would be studying the Kreutzer études, but though I remained with him for seven years, until I graduated from high school, aged sixteen, I had not yet looked at any of them. Nor did he stretch my capacity with the repertory he assigned to me; one of the Seitz student concertos was as far as I got.

It was not long before classical music recordings began to appear in the house, as if by magic. It was my mother's way—she said nothing, didn't tell me or ask me what I wanted to hear—she knew that I had not the slightest idea of the repertory. I abandoned Don Messer for this headier fare: Kreisler playing several of his own pieces; Casals playing *The Swan;* Elman's *Zigeunerweisen* (recorded in about 1906); Menuhin's Lalo *Symphonie Espagnole* and the Mendelssohn Concerto—I cried throughout the middle movement—and the early D minor concerto; Heifetz playing the two Beethoven *Romances*; Heifetz and Emmanuel Bay's Beethoven C minor Sonata Op. 30, No. 2; Cortot, Thibaud and Casals playing Beethoven's 'Archduke' Trio and Schubert's Piano Trio in B-flat; Heifetz playing both parts of Bach's Concerto for Two Violins; Heifetz, Primrose and Piatigorsky playing Beethoven Op. 9 Trios; Milstein's Mozart A major Concerto; Oistrakh's Khatchaturian Concerto; Szymon Goldberg and Artur Balsam's Brahms D minor and Schumann A minor sonatas (years later, after having played the Schumann work myself several times, I listened to this recording; it seemed less passionate than I had remembered—expressive, yes, but suffused with aristocratic restraint. Is one's aural memory refracted, distorted even, over the years through the lens of one's own interpretation of a piece?).

My brother and I would listen to a wonderful ancient recording of the ballad 'Lord Randall', in which the singer declaimed the final refrain *sempre morendo*: 'O make my bed soon, for I'm weak i' the heart, and fain [voice getting weaker] … would lie … [gasping, hoarse whisper] doon.' It was an early lesson for me in how an interpreter can transform a piece of music.

We listened together to an adapted version of Humperdinck's *Hansel and Gretel* (several 78 rpms) with Basil Rathbone as the Narrator and the Witch. At the precise moment when the witch was shoved into the oven, we turned up the volume to full blast, timed to the second, and screamed in unison with her: 'There's nothing wrong with the oven … AUUUUGH!' There was also Basil Rathbone (as Scrooge) and others in *A Christmas Carol* (78s), the ghost scenes particularly hair-raising and, best of all, Olivier's *Hamlet*, with Walton's music (excerpts on bright red 45 rpms). I still amuse myself reciting what I can remember of the soliloquies in a wretched attempt to imitate Olivier, which irritates or amuses my English wife Susan (depending on her mood), who says my bogus accent sounds more Irish than English. All of these recordings, and others, were simply there in the house—we took them for granted. It did not occur to my brother or me to wonder why most of them were English, not American. We were used to English accents. The organist and choir director of our church, who also taught music at the high school, was English. For several years in the 1950s, I listened to *The Goon Show* late at night in bed, my ear to the radio, trying to follow those manic British voices coming through distant waves of static on the BBC. When I moved to New York City in 1963, one of the first things I did was to go to *Beyond the Fringe*.

Speaking of accents, friends have pointed out to me that some of my vowels are peculiar. I say 'egg' and 'leg' to rhyme with 'laid' and 'made', 'merry' with 'marry' and 'Mary', 'cot' with 'caught'—in general a rather brutal flattening of distinctions, a homogenizing of vowels. It is still not clear to me whether this is Canadian, or Maritime Provinces, or my parents, or just me.

At some point, I began to play in competitive music festivals, first in Moncton and Saint John, then, when at university, in Halifax. Sometimes Harold and I played a duet. Once, the adjudicator complained in his report that we turned away from each other as we played. 'What's the matter? Don't you two like each other?' I still have *Dance of the Dwarfs*, a duet by H. E. Davey, that we played in the thirteen years and under class in the 1954 Moncton Festival. We both wrote 'Hold violin up' at the top of the page in our parts. My mother printed in ink on the cover of Vaughan Williams's *Fantasia on Greensleeves*, 'Warwick Lister, Feb. 18, 1957, Moncton, N.B.' and, in pencil, 'Class 268—Parent-Child Class'. I still have Kreisler's *Liebesleid*, with 'WARWICK LISTER October 1955' on the front cover in her large, bold hand. It was surely my mother's idea that I study this piece.

Warwick, about 1955. The jacket and tie suggest that I am about to leave for or have just come home from a performance, perhaps in a music festival. I am holding the bow as if posing for Baillot's *L'Art du violon* of 1835. Later in life I adopted a less bent-wrist position at the frog.

At the Saint John, New Brunswick, Music Festival, May 1956. The violin is not the Rigat Rubus. Photo: *Saint John Evening-Times Globe*.

I came to appreciate a string quartet by Beethoven in a roundabout way. One night (I was about fourteen), before going to bed, I chanced to look out the bedroom window. It was a cold, moon-lit night. Across the drive, I could see two young women, boarders in the house next door, who, at that moment, were undressing for bed. I watched with secret, excited fascination; it was the first—certainly one of the first—pangs of sexual feeling I had experienced. My mother came in, asked me what I was looking at. I made up some lame pretext; she went to the window, saw what it was, and the next night I was put in another bedroom. It was there that I listened for the first time to a recording of Op. 132 played by the Paganini Quartet. I played the record quietly in the silent house. The music was too strange at first for my ears, but then I was quite literally overpowered physically by the monumental passage towards the end of the last movement, when, in a welter of fragmentary motives, Beethoven seems to be searching for the theme, which finally emerges at the end of a *crescendo-accelerando*, as if freed from its chains. It was a moment of triumphant recognition, an awakening, which I suppose sounds pretentious, but I know others who have had similar experiences at that age. I cannot say whether, as a result, I subconsciously associate Beethoven with sex, or with my mother, or both, but I have performed Op. 132 several times as an adult, both second and first violin, and that passage always exerts a strangely powerful effect on me.

Around the same time, I played in the orchestra for a Mount Allison University student production of Gilbert and Sullivan's *Patience*. That night, there was a blizzard; those of us from out of town were stranded. We were put up after the performance at a local hotel, the Marshlands Inn—an adventure![3] A few weeks later, I received a cheque for $5.00 in the mail—my first professional engagement.

My mother often rehearsed with a contralto, a young woman whom I secretly admired—'lusted after' would be putting it too strongly—I was fifteen or sixteen. To prepare herself, Mum would enlist me to play the vocal line of many of the *lieder* with her—Schubert, Brahms,

---

[3] I recently learned that there were three performances: one on Friday, 16 March 1956, and two the next day.

Beethoven: Op. 132, last movement, bars 266–287.

Strauss, Wolf, Duparc. I would stand behind her, looking over her shoulder at the music. I did so not with an especially good grace, such was my adolescent indifference. Now I am aware of what an enriching musical experience it was for my undeveloped, recalcitrant musical sensibility. My memory of playing the magnificent melodies of

Brahms's 'Sapphische Ode' and Strauss's 'Breit' über mein Haupt dein schwarzes Haar' remains indelible, though I had only the vaguest understanding of the texts.

Once, at a party given by my parents, someone suggested that I play a few tunes to add to the merriment. I refused, though I would have liked nothing more than to comply, but I was, and still am, completely incapable of doing this sort of thing. One of my father's friends, an optometrist and amateur violinist, took my violin and walked around playing popular melodies—the life of the party. My father gave me a look of disappointment, close to contempt, that mortifies me still. But why, after this experience, to gratify my father, did I not take the trouble to memorize a few popular melodies so that I would be prepared for the next time?

Michael Rabin came to play in Moncton in January 1956. I turned the pianist's pages. The backstage area was the high school gymnasium. Just before the concert, both Rabin and his pianist (whose name I have unfortunately forgotten[4]), seeing that I was nervous, were kindness itself. Rabin took his violin in both hands and, with a sweet, conspiratorial smile, made as if to toss it up at a basketball net—an underhand foul shot. He was scarcely twenty years old, supremely gifted; the severe psychological difficulties that blighted his career were three or four years ahead. I managed to get through the recital with no mishaps; as a result, I remember almost nothing of their playing—a missed opportunity that I deeply regret. But Rabin's boyish gesture touched me; I was convinced that he had done it to put me at ease.

The next day, my Grade 11 Physics teacher, Mr Kierstead, stopped me in the hall and asked me whether I read the piano part or the violin part when turning pages. I told him (of course it was the violin part, easier to follow, which is always printed in the piano part), but was it with condescension, towards a man who was willing to place himself in the position of learning from one of his students? I noticed recently that for years the principal second violin chair of the Symphony New

---

[4] Possibly David Poliakine. See Anthony Feinstein, *Michael Rabin: America's Virtuoso Violinist* (Milwaukee: Amadeus Press, 2011), pp. 119, 131.

Brunswick has been the Miles and Eunice Kierstead Memorial Chair. So
he and his wife were music lovers, something that I hadn't bothered to
discover. It was Mr Kierstead who, one day in class, explaining the
refraction of light through water, compared it to a column of soldiers
entering a muddy field at an angle—those entering the field first are
deflected before the others, so that the whole column bends or changes
direction. He told it with such relish that none of us could forget it.

Byron Janis and Rudolph Firkušný also came in the 1950s. They
both practised at our house on my mother's piano. My mother thought
that Firkušný was extremely handsome. I was untouched by these
celebrated presences. I do not recall what Janis and Firkušný practised,
I didn't listen at the keyhole, enthralled. No, they were pianists, I was
not interested. Had they been violinists, perhaps I would have
condescended to listen.

In the summer of 1957, I attended summer school at Acadia
University in Wolfville, Nova Scotia, directly across Minas Basin from
Parrsboro. I took an Introduction to Philosophy course and violin
lessons from Janis Kalejs. I still hadn't decided on whether to attend
Mount Allison University (my parents' alma mater) or Acadia. Finally,
because of Mr Kalejs, I decided on Acadia. I enrolled in the four-year
Bachelor of Arts programme, with a major in music, not the Bachelor of
Music—unsure whether I wanted to enter the music profession, I was
hedging my bets.

Janis Kalejs was Latvian, a pupil of Georg Kulenkampff. With his
wife, Felicita (a pianist), and their infant son, he had escaped from the
Red Army towards the end of WWII. He put me on a diet of Hřimalý,
then Flesch scales and arpeggios, Hans Sitt position studies, Dounis trill
exercises, some of the Flesch silent stretching *Urstudien*, Kayser and
then Kreutzer studies and one concerto each year: Vivaldi A minor,
Accolay No. 1, de Bériot No. 9 and Viotti No. 22, along with a very few
easy sonatas. I was an undisciplined player, and Mr Kalejs no doubt
imposed this rather lean, remedial regime in an effort to bring my
technique up a few notches. But when I graduated in 1961, I had never
so much as glanced at any of the standard concertos, nor any of the Bach
unaccompanied works—the most ambitious sonatas I studied were the

Tartini Sonata in G minor, the Dvořák Sonatina and, in my last year, the Vivaldi–Respighi Sonata in D. Mr Kalejs fingered and bowed every piece I studied with him in great detail, which could be justified on the grounds that I was abysmally inexperienced, but it did not encourage curiosity or ambition to find my own solutions. There was only one other degree violin student at Acadia, and no other degree string students. I had never played a string quartet, string trio or piano trio. But Mr Kalejs promoted me in every way possible. He had me play in the Halifax Music Festival in the spring of each year, an important goal outside the closeted university environment. Whatever one thinks of competitive music festivals, and I have mixed feelings, they do inculcate in young musicians the discipline, crucial in the profession, of preparing for a public performance on a certain, non-negotiable date.

For some time before going to Acadia, I had also pursued another 'unofficial', extracurricular repertory outside of lessons. I have already mentioned playing lieder with my mother. And I had worked on three or four of Mozart's sonatas with her, for example. More than a year before going to Acadia, we had played K. 301 in G major in a Jeunesses Musicales concert in Moncton. I had also begun practising the Poulenc Sonata with my mother (this must have been her idea), which at that stage of my life was too difficult for me. In the summer of 1957, I often played through Mozart sonatas with another student. Looking back on it, I was remiss not to have asked Mr Kalejs if he thought I should be doing this.

In my freshman year at Acadia, James Stokesbury, an American, seven years older than I, was assigned to me as my roommate. I would be interested to know how this was decided. As a matter of fact, Jim and I had a few things in common, chief of which was our fondness for classical music. Once, we listened together in our room to an orchestral piece on the radio. Neither of us knew what it was; we tried to guess, without success; it was Brahms's *Variations on a Theme of Haydn*. I have played this piece a dozen times since, both the first and second violin part, never without remembering that half hour in Willett House in the autumn of 1957. But in other ways, we were badly mismatched. I was sixteen—a very young sixteen at that; he was a navy veteran of the Korean War. He was a serious student, majoring in history, and graduated a year early with honours and was immediately given a position on the faculty. I was an inconsistent student, already feeling the pressure of time; there never seemed to be enough hours in the day, with the course work, for practising the violin. This became a recurring pattern in my life. I remember Jim's impatience with me at my poor marks in the European History survey course. My interest in history was, to put it mildly, still dormant. Jim called me 'Kid', a name that stuck for more than a year, which I pretended not to mind, but I did mind. It was only in 2011, at the fiftieth Class Reunion, that I learned of his untimely death in 1995. And it was only after that that I began to read his books: *A Short History of WWI*, *Navy and Power* and others—all of them very well written, models of their kind.

Whatever the reasons, I now realize that I suffered from a lack of self-esteem that year. I remember my feeling of relief—more than that—exaltation, when a boy I knew only slightly, a geology student, asked me to be his roommate for the next school year. I had not had the courage or confidence to ask anyone myself.

One very cold night, in the winter of 1957–58, heavy snow on the ground, four or five of us walked home from the movies downtown, so cold no one said a word, trudging up in single file through the silent campus to Willett House, the sound of our boots squeaking on the packed snow. Why do I still remember this?

I never, or all too rarely, expressed gratitude to my teachers, or for that matter, to anybody to whom it was owing, including my parents. My mother was aware of this deficiency. Towards the end of my first year at Acadia she wrote to me:

Be sure to go up Sunday to say goodbye to Mrs. Kalejs & her mother—they have been very kind to you, and also shake hands & say goodbye to Mr. Collins [the dean of the School of Music]. Try to develop a few of the friendly social graces—it makes people a little happy. I watched Morley [her cousin] this trip—and he tries to be so friendly and people do like him for it.

And, in the same letter:

> Warwick, please run in to see Aunt Clare this week, for just a half hour.
> … If you go to see Aunt Clare & Mr. Hemeon it will be your Mother's
> Day effort for me!! Please do. It will be a good little walk for you.

I heard Alfredo Campoli play a recital in Halifax in the early spring of
1958. I wrote to my mother:

> Campoli was a terrific player. He has magnificent control over the bow
> especially, and can bounce it, flip it, jerk it, slash it, or ooze it any way
> he pleases. He is a fat, roly-poly man, and he was so relaxed that he
> seemed to be sharing a little joke with the audience while he played—
> completely detached from his fiddling. The Handel sonata (see
> program) was mere child's play to him, of course—he just used it to
> warm up on. In some places I liked his playing of Beethoven's C minor
> sonata better than Heifitz's [*sic*] record. His tone is fuller and more
> luscious than Heifitz's, but not as clean or clear-cut. Gordon
> MacPherson was his accompanist [*sic*], and did very well. It must have
> been quite a thrill for him to play with Campoli, who is certainly
> among the top 10 violinists in the world. He played 4 encores—La
> Chasse (a hunting song), Variations on a Theme of Corelli by Tartini,
> Bach Arioso, and a piece by Ravel. I stayed overnight [with my uncle]
> and came back Monday morning on the bus, and only missed one
> class.

Joseph Szigeti played at Acadia University in the spring of 1959, with
the pianist Roy Bogas.[5] I remember his Bach *Chaconne* and the Debussy

---

[5] Bogas is called the 'Accompanist' on the programme, which also included the
Sonata in A major, Op. 100, by Brahms. This deplorable solecism, unfortunately and
unbelievably still with us, is roundly condemned by the pianist Susan Tomes, in a
chapter of her *Beyond the Notes* (Woodbridge: Boydell, 2004), pp. 179–182. One of
the most blatant recent examples of this 'star'-centred syndrome, no doubt
commercially motivated, is the publicity for many of the violinist Anne-Sophie

Sonata, the first an Everest conquered after an epic ascent, almost a struggle (technical obstacles were for him, not something to be glossed over with a veneer of slick *sprezzatura*); the other a kaleidoscope of shimmering, gossamer colours. Szigeti was past his prime—though only sixty-six years old, he had developed arthritis in his hands and stopped playing in public very soon afterwards. His vibrato was slow, his long arms seemed ungainly,[6] but his bow was masterly, above all, his gliding full bows in certain passages in the first and second movements of the Debussy sonata (*sur la touche* and *expressif et sans rigueur*) in which he achieved an expressive *parlando* (literally 'speaking') quality of hypnotic, ethereal eloquence. After the concert, Mr Kalejs introduced me to him. Perhaps he shook my hand. His bearing was patrician, almost aloof. I believe they spoke German to each other; I was too shy to offer even the tritest commonplaces and withdrew as politely as I could. I was only dimly aware of Szigeti's distinguished career. I had not heard of, let alone read, his autobiography, *With Strings Attached*, published a decade earlier. I was unaware that he had played the Chaconne at his debut in Berlin in 1905, aged thirteen, and a few years later, privately, for Ferruccio Busoni, whose performances of his piano transcription

---

Mutter's recordings and television performances. See, for example, the covers of her Deutsche Grammophon sonata recordings with the pianist Lambert Orkis, in which her name is about three times as large as her collaborator's and which are dominated by a glamorous picture of her—her alone. As to my perceptions in this regard in 1958–59, I can only repeat the immortal words of Samuel Johnson, who, when questioned about one of the incorrect definitions in his dictionary, is said to have replied, 'Ignorance, Madam, sheer ignorance'.

[6] Carl Flesch (*The Memoirs of Carl Flesch* (London: Rockliff), p. 330) asserts that he held the bow with the upper arm in the old-fashioned low position near his body. This, at least to an extent, is refuted by Canadian Broadcasting Corporation television videos of Szigeti in 1954, 1955 and 1960. Flesch also observes that 'allegedly, his arms are too short for the modern posture' (*ibid.*). Either Szigeti's arms had lengthened since the 1930s or Flesch was not wearing his glasses. At any rate, short arms would have precisely the opposite effect: the bow would not be able to reach the frog with the upper arm held close to the body, especially on the D and G strings.

and explanations of the work had marked a turning point in Szigeti's career. Nor did I know that Szigeti had been playing the Debussy Sonata since 1918, a year or so after it was composed, and that he had recorded it with Béla Bartók. If I had, would I have listened more attentively? At least I could sense something extraordinary, an aura, the memory of which, after more than sixty years, is with me still. I recently came across a YouTube recording of Szigeti playing Elgar's *Serenade*, arranged by him from the original for piano. It is a sentimental little trifle, played with unsurpassable charm and warmth, giving the lie to Szigeti's one-sided reputation as a severely intellectual musician, which he was, or rather he could be.

The fourteen-year-old Itzhak Perlman came to Moncton in 1960, with an entourage including his mother; my mother accompanied him at the piano. In her diary, 19 April, she wrote, 'Itzhak Perlman came tonight—we practiced here for about 2 hours'. And the next day: 'Young Perlman, crippled 15-year-old violinist came in morning to practice, then for a while in Hotel this afternoon. Concert tonight at Brunswick [Hotel]—I accompanied, Gwen and I assisted. He is a genius I am sure.' Of his programme (I was home for the college spring break) I remember only Wieniawski's *Scherzo Tarantelle* and Saint-Saëns' *Introduction and Rondo Capriccioso*, both virtuoso pieces of the highest order, and possibly the Mendelssohn Concerto. I listened, a nineteen-year-old to a fourteen-year-old on another violinistic planet, with mixed feelings: self-pitying discouragement, yes, but also awe-struck admiration and inspiration. It was inevitable that I would compare his rendition of the *Scherzo Tarantelle* with Jaime Laredo's recording, with which I had recently become acquainted. I stubbornly preferred Laredo's, although this was based on nothing more than my familiarity with it. As for my mother, I dare say there are many pianists who would jump at the opportunity of rehearsing (three times!) and performing with Itzhak Perlman. I am pleased beyond measure for her. What did they say to each other? He had only just begun learning to speak English. Did someone translate? But my mother was an intelligent, resourceful woman, and he was an outgoing, cheerful boy. Did she make suggestions? Ask questions? The *Scherzo Tarantelle* begins with a brief piano introduction, establishing the tempo. He would have wanted it played at a certain speed. I recently came upon a letter to my mother from the Moncton chapter of the Hadassah Organization of Canada, which had sponsored the concert, informing her that 'As a token of deep regard and appreciative thanks, we are planting a Tree in Israel in your name, a certificate for which will be forthcoming shortly.'

I include, chiefly for its meteorological interest, my letter of 7 February 1960:

Sunday nite, 9.30 p.m. (while listening to Isaac Stern play Prokofiev Concerto in D on radio)

Dear Mom,

Yes, I went down to Halifax Thursday [to play in the Halifax Music Festival final concert] and thereby hangs a tale. As you may know, on Thursday Halifax was smitten by the worst storm of the century, so said the papers, so there was some doubt as to whether we would go. However, Mr. Kalejs decided, after listening to latest road reports, that we would go. So! At 5.30 p.m., our brave little party set out, including Mrs K., in little green Austin. All was well until about Mount Uniacke, then snow on ground got deeper and deeper, and roads worse and worse as we approached ze beeg citee, but finally we made it—But!—Halifax was unbelievable—only half the streets were plowed, and the snow was piled in great mountains on either side of the streets that were plowed. It was really a beautiful sight, even though it was hard driving for poor Mr K., and Mrs K. didn't help things much as you can imagine. Anyway, we made the Queen Elizabeth School in lots of time (20 mins) and I played the De Bériot Concerto [No. 9] all right—with more spirit than in the YMCA, but not as good technically. Also I am getting a $50 prize. *But* here is the jest of the matter, or the matter of the jest: Mr K. decided that we had better not risk trying to go back that night, so we bunked down in the Scotian Hotel ($9.50 per room) for the night like a bunch of wild gypsy musicians with no luggage nor nothing no-how. We left Halifax at 8.30 next morning and got to

Wolfville all right. Quite a trip, but it was worthwhile seeing Halifax the way it was.

The experience of playing in the newly formed Canadian National Youth Orchestra in Stratford, Ontario, in the summer of 1960, was the first I had had of anything like a full symphony orchestra. I still feel a frisson at the memory of the beginning of the first rehearsal of the session. It was Schumann's Symphony No. 4; I was in the second violins—the dark, foreboding D minor theme of the slow introduction, *pianissimo* on the G string, with the violas and bassoons, surrounded by the all-enveloping pedal in the rest of the orchestra, was so overpowering that I was almost unable to play.

I returned for three more sessions, winter and summer. We violinists were fortunate to have the likes of Oscar Shumsky and Josef Gingold as string coaches. During the December 1960 session in Toronto, I wrote home that Shumsky was 'a magnificent violinist and a patient and painstaking instructor'. And I remember Gingold in the December 1961 session in Montreal having the violinists stand in a semicircle and leading us, exhorting us, in scales—different bowings and tempos. Once, Glenn Gould, the idol of many young Canadian musicians in the late fifties and sixties, said a few informal words to the orchestra during a rehearsal. And I heard two or three chamber music concerts given by Gould, Shumsky and Leonard Rose at the Stratford Festival. They were a revelation to my provincial ears. I had never heard chamber music in the flesh even remotely at that level (except, of course, for Serkin and Busch in 1947!).

Intermezzo: sporting life

I started to play golf when I was twelve or so, and at the age of fourteen or fifteen became quite serious about it. I was given a few lessons in Moncton, but for the most part I was self-taught. I studied my father's copy of *The Nine Bad Shots of Golf* (the only book I ever knew him to read) and Ben Hogan's *Power Golf* (of which I had a battered paperback version, published in 1953) and one or two others. My golf was almost entirely limited to the months of July and August, when school was out and we were at the cottage. The nine-hole Parrsboro Golf Course, though extremely scenic, overlooking Minas Basin from a high promontory, was not much of a course on which to become a good golfer. It was a par 34, but the longest hole is (or was) marked as 379 yards long ('par 5', ridiculously, on the scorecard in my day) and there are no sand traps. For most of those three or four summers, until I started university in 1957, I played almost every day, usually by myself. (I cannot remember how much violin practising I did in the summer those years, if any; very little, I think). In the mornings, I walked with my clubs across a field and a few hundred yards up the road (in those days, unpaved) to the course, which I almost always had entirely to myself. Often, halfway through the round, I would choose a spot and lie down on my back, looking up at the scudding clouds. I had no desire to play with anyone else, though occasionally I did if there was someone to play with. I was trying to improve my skill as a player, but I remember it now as more of a communing with nature in a spectacularly beautiful place. Walking back to the cottage, rounding a curve on the downhill road, the view of Parrsboro Harbour opens up, then the lighthouse, Partridge Island and finally the frowning brow of Cape Blomidon across the bay; for me, it was, and still is, the prettiest sight in the world.

My father and I often played together when he was in Parrsboro. My relationship with him was chiefly through golf. I think Dad enjoyed playing with me, just the two of us. Some of my warmest memories are of playing with him on the Parrsboro course, in all kinds of weather, talking about nothing in particular, sometimes joshing each other: 'Great drive, Dad', when I had out-driven him, or 'Nice approach Warwick, too bad you can't putt'. I have kept three or four scorecards from those years. On one of them, dated 30 August 1956, my score for nine holes is 37, under which I proudly wrote 'Lowest score to date'. Dad's score for eighteen holes is 67 (34 + 33). He pencilled on the card, 'Course record' and 'Certified by', with my signature. It was an educated guess on our part, but I think it highly plausible that it *was* the course record. The next year, after I had come back from attending summer school at Acadia University, he shot a 66 and I had 85 on 16 August, and on 21 August he had a 31 on the first nine. We both knew the course as well as anybody, but he could play it as well as anybody.

My father, Ralph W. Lister. Parrsboro golf course, summer 1965.

The Parrsboro Golf Club had a traditional friendly one-day tournament each summer with the Sackville, New Brunswick club. A few players would make the hour-long drive, eighteen holes were played, followed by a driving contest, supper and 'blue' films. There was quite a bit of drinking. When I was about fifteen, I went along on one of these junkets. Out of consideration for my tender age, I was not allowed to see the films. The ride home was filled with drink-fuelled, raucous storytelling. It was my first experience of this kind of strictly male mateyness. It was fun, but once was enough.

In the summer of 1959, between my sophomore and junior years at Acadia, I won—by a one-stroke margin in a three-round round elimination tournament in Moncton—a place as one of four players on the New Brunswick–Prince Edward Island provincial junior team at the inaugural national junior championship held at the Montreal Kanawaki course. I remember vividly the last nine holes of the final round in

Moncton—almost every shot. A few months ago, I read, for the first time since I had written it, a stroke-by-stroke account of this back nine I had sent to my mother the next day. I remember nothing of the front nine, nor of the other two rounds. It was surely the act of writing the description, not the experience itself, that impressed those moments on my memory. Or was it? Why did I describe only the back nine? My front nine was much better—37 as opposed to 43.

In Montreal, underqualified, unprepared and ill-equipped (I had a driver, a three wood, four irons and a putter in my bag), I was overwhelmed by the sheer length of the course, by the sand traps and by the sight of so many other players who were vastly superior to me. I remember it now as a nightmare, all details blotted out. I played terribly, far below my usual level, which at best was not remotely at a national standard. When I got home, my father had left the Moncton newspaper for me to see. It had the listing of all the scores. Mine was the worst of all the players. My parents said nothing, no doubt to spare my feelings, but it would have been better had we talked about it.

A few weeks later, at Acadia, I bumped into a student whom I did not know very well, and who either had a nasty disposition or for some reason didn't like me. He said, 'You had the worst score at the national tournament, didn't you.' He clearly enjoyed my discomfort, and instead of replying, 'Yes I did, I played like a pig, but even if I had played my best I still might have had the worst score', which perhaps would have given him pause, I squirmed and murmured, 'I don't remember', a craven lie. I hadn't yet learned that to admit failure is the best defence for both one's self-esteem and the esteem of others.

I continued to play golf in the summers, with my father, during the few weeks when I was in Parrsboro. After his death, I stopped playing and got rid of my clubs. By then, I had taken up tennis.

CHAPTER 3

Professional beginnings: Eastman, NYC, Santa Fe

In the spring of 1961, I applied to Juilliard in New York City for entrance to the Master of Music programme, and to Eastman in Rochester, New York, recommended by a friend who had gone there a few years earlier. But I wanted to go to Juilliard, drawn by the bright lights of NYC and by the famous Ivan Galamian, teacher of everybody who was anybody. The audition at Juilliard was a disaster. I don't remember what I played; at one point, while playing, out of the corner of my eye, I saw Galamian shaking his head negatively to a woman (possibly Dorothy Delay, his highly regarded assistant) beside him. I knew instantly that the axe had fallen. And so, by default, Eastman it was.

I am at a loss to explain why I did not consider furthering my studies in Canada, at the Toronto Conservatory, for example. It is true that neither New York nor Rochester is as far from New Brunswick as Toronto. But that I did not even consider Toronto surprises me. As it turned out, my decision to go to the USA in large measure determined my future career. Professionally, I had turned my back on Canada irrevocably, except for two or three brief excursions.

When, in September 1961, I arrived at the Eastman School of Music for the two-year MM degree, there were dozens of undergraduate violinists who could play circles around me. I was two or three years behind in technique and repertory. On the one hand, it was stimulating to be surrounded by so many young musicians, on the other, I realized how far I had to go before I could hope to compete even for an orchestral position. It was sink or swim. I practised the Josef Gingold volumes of orchestral excerpts, outside my violin lessons, with a kind of desperate intensity.

That I did so outside the purview of my lessons was typical of the traditional training of string players. Young violinists were taught the standard concertos, which the overwhelming majority of them would never play, except, ironically, as an audition piece for an orchestral position. It was a form of deception, that the pupil would someday become a soloist. The probability that she/he was destined to be an orchestral player was ignored; the notion of an orchestral career was tacitly reduced to that of a dustbin of failed soloists. Worse still, this attitude was often the psychological burden of violinists who eventually joined an orchestra—exacerbated by the fact that there are upwards of thirty violinists in a symphony orchestra—far from being soloists, as the wind players in effect are, they are cogs in a wheel and often grow to resent it. In recent years, this long-entrenched system has gradually changed, partly by conservatories offering courses in orchestral playing, on the assumption that an orchestral career can be a dignified and reasonably fulfilling life's work, partly by the enlightened practice in some orchestras of promoting opportunities for the players to participate in various chamber combinations, partly by more generous contractual conditions, and partly by the demise of the all-powerful tyrant-conductor.

I wrote to my mother that first autumn: 'I'm working pretty hard on the violin—never less than 4 hours a day. So far, I have lots of time to practise, but soon my courses will start to take up more time.' In fact, one of my enduring memories of Eastman is never seeming to have enough time to practise, as the degree required a number of academic courses.

My boarding house, 30 Vick Park A, was run by Mr and Mrs Carpenter, who, though very elderly and quite decrepit, gave us a big cooked breakfast, prepared by Mr Carpenter, and a very fine evening dinner, not only for the six or seven of us graduate student boarders but often also for two or three guests, cooked by his wife, while he served the tables. They seemed too old to be doing this great amount of work (they must have washed the dishes as well) all for $20 a week. After supper, I and one or two others would return to the School and practise until it closed, I don't remember at what time. Then we sometimes would repair to a bar for a beer.

Once, on a Sunday, I took the better part of an afternoon to scrub off the considerable amount of mould that had accumulated on the walls and ceiling of the bathroom we boarders shared. Mr Carpenter was touched and thanked me. In my entire life, it is this one unsolicited act of generosity of which I am proudest.

In the first year, I shared a room with Greg Woolf, a composition student. One late night he came back to the room, breathless with excitement, waking me up to play a new recording of Elliott Carter's Second String Quartet, played by the Juilliard String Quartet. Another time, again late at night, it was the fresh recording of Bernstein's *West Side Story*. The exhilaration of sharing his enthusiasm!

In the second year, I roomed with Ernesto Lejano, a wonderful pianist who had a fellowship as a *repetiteur* with the opera department. Ernie generously played my graduation recital with me and, even more generously, offered to come to NYC to play for me when I auditioned for Raphael Bronstein (did I thank him?). After introducing myself I said to Bronstein, 'This is my pianist.' Bronstein smiled at that.

My violin teacher at Eastman was Millard Taylor. To begin with, he put me on the Rode and Fiorillo studies, the Bruch Concerto and the Bach E major solo partita. His star pupil at that time was a young woman named Marie Koczak. At the weekly class in which Taylor's pupils played for each other, I remember that she played the Brahms and Sibelius concerti and Beethoven's Kreutzer Sonata. She was an inspiration to me and, I dare say, to the others. She went on, as I did, to study with Raphael Bronstein, who once told me of his regret that such a talented musician did not pursue a solo career.

I attended as many concerts as I could and wrote enthusiastic letters to my mother about them.

November 1961:

I saw the Boston Symphony (Charles Munch) and they were faaabulous, in fact I've never heard anything anywhere that impressed me so much. They played Brahms's 1st Symphony and it was really breath-taking.

Again in November 1961:

Yes I saw Milstein rehearse [with the Rochester Philharmonic]. No he doesn't do a few bars over and over—he is sort of a character—very humorous and a showman during the rehearsal. I will tell you all about him when I get home [for the Christmas holidays]. ...

[On a Thanksgiving weekend trip to NYC] to the Guggenheim Museum and the Metropolitan Museum, where I saw the Rembrandt which they just bought—they paid 1½ million [actually 2.3 million] dollars for it, really. Have you heard about it—'Homer Contemplating a Bust of Aristotle' [sic] or something like that. The only trouble was I couldn't appreciate it very well with my weak eyes because they had it all roped off—about 50 feet away, but it was still all very awesome. I stayed in the YMCA on 34th St., which is very nice and central, but about 90% of its inhabitants are homosexuals, as far as I could tell.

I began to remedy, partially, my ignorance of Classical history and culture only after my first trip to Europe in 1965, when I began to buy books on history and after taking art history courses at Boston University.

Early 1962:

Did I tell you that I heard Rubenstein earlier this year? Also Rudolf Serkin, just last week, also Segovia 2 or 3 weeks ago. All three are magnificent, but I thought I would die at Segovia's recital—it was so beautiful.

Autumn 1962:

Heard the Philadelphia Orchestra last night, with Eugene Ormandy conducting. By far and away the best orchestral playing I have ever heard, live or on records. Enjoyed it even more than the Boston Symphony last year. They are so good that it is almost depressing. Most gorgeous, lush string section imaginable.

The Leningrad Orchestra also came to Rochester. I remember being bowled over, as were most of my violinist friends, by the virtuosity of the violin section in the *Rusllan and Ludmilla* overture, taken at breakneck speed.

In the spring of 1962, I played the Brahms Horn Trio in the graduation recital of a graduate horn student. Afterwards an acquaintance said to me, 'I thought your playing was the best thing about the recital.' I replied, 'Well, that isn't saying much.' I was twenty-one years old. How was it possible to be capable of such a crassly offensive, loutish remark?

I spent part of the 1962 Christmas vacation in New York City where I heard a memorial concert for Kreisler in Carnegie Hall for the benefit of the Musicians' Emergency Fund. The soloists were Francescatti, Milstein, Morini and Stern—a feast of violin playing. I remember thinking that in their performance of one of Vivaldi's Concertos for Four Violins, Erica Morini outshone the other three—energetic, scintillating, full of *joie de vivre*. The next day, my birthday, I played for Raphael Bronstein in his apartment. I also played for William Kroll, the distinguished violinist, composer and quartet player. He played a rich, sonorous chordal accompaniment on the piano to my Bach G minor unaccompanied sonata Adagio.

Spring 1963:

Earlier this week I had a most unbelievable, in fact faaabulous three musical evenings, namely, to wit (1) On Sunday afternoon a few of us drove to Buffalo (50 miles) and heard Isaac Stern play the Beethoven

Concerto with the Buffalo Symphony, and he was magnifique, and, furthermore, we got in free at intermission time. (2) The next night (Monday) I heard Glenn Gould play a Bach, Beethoven and Hindemith recital, and he was magnifique, complete with shirttail hanging out and shirt cuffs hanging loose and flapping with each conductor-like swoop of his hand. Then to cap off this great orgy of music we (3) traipsed off again Tuesday nite to Buffalo and heard the Budapest Quartet play Mozart and Schubert and joined by Heifetz's brother Benar, a cellist, play a Schubert quintet, all of which was just too much for me to take, and I was still in a daze when you phoned.

A young man from the provinces soaking it all up. I neglected to tell my mother that the conductor in the first concert was the great Josef Krips. Gould's recital at Eastman was one of the last public recitals he gave. It pains me to see that I seemed not to be familiar with the ('a'!) Schubert Quintet.

In the weeks before my graduation recital (the first two movements of Bach's G minor solo sonata, Debussy Sonata, Brahms D minor Sonata) I would try to go through the two Bach movements from memory while bicycling from the boarding house to Eastman.

Afterwards I wrote to my mother:

As for my recital—it's very hard to remember or to judge how it sounded. I'm dying to hear the tape. The first movement of the Bach went quite smoothly, if I'm not mistaken, although my tempo might have been a little hurried. The fugue was rather rough—scratches and forced tone production because it is that sort of piece, with big, massive, difficult chords. Also, in the fugue, in one spot I left out 2 or 3 notes, and had a momentary memory slip in another place—although I didn't stop playing, even for an instant—just sort of on the brink— maybe a person who didn't know the piece wouldn't even have noticed it, but that remains to be heard.

As for the Debussy and Brahms—a lot of things didn't come off as well as they did in rehearsal, as usual, but I think I did a few good things and that it wasn't a complete loss.

Now I want to work on the Mendelssohn concerto and also, lo and behold, the Tchaikovsky concerto at the same time. Since my repertoire, especially concertos, is so small, and since I seem to learn things so slowly, I'm going to try and learn these two concertos by the end of school—work on both of them at the same time to try and speed up the learning agonies. What think you on this? Penses-tu qu'il est une idée intelligente?

Yes, I did get the black pants and the corduroy jacket. I don't know what made me say I didn't—just stubbornness, I guess.

That I thought I would be able to learn two such formidable pieces in two months now astounds me. Was I trying to impress my mother? I must have abandoned the idea and more modestly and sensibly confined myself to the Mendelssohn. In the summer of 1963, I returned to Acadia University to take violin lessons from Mr Kalejs. We worked on the Mendelssohn Concerto and Wieniawski's *Scherzo Tarantelle*.

I studied with Raphael Bronstein in NYC for three years through the Mannes College of Music on East 74th Street, where I took a conducting course with Carl Bamberger and chamber music with Paul Doktor, and played in the College orchestra conducted by Bamberger. In the first year, I also took a course in orchestration at Columbia University and played in the Columbia University Orchestra. I thought that the orchestra experience would do me good, but, not for the last time, I was spreading myself far too thin.

I lived for two years in International House, a large residence for graduate students on Riverside Drive, not far from Columbia University and the Juilliard School of Music. It was exhilarating to live among people from all over the world. There were several Israeli students, and several Palestinians, who seemed to co-exist peaceably, at least on the surface, in the atmosphere of friendly international relations engendered by the residence. But I do recall one incident in which the two groups confronted each other in one of the public spaces of the House. There was angry shouting, but they were separated before coming to blows. There were also several Russians, who kept to themselves, and some of us were convinced that they were spies. And there was an extremely unpleasant German cellist, a Juilliard student, who was openly and unabashedly anti-Semitic. Once, at table in the dining room, he gave a ranting monologue about how highly placed Jewish musicians were preventing Gentiles from getting ahead in the music profession in New York City. How he came to be living in International House is a mystery. On the other hand, to my knowledge, no one, including me, ever challenged him, which I regret deeply to this day.

Concerts were often organized in International House, in several of which I participated as a violinist and as a conductor. After a concert in which I conducted a chamber orchestra in performances of Bach's Violin Concerto in E major and Quantz's Flute Concerto in E minor, I received a note from a young Turkish woman, a friend and fellow resident, not a musician. It came at a time when I was depressed in general about my progress as a musician. I treasure it still.

Nov. 15, 1964

Sunday

Warwick,

That was very good. I was very proud as I listened to both pieces. I think things are going to be very bright for you.

Engin

The other piece on the programme, Mozart's Piano Concerto, K. 175, was conducted by Catherine Comet, a Juilliard student, about twenty years old, who afterwards enjoyed a distinguished career as an orchestra conductor.

In a production of Samuel Beckett's *All That Fall*, I acted the role of Mr Tyler, and I edited two issues of the House newspaper, the *International House Student Voice*. In one of them, I had wanted to include interviews with students concerning the political situation in their native countries. I put out feelers to prospective interviewees, one of whom, a Haitian, came to my room one evening and told me apologetically that he could not talk to me as he had a wife and family in Haiti and was too frightened for their welfare to speak freely.

For my audition for entrance to Mannes, I played the opening pages of the Mendelssohn concerto. The piano accompanist, with whom I had never played before, took an extremely fast tempo in the opening bars, much faster than I was used to. But the effect was miraculously positive. In my surprise and my supreme effort to keep up, I forgot to be nervous, and the faster tempo forced me to play with an unaccustomed lightness and fluency. I now am convinced that this is a very effective way (not enough in itself, of course) of improving a passage that sounds laborious or heavy-handed—simply play it, or try to play it, at a much faster tempo; then, when playing it at the normal tempo, try to recapture the feeling.

Carl Bamberger was Viennese, then in his mid-sixties. He was a loveable man, a dedicated teacher as well as a very fine musician with international experience. He conducted our rehearsals with warmth and quiet, avuncular authority. I remember how much I enjoyed playing Mendelssohn's *A Midsummer Night's Dream* incidental music and Bruckner's Fourth Symphony under his baton. We also played for a production of Janáček's The Cunning Little Vixen, which, if I am not mistaken, was one of the first, if not the first performance in the USA. The conducting class was small—only six or eight of us. He took us through several scores, with special attention to the phrase structure, unusual orchestrational features, problems of balance and clarity of gesture, pointing out traps for the unwary conductor. He enjoined us to be scrupulous about what he called 'bookkeeping', meaning the beating of bars of rest in accompaniments, or, for example, the fifth bar, with its fermata, of the first movement of Beethoven's Fifth Symphony. One day, he brought a shy sixteen-year-old boy in to join the class. He was a very fine pianist, and very generously played from piano scores some of the repertoire for us to conduct. I remember, in particular, one day when he patiently played a big, ascending solo scale passage from one of the Beethoven piano concertos, several times over, to give each of us in turn a chance to conduct the entrance of the orchestra at the top of the scale, the problem being to time it exactly. His name was Murray Perahia.

I was rehearsing the Dvořák Piano Quintet in A major at the Mannes School when someone burst in with the news that JFK had been assassinated. I wrote to my mother, 'Classes were cancelled, so I just went home in a daze, there was nothing else to do.' On the walk to the subway station, there was an eerie atmosphere, not of panic, but of palpable tension. On the train, I saw a young, seated woman crying silently.

In my student years, I lived in a kind of cocoon, largely untouched by outside events. This one event, of course, impinged on me indirectly. But in general, I took very little notice of the world beyond my daily routine. The Cuban missile crisis, a little over a year earlier, in which for two weeks the USA hung on the brink of a nuclear war, I seem not to have noticed. I have no recollection of it, and my letters home make no mention of it. I rarely read a newspaper, listened to a radio, or watched television. I was too busy trying to become a musician.

Raphael Bronstein lived in a spacious apartment in the Upper West Side. One waited in an anteroom for the previous lesson to finish. His studio was large and furnished in what seemed to me pre-revolutionary Russian style. His elegant, silver-haired wife would sometimes make an appearance. Once, during a lesson, I had a brief fainting spell. Mr Bronstein, with amazing alacrity, grabbed my violin and bow from me and eased me into an armchair. He called his wife, in Russian, who brought a shot glass of brandy (or was it vodka?) and administered it to me. They both were unforgettably gentle and solicitous (I recovered quickly and have never had a fainting spell since). When she died, I think it was in 1965, he was bereft: 'All I have left now are my pupils.'

He was a man of extraordinary warmth and empathy. He once expressed nostalgia (as much with his large, expressive eyes as with words) for the vast, wintry Russian spaces of his youth and asked me if I felt the same for Canada. He kept a battered violin and a sparsely haired bow on the piano, which occasionally he would use to demonstrate. With him, I studied the Dont études, Op. 35; two or three Paganini Caprices; Bach's unaccompanied Sonata in A minor and Partita in D minor (at the top of every page of the Flesch edition of the A minor fugue I pencilled in the words 'VIOLIN UP', just as I had done ten years earlier in 'Dance of the Dwarfs'; Bronstein had reminded me several times that I was letting the violin sag from the horizontal—it had become an ingrained bad habit). He took me through several of the Classical and Romantic violin concertos, including Mozart D major, Beethoven, Brahms, Tchaikovsky, Lalo *Symphonie espagnole* (first movement), Glazunov and Sibelius, and some of the standard virtuoso pieces such as the Saint-Saëns *Introduction et Rondo Capriccioso* and the Ysaÿe Sonata No. 3 (*Ballade*)—mostly not to performance level but sufficient to become acquainted with them and to be aware of the challenges each work presented. It was a pragmatic approach in that he knew that I was not going to be a virtuoso soloist. But I did subsequently play the *Scherzo Tarantelle* a number of times in public, for the first time at the Liederkranz Foundation in 1966, and in 1981 (finally!) I played the *Ballade* in a recital in Ville-d'Avray, near Paris.

Bronstein was a pupil of Leopold Auer (he had been Auer's assistant in the 1920s), but he had his own personal ideas about certain aspects of violin technique which he had developed over the years. Some of these I still find helpful: the notion of playing with 'space', that is, of giving sufficient time for a phrase to end without anticipating the next phrase; the idea of the fingers 'speaking', the bow 'painting'; the notion of 'visual intonation', which he elaborated in great detail; and his use of certain phrases invested with special significance: 'second notes' (indicating the notes on the weak part of beats or the second of two repeated notes), and 'preceding note' (the note before a shift or a string crossing), both needing to be played with special attention. He used poetic images to arouse his pupils' interpretive imagination. Some of these may sound hackneyed, but when he used such language you sensed his utter sincerity and his deep feeling for the piece. He urged me to think of entering a great cathedral when beginning the opening Adagio of Bach's G minor unaccompanied sonata, and of a swan gliding smoothly on serene waters for the opening violin solo over the gently rippling orchestral accompaniment of Sibelius's concerto. His book, *The Science of Violin Playing,* sets forth his principles of violin technique, along with a detailed bar-by-bar interpretive and technical lesson for each of several concertos and concert pieces. Some may find this approach too prescriptive, but it not only is the fruit of many years of thought and experience with these works, but also provides a precious, if personal glimpse, from the inside, as it were, of the great Russian school of violin playing stemming from Auer. During one lesson, he told me that he admired David Oistrakh's playing, that he played with 'space'. Another time, I asked him who he thought was the greatest of all the violinists of the past that he had heard. He answered without hesitation: Ysaÿe.

I did have one moment of disagreement with Mr Bronstein during a lesson. He said that he thought the Soviet system of musical education in place at that time—the practice of choosing the most promising musicians and rigorously grooming them at state expense from childhood—was superior. I, without knowing anything about this system, presumed to protest that it was a violation of civil liberties. Bronstein heard me out respectfully. Now I see his point. The proof of the pudding was in the eating, as was shown time and time again in international competitions.

Early in January 1964, I played the first movement of the Lalo *Symphonie espagnole* in the national CBC Talent Festival in Halifax, with the Halifax orchestra conducted by Sir Ernest MacMillan. About two months earlier, I wrote to my mother: 'I've already had a couple of lessons on it. It's not too terribly difficult and it is very effective, as you may remember, and I should be studying it anyway for my repertoire. Bronstein is magnificent on this piece—lots of ideas.' During the break in the rehearsal with the orchestra, the concertmaster took me aside and very courteously told me that I was rushing the triplet passage in the middle of the movement, so much so that the orchestra was having difficulty keeping up. I don't remember whether I tried to correct this fault on the spot, as it were, but some time afterward I listened to the tape (the concert was broadcast), and those triplets are indeed rushed, very rushed, and indeed the orchestra scrambles to keep up. Mercifully, I seem to have lost the tape. I recently obtained from Library and Archives Canada my adjudication form with Sir Ernest's remarks: 'I was rather worried at his first "run-through", but he pulled himself together and gave a good account of himself, although the work is really too difficult for his present abilities.' These comments must have been intended for internal use only, as I do not believe the participants were given them.

On 10 June 1964, I gave a recital in the New Brunswick Museum in Saint John, New Brunswick, King George VI Hall, with the pianist William Aide, who was then between positions on the faculties of Mount Allison University and Acadia University. The programme included the Sonata by Franck, which Mr Bronstein had suggested I play. Bill went on to a distinguished career as pianist, pedagogue and poet, but here I want to praise his splendid *Starting from Porcupine*, a brilliant, poetic memoir, published in 1996, full of wisdom, humour and probing musical insights, all expressed in his inimitable, highly individual prose. I had lost touch with Bill; I am glad that after fifty-seven years I finally had the wit (the courage?) to write to him and renew our acquaintance.

My first proper professional job as a violinist was in the second violins of the Santa Fe Opera orchestra in the summer of 1964. I had written to my mother:

I'm signing the contract tomorrow. I played the Braaaawaawhms Concerto—2 or 3 pages of the first movement for the audition—only one man was there to listen—not the conductor.[7] Then he asked me to

---

[7] It was one of the staff conductors, Robert Baustian.

play some of the second movement and that was all. He phoned me up the next day and said I had the job.

It was a summer of awakening, musical and otherwise. Among other things, it was my first taste of Mexican food. I had never heard of guacamole, let alone eaten it. It was my first 'total immersion' in the operatic repertory, ten weeks of it, from late June to the end of August, from *The Marriage of Figaro* (I have always thought that the second violin part is more difficult, certainly more tiring, than the first violin part) to Strauss's *Daphne* and Berg's *Lulu* (Acts I and II). I returned in the summer of 1966; eight operas were given each season. The salary was $85 per week, to me a princely sum. Two of the clauses in the 1966 contract may be of interest.

6 The Musician agrees to be present for rehearsals and performances at least ten (10) minutes before the appointed hour, and will be in his chair at least five (5) minutes before the appointed hour.

7 The musician owns or controls a suitable instrument and will always furnish and use such instrument to perform upon, and will play to the best of his ability. The musician agrees that the Conductor shall have full power to regulate the pitch of the Orchestra, and the Musician agrees that he will accept the wishes of the Conductor at all times concerning his services.

Orchestral musicians' contracts have changed very little over the years. Here are two of the clauses of a typical contract of the Teatro Regio opera theatre in Turin, dating from September 1775. One of the musicians who signed it was the twenty-year-old Giovanni Battista Viotti, in the second violins.

2 It is expected that everyone will appear equipped with instruments of the highest [*ottimo*] quality, with the understanding that they will be inspected carefully at the first rehearsal, and second-rate ones will be rejected. As regards violins and violas, it is required that they be strung

with thick strings [*che siano montati di grosso, cioè armati di corde grosse*].

[The directors of the Teatro Regio are to be commended for their scrupulous attention to detail—more than in the Santa Fe Opera contract, and indeed than in modern orchestra contracts in general. Thicker strings, with the greater bow pressure required to make them vibrate, produced a more robust, more substantial sound, as recommended by Leopold Mozart in his 1756 treatise on violin playing.]

   3 For the rehearsals as well as the performances, everyone is required to be
      present in good time in the orchestra to play diligently each his part
      with attention and precision, subject to the discretion of the first
      violinist [Gaetano Pugnani].

For this particular series of performances, Pugnani was paid 400 lire, Viotti, 60 lire (the analogous difference in 1966 in Santa Fe was, to my knowledge, not so great!).

   The atmosphere in the orchestra and in the company in general was informal, relaxed, but at the same time committed and hard-working. There was a swimming pool on the grounds which we could use, and there was an occasional lavish post-performance party in which audience and company members mingled. The theatre, situated about ten kilometres from Santa Fe, commands a magnificent view of the surrounding countryside as far as the city of Los Alamos. At that time the building, including the opera pit, was largely open to the elements (replaced twice, subsequently, by much larger and more enclosed theatres).

   John Crosby, the founder of the company in 1957, and its director, was a brilliant entrepreneur but also a thoroughly competent and well-prepared conductor. He had a knack for putting together excellent casts and creating conditions for fruitful collaboration among singers, stage directors, and scene and costume designers. He himself led the performances of *Rigoletto* and *Daphne* (the American stage premiere) in 1964, and *Rigoletto* and *Capriccio* in 1966.

Santa Fe Opera, the first rehearsal of the 1964 season: Rigoletto, opening bars.
I am seated just beyond John Crosby's desk, waiting with nervous excitement for
the entrance of the (five) second violins.

Once, in a rehearsal of *Lulu*, conducted by Robert Craft, during a
notoriously loud passage, some of the wind players complained bitterly
that the noise of the trumpets directly behind them was unbearable. The
rehearsal atmosphere, normally collegial, was in danger of becoming
rancorous. At first, Craft seemed out of his depth, at a loss for words, but
showed sympathy and managed to restore calm. At the next rehearsal of
Lulu, the orchestra seating had been rearranged.

I wrote to my mother on 6 August 1964:

Tonight we have the second dress rehearsal of Lulu with Robert
Craft—I think you have heard of him—he is Stravinsky's great
confrère—records his works and wrote a book with him. He is
marvellous—very witty and absent-minded, and a gigantic musical
intellect—just staggering—knows the complicated Alban Berg 'Lulu'
like you know the piano accompaniment to Liebesleid, for instance
(not meaning to belittle your musical attainments, mind you). The only

thing is, he is a horrible conductor, absurdly horrible in fact, with great swooping, clutching, flailing, scooping motions, like a porpoise, and puffs and blows his cheeks out and his glasses get all steamed up and fall down on his nose and he's just marvellous, all in all.

My tendency to focus unduly on a conductor's technique, already apparent in this letter, will be noticed in the pages that follow. It is the thing that impinges most directly on an orchestra player's experience of a conductor, the easiest, the most noticeable thing to criticise. How many times have orchestra musicians said, 'his beat isn't clear'? But at least in this case, I was able to see beyond the superficialities to the musicianship. It was only after beginning to write this memoir that I read Craft's *Stravinsky: Chronicle of a Friendship* and learned just how gigantic his intellect, not only his musical intellect, was. At any rate, besides *Lulu* in 1964, I had the pleasure of playing Berg's *Wozzeck* and Stravinsky's *The Rake's Progress* with Craft in 1966.

For *Carmen,* in 1964, the designated conductor was Werner Torkanowsky, a name familiar to me as Mr Bronstein once told me that Torkanowsky had been his best student. Unfortunately, he got off to a bad start with us on account of his cold podium manner. Then, when there was a problem keeping the stage chorus and the orchestra together (a common enough problem in opera), he told us he would conduct the orchestra with one hand, the chorus with the other—an absurdly impractical idea which didn't work. After two or three rehearsals, in which relations did not improve, Crosby read a carefully worded notice aloud to the company that it had been mutually agreed that Torkanowsky's contract with the company had been terminated. His place was taken by one of the other conductors. Later I told Mr Bronstein about this. Perhaps I should not have.

I remain puzzled by this incident. Werner Torkanowsky had a national reputation, with considerable operatic experience, and since 1963 had been the conductor of the New Orleans Philharmonic Symphony Orchestra. But he left that orchestra in 1977 to become the conductor of the Bangor (Maine) Symphony Orchestra, a step downwards, surely, in his career.

One early morning, I woke up to the sound of voices outside the house. The Spanish-American landlady, her daughters and their friends were picking the apricots from the tree beside the house, a sweet, gently chirruping female chorus. It was one of the enduring sound-memories of my life, and one of the most pleasant. Afterwards, the landlady gave me a jar of her apricot jam.

As I have said, I was shy and inept with the opposite sex. On the few occasions when I summoned up the courage to ask a young woman out, I was intractably, excruciatingly gauche. Unable or unwilling to make conversation, I would sometimes go through an entire evening without saying a word, or I would blurt out a wildly inappropriate comment in an attempt to be clever. This lasted well into my twenties. I felt secretly that females found me not unattractive; my shyness, in fact, was mixed with, or perhaps was even produced by, a kind of arrogant standoffishness which, dimly aware of it though I may have been, almost crippled my social and sexual development. This situation was at least temporarily relieved in the summer of 1964. I met a local Santa Fe woman who was a few years older and infinitely more experienced than I. She saw the discrepancy and generously remedied it. Her house was only a few hundred yards away from the one in which I lived, on the outskirts of town. After opera performances, late at night, I would walk through a field (were there rattlesnakes lurking in the desert vegetation?) and knock softly on her bedroom window. It was beyond my wildest twenty-three-year-old dreams.

We went on excursions together in her car, to an Indian Pueblo reservation, to Taos to see D. H. Lawrence's paintings, to the lovely, forested mountains near Santa Fe. It was idyllic; we both understood in our different ways that it was only for the summer. In 1966, I met up with her once early in the summer, but by tacit agreement we did not see each other again. The magic was gone.

Towards the end of the summer of 1964, I wrote to my mother:

I've decided what I'm going to do. I'm going straight back to NYC and try to get into some orchestra. I already have some contacts and I think I could get into some orchestra like the Brooklyn Philharmonia or the

American Symphony Orchestra of Leopold Stokowski, which pay quite well. I have the Mannes scholarship to pay for my lessons, and if necessary I can be a waiter in International House—2 hours a day— which pays for all my meals. If I can't get an orchestra job in NYC then I will play in the North Carolina Symphony for their annual tour— March to May—for $100 a week. I have already been offered this job if I want it and so I can be sure of it, and it would more than pay for my expenses in New York. Then I could go back to NYC for May and June and take more lessons, before going back to Santa Fe in the summer (as I intend to if I get the job again), although May and June would be a good time to go to Europe, n'est-ce pas? Well I might do that too, who knows? In any case I want to be completely financially independent, and I don't think I will find it very hard. ... I desperately need the experience of playing in a professional orchestra—there is no substitute for it, and it's about time I started getting it. In fact, I would probably try to get into a professional orchestra this year even if I didn't want or need to earn the money. And it would probably only involve about 8 or 10 hours a week. I'm preparing right now for orchestral auditions, which I hope to take immediately upon getting back to NYC. I'm practising orchestral passages, etc.

This harping on my 'need' to earn money protests too much, it now seems to me. My parents had always been generous. It is true that though they had paid for my tuition and costs at Acadia and my first year at Eastman, from then on, I had scholarships and jobs. For the second year at Eastman, I had a full tuition scholarship, and for my first year in NYC, I had a Canada Council grant (as I recall it was for $1200). But my mother often sent me money—$20 or $50 or $100—and continued to do so even after I had taken full-time jobs in Holland and the USA and no longer needed help.

I did, however, as I said I would, take on a job as a waiter for a few weeks in the International House dining room, clearing trays. And I did audition for as many orchestras as I could, partly in order simply to gain experience auditioning. I played for the conductor of the Brooklyn Philharmonia (as it was then called), Siegfried Landau, who told me that

I should not have attempted to play the first movement of the Brahms Concerto, but something less formidable. Of course he was right. I had been studying that work, and I had managed to get into the Santa Fe orchestra with it, but I had not brought it up to a reliably consistent level. I forget what I played for the artistic director of the Concertgebouw Orchestra, who was recruiting players in the USA. He offered me a contract, but, though tempted, I decided that I needed more work on my violin playing.

Nor do I remember what I played for the New York Philharmonic audition, but I do recall that it was behind a screen. After I had played one piece, someone came around from behind the screen and asked me what make my violin was. I replied that I didn't know, that it was 'anonymous'. He asked me if he could show it to the panel, I agreed, he took it round and I heard murmured conversation; one voice said, 'Maybe it's an anonymous Strad.' At the time I thought nothing of all this, but now I flatter myself that they liked the sound of my violin. I regret that I cannot recall how or when I obtained this violin, which I had played from at least as far back as the age of sixteen (it must have been my mother who arranged it), and which I must have traded in when I bought another instrument in 1970 in London. I am certain it was not the Rigat Rubus, whose fate I am now ignorant of. At any rate, I was not invited to play in a further round of the auditions.

Soon after arriving back in NYC, I wrote:

I phoned Mr Bronstein today. My first lesson on Friday. He said I should have 25 lessons instead of 20 which I had last year, and was his usual big-hearted, embracing-the-universe, open-souled, Russian Jewish self.

Did I tell you I heard Heifitz [*sic*] twice in Carnegie Hall, playing chamber music with Piatigorsky and others—and it was wonderful to hear his unmistakable thrilling, thrilling tone. He doesn't seem to have aged much and what a contrast he was with Piatigorsky—great lumbering big-faced, whereas Heifitz is so compact and lithe-looking—both magnificent artists though.

And in another letter:

> Heard Serkin and Alexander Schneider and a cellist (who was very good) play Haydn trios the other night. Magnificent, perhaps the best concert I've been to in my life. Surely Serkin is the greatest pianist alive, and he and Schneider are an unmatchable twosome.

Perhaps I may be forgiven for not naming the cellist—in Haydn's piano trios, the cello simply doubles the left-hand part of the piano for most of the time, not, however, as simple a task as might first appear, as any cellist who has played these works can tell you. It was Leslie Parnas, not a familiar name to me then. Serkin and his two colleagues were performing all of Haydn's piano trios in a series of nine concerts over a period of four years in the Metropolitan Museum.

More concerts, duly reported to my mother:

> I was extremely moved by Gerard Souzay. He has a magnificent voice and is an impeccable and passionate musician.

> Tonight I am going to hear the Vienna Symphony, last night I heard Francescatti, who I think is superb, certainly the most luscious tone of all the players, and a terrific technique, refined Gallic manner, even walking on and off stage and taking bows—ever so gracious.

> I was at another recital a couple of weeks ago and heard a terrifically elegant French, French, French voice in animated but refined conversation and it was none other than Monsieur Francescatti with sparkling eyes and elegant cuffs and immaculate manners, and at the same concert (recital by Henryk Schering) at intermission I saw Rubenstein, surrounded by hordes of big fat rich ladies, and he was entertaining them with *his* special brand of charm, with sensuous, heavy eyelids and huge emerald rings on fingers and nodding and bowing and laughing—all very awesome for a young man from the provinces like me.

CHAPTER 4

Stokowski, Siena

For two seasons, 1964 to 1966, I played in the American Symphony Orchestra, conducted by Leopold Stokowski, then in his mid-eighties. For the audition, I went, as many others must have done, to his Fifth Avenue penthouse, reached by a private elevator. Afterwards, still glowing with excitement, I wrote to my mother.

> What an experience! He has a beautiful suite on the 14th floor on 88th and 5th Ave, right beside the Guggenheim Museum, with a view of Central Park with a beautiful lake. It's the [doubly underscored] most plush area in Manhatten [*sic*]. His secretary showed me into a studio with piano …

> I warmed up a little and looked around the room: pictures, dramatic photographs of him conducting and many recordings—mostly of him conducting. After about 10 minutes the great man came in—swept-back, flowing white hair, bright blue eyes, and long white blue-veined hands, wearing a blue double-breasted suit with stripes. He extended one of those famous hands, and I was almost afraid to touch it for fear of being sued for $800,00500065 if I squeezed it too hard. He has absolutely no accent whatever, just sounds like an American and very modest and unassuming with a quiet refined voice. He asked me a few of the usual questions—he had heard of Bronstein—he uses a lot of his

pupils in the American Symphony and is very impressed with them. He said he would like to meet Bronstein. Then I played the unaccompanied G minor Bach sonata, 1st mov. He heard it all the way through, then asked me to do some sight-reading of orchestral music. I wasn't too nervous in the Bach, got through it without any memory slips and my sight-reading was all stuff that I had played before, so I got thru it fairly well. Then he ushered me over to a table beside the window overlooking the park and he sat opposite me and we chatted awhile. While I was playing he had marked down on a piece of paper what he thought of my playing under various categories, like Tone, Intonation, Interpretation, Bowing, Technique etc. and opposite each category he had graded me—so many points out of 10, and I got 10 on everything except one of them, I couldn't see which, maybe intonation or sight-reading—on that I got 9. So he seemed to think my playing was good. He told me, 'I like your playing very much, and I would like you to play with us in the symphony.'

So it was a success—I'm on the waiting list—and will probably get to play in a few of the concerts, but maybe not until next spring, I suppose. He said a number of things to me—advice on practising etc. He said one thing though, which sticks in my mind, it seemed somehow typical of him: 'I want you to continue with Mr Bronstein, he's an excellent teacher, but I also want you to study with someone else—you know him quite well, and you can learn a lot from him too—his name is Warwick Lister.' Coming from anyone else this would have sounded awful and melodramatic, but from him it sounded perfectly natural. Then he got up and cordially said goodbye, we shook hands (again the long blue-veined fingers) and he left the room. I packed my fiddle and as I went out the door I caught a glimpse of him sitting in an adjoining room. He was drumming his fingers lightly on a table and was looking out the window, seemingly lost in thought. I'm sure he had forgotten about me completely and was deep in reverie of one sort or another. Anyway, to see him sitting there like that was something of a revelation to me. It was as if I were seeing a character out of a 19th cent. novel, a reminder of an era we'll never see again I don't suppose—like a Viennese waltz—beautiful but sad. And he seemed almost to be aware of it as he sat there (or so I imagined)— aware that he is one of the very few of that era still left, and that he will soon die (he's well over 70) [*sic*] and it seemed all the more so when I stepped out in the bright sunlight on Fifth Ave and got into a crowded bus—incredible that there could be two such different worlds only 50 yards apart!

He's a remarkable man, maybe even a great man and I'm glad to have met him at least. I was elated, of course, that he liked my playing, but still, I somehow felt more sad than happy when I left him—very strange, eh?

Stokowski, far from dying soon, lived to be ninety-five, conducting to the end, very much of the contemporary twentieth-century world. Now that I am 'well over seventy' (in fact I am exactly the same age as Stokowski was in the autumn of 1964), I wish I could have a word with my twenty-three-year-old persona about those fanciful philosophical-cum-historical-cum-sentimental musings. Perhaps I was dramatizing for my mother.

When Stokowski spoke to the orchestra, he had a vaguely European accent. Could it be that in private conversation he toned it down? I think so. I learned recently that I was not the only musician whom Stokowski advised to study with himself, which somehow disappoints me, though it is admittedly too good a piece of wisdom not to spread around.

In the event, I was called by the orchestra manager a few days later and joined the orchestra within a week or two. The American Symphony Orchestra consisted mostly of young players like myself, at the beginning of their careers. Our rehearsals and concerts were in Carnegie Hall, itself a thrill for a young musician. For each concert there were four rehearsals, lasting two and a half hours each, and usually two performances, on Sunday afternoon and on Monday evening. Mischa Elman played the Tchaikovsky Concerto with us. All of us in the violin section were aware that we were witnessing one of the great links with the past. Elman had studied the work with Leopold Auer in the first decade of the century and had made his American debut with the same work in the same hall in 1908. It was decided in rehearsal to open a cut in the third movement that is traditional in the Auer version. In the concert, Elman's memory failed him at that very spot; there was a moment of stunned silence, he walked over to the conductor (David Katz, who was also the manager of the orchestra), who pointed to the score. Elman returned to his place, we started again, and the movement finished without a hitch. It should be remembered that he had been playing the concerto for nearly sixty years with the cut. He seemed old to me (he was in his mid-seventies), but his ravishing tone was just as I remembered it from his *Zigeunerweisen*. He died about two years later.

Ruggiero Ricci played a series of four concerts with the American Symphony Orchestra—fifteen concertos over the span of a month, a staggering feat. I played in the last three concerts. My letter of 30 November 1964:

> I am playing in three concerts with the violinist Ruggiero Ricci. He is giving a series of concerts of the major violin concertos. We had a rehearsal this morning, concert tomorrow night in Philharmonic hall: Mozart A major, Bartók No. 2 and Tchaikovsky concerti, also a concert Dec. 8 and Dec. 16—not on the regular American symphony series but using players from it. What a thrill to hear Ricci, let alone play with him!

Stokowski's attributes are well known. He conducted without a baton, moulding the sound with both hands, the right with the forefinger curved downwards and pressed against the tip of the thumb, the other three fingers extended straight out, the left hand often swooping in grandiloquent arcs, both wrists flexible as if laying paint thickly on a canvas. He was chiefly concerned with instrumental balance and colour, less with rhythmic precision or intonation. He would adjust the printed score to allow some instruments to come through—often asking the brass to come down to *piano* in favour of the strings, with, however, one significant exception that I can remember: he told the strings in no uncertain terms not to overpower the theme in the winds in the second movement of Schubert's 'Unfinished Symphony' (the first *forte*, beginning in b. 33). He eschewed uniform bowing in the string sections, down bows and up bows in military unison, in favour of 'free bowing' in which we were encouraged to bow as we saw fit as individuals. The result was a continuous, rich sound, not precisely articulated—ideal, many thought, for Romantic music, though others, including at least one distinguished musician, Nathan Milstein,[8] considered it unmusical and unnatural, since bowing is equivalent to breathing in the singing voice and should be unanimous. He experimented with the orchestra seating; for one of his arrangements of a Bach organ piece he placed the woodwinds in a steeply banked setup to his right, behind the cellos. He was perfectly content to have the violins tune down their G strings to F sharp to finish their last phrase towards the end of the last movement of Tchaikovsky's Symphony No. 6.

Stokie (as orchestra musicians often called him) was famous for his glamorous, flamboyant podium presence, but he had a methodical side as well. During rehearsals, he would often continue beating time with one hand while jotting down a brief pencilled note with the other— reminders to make some adjustment at the next rehearsal. He would give instructions, more like commands, to the orchestra in a very crisp, almost telegraphic manner, and then call out the rehearsal number or letter to begin again, but give us only a second or two before starting to conduct the passage. He did this not only to use time efficiently but also to keep us on our toes. He could be hectoring in his vocal corrections in rehearsals, which I think was partly because most of us were young and he could adopt the role almost of a disciplinary parent.

One winter's morning, as we were taking our seats for a rehearsal, some of us found on our music stands an envelope with a player's name on it. It was a type-written letter, signed by Stokowski, taking us to task for not arriving in good time to warm up before the rehearsal in the cold weather. Since I was punctilious about this very thing, I was offended.

---

[8] Nathan Milstein and Solomon Volkov, *From Russia to the West: The Musical Memoirs and Reminiscences of Nathan Milstein* (New York: Henry Holt, 1990), p. 253.

Besides, not all of us had received this letter. How did he know which of us were guilty? Just before the next rehearsal, I took my courage in both hands and spoke to him, seated as usual on the podium well before the rehearsal began. He listened to my (polite) protestations and replied, 'Well, you know, even a conductor can make mistakes,' disarming me utterly. But he could crack the whip when necessary. Once, in a rehearsal, when he thought one or two players weren't giving their best, he said, 'If you aren't willing to practise this passage, there are others in the wings who are.' Yet his generosity and encouragement to young musicians were well-known. He wrote for me a handsome letter of recommendation when I applied to Boston University for a fellowship.

One highlight was the world premiere of Ives's Symphony No. 4 in 1965, which we recorded. Stokowski stood on the podium to conduct the main body of the orchestra and had two assistants deployed to conduct the smaller sub-groups. Stokowski was not always completely in control of this very complex work. At one point in the recording session, the producer came out from the control room to confer; he watched us go over a passage in which the score directed the first violins to make a diminuendo, the seconds, simultaneously, a crescendo, but this was not being done and the producer pointed it out. Stokowski, unfazed, simply said, 'Please, violins, do what is printed,' and we did.

In March 1966 we recorded Beethoven's 'Emperor' Concerto with Glenn Gould. The recording took place over two days in two three-hour sessions in the Manhattan Center, a vast, dreary space in West 34th Street. On the face of it, two more different musical personalities than Gould and Stokowski could scarcely be imagined; in fact, they seemed to get along extremely well, and the rehearsals and recording sessions proceeded with utmost collegial cordiality. During a break, Gould, as if in a reverie, began to play the opening bars of Schubert's B-flat Symphony, No. 5. It was an invitation; several orchestra players joined in—a moment of genuine musical camaraderie, contradicting the notion people used to have of Gould as a remote, anti-social eccentric. No one seemed surprised that he could play this little-known work from memory.

One night, when I was returning late from an American Symphony

Orchestra concert on the subway with my violin, an extremely scruffy, thuggish-looking young man got on my carriage. There were very few people around. He glared at me menacingly. I averted my eyes. After a few moments he began to whistle. I thought, 'This is it, the prologue to an assault; now he's going to come at me with a knife.' Then I became aware that he was whistling the opening violin solo of the Saint-Saëns *Introduction and Rondo Capriccioso*, with unerring precision and musicality. He got off the train at the next stop.

In the summer of 1965, I attended the Accademia Musicale Chigiana in Siena. I had been longing for some time to go to Europe. I got a passage, with an American fellow of my acquaintance, for fifty Canadian dollars, on a very small Danish tramp steamer, the *Anne Reith*, carrying a load of lumber from Parrsboro Harbour. My mother saw us off, waving from the wharf. I had a duffel bag and my violin. I slept in a bunk in the captain's tiny cabin. The three or four officers were German, all men in their fifties; we ate with them. They all said that they had served on minesweepers in World War II. My friend, who was more outgoing and confident than I, got into a discussion about the war with the engineer, who opined that Churchill (or was it Roosevelt?) was just as much of a gangster as Hitler. There was a moment of shocked outrage, but we all remained calm, and the war was not mentioned again. The crew were Spanish and very friendly. We ran into dense fog off Newfoundland; the captain stayed on the bridge for what seemed an eternity, without sleep, his face glued to the radar. We were ten days crossing the Atlantic, which was like a mill pond—just as well, as the ship was alarmingly small. I whiled away the sunny hours reading in a nook in the bow, the lumber stacked behind me.

We put in at Galway Bay; my companion and I were let off on a small boat, and we were greeted by a charming Irishman who turned out to be the immigration officer. He took us to his house, stamped a few papers and drove us to the railway station, from where we took the first train to Dublin, then the overnight ferry to Liverpool. It was a cattle boat, quite literally, reeking overpoweringly of cow piss. We stood up all night on the deck, buttonholed by a red-haired young Irishman who

The lumber freighter *Anne Reith*.

never stopped talking. I remember nothing of the train to London, where I bade my companion goodbye.

I stayed in a hostel for three or four nights and explored the sights of London. On 10 July at 9.45 a.m., I wrote a postcard to my mother:

I'm standing in a long line at the Old Vic Company Theatre to get a gallery seat for Othello with Laurence Olivier. I hope I get one, but there's an awfully long line—people slept overnight on the sidewalk in sleeping bags. Can you imagine that? ... have seen all the touristy things—Changing of the Guard, Westminster Abbey, Tower of London, St. Paul's Cathedral, etc., etc., also plays (very cheap in London): The Mousetrap by Agatha Christie, The Circle by Somerset Maugham, Orpheus in the Underworld by Offenbach at the Sadler's Wells Theatre, and, I hope, Othello this afternoon. Tonight I leave at 10.30 p.m. on train for Florence—will get there tomorrow sometime and then immediately on to Siena ...

It must have been a few minutes after writing this that I bought a ticket from scalpers: two shady characters who took me around to the side of the theatre and named the price as so many 'quid', a word I had never heard before. I was eager to see Olivier. He played the role in blackface, rolled his eyes, gestured and walked with a rolling gait that he must have thought was like that of a black man, and affected an unnaturally deep voice. I didn't know what to think. But he dominated the stage, such that I scarcely remember the other roles, though they were played by distinguished actors. Mannerism and artifice notwithstanding, I left the theatre moved by the tragic figure that Olivier created. Nowadays, such an interpretation would be unthinkable. In fact, I am surprised that the play itself is permitted to be staged unexpurgated, so grotesque has the wave of 'political correctness' become.

My interest in Italy had been aroused by one of my mother's books, Bernard Berenson's *The Passionate Sightseer*, an illustrated edition of which I had pored over in the weeks before leaving Nova Scotia. There is very little about Siena in the book; it was Berenson's intensity of feeling for all that he saw in Italy, both works of art and in nature, that struck me. How was it possible that someone could react and write so passionately, could 'burn', in Walter Pater's potent phrase, with such 'a hard, gemlike flame'? The danger for lesser mortals is that, inspired by Berenson, Pater and the others, the would-be aesthete sets out determined to be sensitive, to be deeply moved—a caricature in the mould of Gilbert and Sullivan's Bunthorne. How was one to know what to be passionate about?

I had somehow conceived the desire to see Mantegna's monumental series of paintings, *The Triumphs of Caesar*, which were languishing in the orangery of Hampton Court Palace, undergoing a long restoration, begun in 1962, not finished until 1975. They were not open to the public. A dignified but sympathetic man met me at the entrance. I am now a little ashamed, but only a little, that I somewhat overstated the urgency of my mission: that I had come all the way from Canada, that all my life(!) I had deeply desired to see these masterpieces. He hesitated. Then, saintly man, he ushered me in. Several of the nine huge canvasses were lying partially rolled up on the floor; some could be seen hanging. He showed me around, said a few things, in fact treated me as if I were an art historian; I thanked him and took my leave. I had burned with a hard, gemlike flame.

In Virginia Woolf's *Mrs Dalloway*, I had read the description of Bedford Place leading into Russell Square: 'beauty pure and simple'. I wanted to see it for myself, and I did, thinking myself duly impressed—another check mark on my list.

The student train to Florence creaked slowly through the night. I remember seeing the Cologne cathedral from the railway station, looming in the darkness, and the moon over the Alps as we left Munich. From my seat in the *treno accelerato* (gloriously obfuscatory name!) to Siena, I caught my first glimpse of the Tuscan countryside. But lack of sleep took its toll; half-dazed, I found a room for the night and slept the sleep of the dead. In the morning, I awoke to the sounds of the street below—not cars, there were none and still aren't, but people out shopping and chatting in the morning sun—there was a fruit stand beneath the window. The sounds of Italy.

I enrolled in the chamber music and orchestra conducting courses at the Accademia Chigiana, but ended up concentrating on the conducting. I do remember, however, rehearsing a Mozart piano and violin sonata a few times with a very pretty Italian girl to whom I was attracted. I was tongue-tied, only partly because of the language problem. Once, I positioned myself as close to her as I dared, pretending to look at a passage in her music, in a ridiculously clumsy gesture, hoping that she would rise up from her bench and offer her lips to me, as in that famous painting used for a perfume advertisement. Of course, it came to nothing; she was not interested in me and had no idea that I was, in her.

Once, in the chamber music class taught by Sergio Lorenzi and Riccardo Brengola, the sixteen-year-old violinist Augustin Dumay played the Brahms G major Sonata with a pianist. He was extraordinarily gifted. I still remember the thrilling way he sustained the rising sixth to the vibrant B's on the E string at the end of the first movement, an effect I confess I have ever since emulated in that passage.

We students ate supper in a very simple trattoria on Via del Porrione: a *primo* and a *secondo piatto* and a fruit or a dessert and a quarter-litre of wine, after which you went to the counter, said 'normale' and plunked down a 500 lire coin (large and heavy).[9] Afterwards, we would pass the

---

[9] The other day, in an excess of nostalgic self-indulgence, I bought one of these at an antique coin stand in the Sunday morning fair in the Piazza Santo Spirito. It cost me ten euros and is disappointingly smaller and lighter than my memory of it.

balmy evenings seated outdoors at a café (always the same one) on the central Piazza del Campo. Sometimes, the violin instructor Franco Gulli, superbly elegant, flowing blond hair, cream-coloured suit jacket draped over his shoulders, would stroll into view, surrounded by an entourage of adoring female students.

The conducting course, held in the eighteenth-century Teatro dei Rinnovati in the Palazzo Pubblico, was taught by Hermann Scherchen, then seventy-four years old. For the audition (musicians invariably remember auditions, not always with pleasure), I conducted the opening few pages of Tchaikovsky's Romeo and Juliet overture. Scherchen was a hard taskmaster. He brusquely dismissed one student from the podium for grimacing, and one day he had several of us conduct the opening of Schubert's 'Unfinished' Symphony, having instructed us to maintain strictly the same tempo after the opening six bars, when the oboe theme begins. No one passed the test—he insisted that everyone had changed the tempo, however imperceptibly. On another occasion, he passed around a score of Schoenberg's *Chamber Symphony, Op. 9*, a complex work at the limit of tonality, and asked us to sing one of the themes. None of us could. Scherchen himself no doubt could have. At the beginning of his conducting career, in 1913, he conducted an early performance of this work in Berlin.[10] In his *Handbook of Conducting*, he gives several progressive sight-singing exercises, reaching a very high level of difficulty. I don't think any of us realised what a distinguished career he had had. He had been a personal

---

[10] See Carl. F. Flesch (Carl Flesch's son), *And do you also play the violin?* (London: Toccata Press, 1990), p. 332, quoting a letter from Scherchen to Flesch senior of 11 September 1913. There is a glaring disagreement between Hans Keller (translator and editor of *The Memoirs of Carl Flesch* (London: Rockliff, 1957) and Willi Reich, *Schoenberg: A Critical Biography* (New York: Praeger, 1971) regarding Scherchen's role in the preparation and first performances of *Pierrot Lunaire*. Keller, *Memoirs* (p. 323, n2): 'Scherchen … played, at the outside, a very subordinate role—that of an odd-job man.' Reich, *Schoenberg* (p. 78): Scherchen not only 'deputised for the composer at some of the [forty] rehearsals' for the first performance on 16 October 1912 but also conducted half of the performances on the tour of eleven cities undertaken by the ensemble immediately afterwards.

friend of Schoenberg and his pupils and was an assiduous and prominent interpreter of their orchestral works for nearly half a century. But he was also a pioneer in the recording of Haydn's symphonies, including the first complete recording of the 'London' Symphonies, dating from 1950 to 1953.

One day, I conducted the opening bars of the Adagietto from Mahler's Fifth Symphony. Members of the Italian Radio orchestra from Turin comprised the group used for the course; there was no harp. Scherchen sat at the back of the orchestra, his piercing blue eyes glinting maliciously, and sang the harp part of the opening bars with an exaggerated, percussive series of 'PING's, clearly doing his best to distract me from the main theme of the passage, to which the harp is rhythmically counterpoised in triplets. I sometimes wonder whether his disappointment and frustration at teaching this course was a contributing cause of Scherchen's death less than a year later.

I wrote to my mother (12 August):

Scherchen seems to think I have some talent ... Today after I conducted he said (in his Italian with a thick German accent) that I 'understood better than any of the others how to make the orchestra sing,' which was a tremendous compliment, especially coming from him, so I am really working hard to try and keep up this good public image.

I now wonder whether Scherchen really said this. My understanding of Italian was rudimentary—perhaps he made some observation about making the orchestra sing, but without the compliment? Doubts assail me. At any rate, in his *Handbook of Conducting*, published in 1933 and never surpassed for its thoroughness, Scherchen stresses repeatedly the importance of singing as the basis of the orchestra conductor's art: 'The conductor's conception of a work should be a perfect inward singing. ... Let every gesture represent singing tone,'[11] and so forth. Perhaps, after all, Scherchen did take a special interest in me. He seemed pleased that I was a violinist (I believe the only one in the class). He himself had

---

[11] Hermann Scherchen, *Handbook of Conducting* (Oxford: Oxford University Press, 1933), pp. 2, 16.

played orchestral viola at the beginning of his career. In his book, he writes, 'It is indispensable that the student should play a string instrument well enough to be able to sit in an orchestra.'[12] And, after all, he chose me to conduct the Adagietto in the final concert, one of the plums, if not *the* plum assignment.

In one of the rehearsals that I conducted of the Adagietto, I ventured to point out (very politely) to the first violins and violas that they had failed to play the long descending *pianississimo* glissando towards the end. The concertmaster (leader), almost apologetically said, 'Si, ma è brutto' ('Yes, but it's ugly'). All I could manage in reply was 'Oh no, non è brutto.' With my beginner's Italian, I was unable to tell them that it should sound like a long, resigned sigh.

Mahler: Symphony No. 5, Adagietto, 7–5 bars before Tempo I. Harp part not shown.

---

[12] Scherchen, *Handbook of Conducting*, p. 4.

To their everlasting credit, they did bring themselves to play the glissando, against the grain though it may have been. Italian orchestras in the mid-1960s were not yet thoroughly accustomed to Mahler's symphonies. The post-war Mahler revival was, I believe, slower reaching Italy than elsewhere.

In the final concert, I conducted the Adagietto far too slowly, as I recall, the four beats to the bar laboriously subdivided, no doubt influenced by Scherchen's own tempo in his recording of the work I had listened to months earlier. I was pleased and relieved, however, that I got through the piece, which is not simple, without mishap, from memory.

About to begin Mahler's Adagietto, Siena, 28 August 1965. Hermann Scherchen, seated in a box, is just visible behind my head. Photo by Grassi, Siena.

At the end of the concert, after a very long delay, during which it was expected that a prestigious prize of 150,000 lire would be presented to the best pupil of the evening, it was announced that the prize would not be awarded because of the brevity of the selections (about twelve or fifteen conductors had participated) and because none of us were considered worthy of the prize. Whatever Scherchen's opinion of my abilities, the Siena newspaper reviews the next day were not deliriously enthusiastic.

La Nazione, Cronaca di Siena, 29 agosto 1965:

The inelegant gestures of the Canadian Warwick Lister watered down the sweet[!] *adagietto* of Mahler's Fifth to a grey pallor, slightly hypnotic.[13]

Giornale del Mattino:

An instructive[?] interpretation; a Mahler, however, not sufficiently sorrowful, as it should have been, for the rest lacking as well that opaque varnish that characterises his 'anguished' and, we might say in today's fashionable term, 'personified' work.[14]

The conducting 'bug' bites many instrumentalists. The classic case is the distinguished musician who has reached a high level on his instrument, enjoyed a successful career, and feels the need to branch out—violinists perhaps most of all, cellists, pianists, even an occasional singer—the list is long. I don't remember exactly when I was bitten by the bug, but it certainly wasn't because I felt that violin playing no longer presented a sufficient challenge—far from it. As a teenager, I went through the motions of conducting the orchestral recordings we had in the house, for the fun of it, but it was only at Eastman that I began to study conducting, with, however, no thought of it as a career. But the bug had bitten me. Those who have never stood in front of an orchestra and would like to should know that, contrary to the impression one might get from watching most conductors, it is not a matter of choreographing the music with elegant gestures, no matter how appropriate such gestures seem. The conductor must (alas, so few of them do!) elicit the music from the musicians, not react to it. This

---

[13] 'Il gesto inelegante del canadese Warwick Lister ha stemperato il soave *adagietto* della Quinta di Mahler in un grigio pallore, lievemente ipnotico.'

[14] 'Docente interpretazione; un Mahler però non sufficientemente desolato, come conveniva, privo, del resto, anche dell'opaca vernice che caratterizza la sua 'sofferta' e diremmo con un termine oggi di moda, 'impersonata' opera.'

fundamental difference is what separates, in various ways and to varying degrees, the charlatan or semi-charlatan from the really competent conductor.

I became friends with a remarkable fellow student, George Wilson, an English mathematician who happened to be an excellent pianist taking the chamber music course. He was extremely thin, with a wispy red beard, very soft spoken, but with a sharp tongue. For some reason, we hit it off and played a few sonatas together, not for the chamber music course but for our own amusement. On the last day of the summer session, at his suggestion, we walked around Siena, visiting three or four of the smaller, less well-known churches, looking at the paintings listed in a guidebook. For the next two or three years, we corresponded (he at Oxford University, I in the USA), but then lost track of each other until some thirty years later.

It was Siena itself, more than the music, that impressed itself most vividly on me: the beauty of its medieval streets, the secret passages, the superb palaces, not least the Palazzo Chigi-Saracini itself, the Piazza del Campo—the most beautiful square in the world, the marble stairs leading up past the baptistery to the cathedral square—perhaps the most striking urban vista in Europe and, most of all, the awe-inspiring skeletal remains of the unfinished cathedral, a melancholy monument to the thwarted ambition of the fourteenth-century city fathers. But my interest in Sienese painting was not yet awakened. The superb equestrian fresco of *Guidoriccio* (I shall return to him later) and Ambrogio Lorenzetti's *Effects of Good Government* fresco, both in the rooms directly above our conductorial strivings, and Duccio's sublime *Maestà* in the Museum of the Opera del Duomo—all of these held little or no interest for me.

I managed to get to Rome for two days. Gazing up at Trajan's Column, I sensed that someone, a priest, was following me. I was being stalked. (The only other time I was followed was years later in East Berlin—altogether a more sinister experience, as I could only imagine his motive—surely not sexual.) In Rome, I succeeded in shaking off my admirer with no serious consequences. One of the things I most wanted to see was Nero's Domus Aurea (Golden House). At that time, visiting the underground remains of this fabled, notorious palace was an

Siena, the stairs leading up to the cathedral square, mid-1970s. Still burning with a hard, gem-like flame.

extremely casual affair. The one caretaker sent me and the five or six other visitors (a French group, as I recall) down a ramp into the damp, cavernous depths. Illumination was dimly provided by an occasional bare light bulb hanging from the ceiling. It was gloomy, cold, oppressive, claustrophobic, fascinating. As I wandered through the roughly excavated, sepulchral rooms, some of them vaulted, here and there a mosaic or fresco, I gradually lost contact with the others. After about an hour, the lights suddenly went out. I realized, to my horror, that the others had finished their tour and that the caretaker, who had not counted us, assumed that everybody was out. I was alone in total, utter darkness, deep underground, without the faintest idea of where I was in that labyrinthian prison. Shivering with the cold and with fright, my first reaction was an overwhelming need to pee, which I did, on the cold earthen floor. When I regained a degree of composure, I felt my way blindly along a wall until I came to an opening into another room, again along the walls of that room to another opening. Turning the corner, I saw the faintest imaginable glimmer of light at the end of a long corridor. It was daylight. I ran towards it, up the ramp to the metal gate which had been locked. By an incredible stroke of luck, I glimpsed the caretaker who was about to go home on his Vespa. His day was over. I rattled the gate and shouted at the top of my lungs. He heard me and let me out. We exchanged glances but not a word. It was about five o'clock on a Friday afternoon. Would I have had to spend three nights down there?

I returned to NYC on the SS *United States* from Le Havre, sharing a cabin with three others in the bowels of the ship. It was a stormy passage; not for one day was it possible to go on deck. When we arrived in New York Harbor I could see that damage had been done to the bridge.

I lived for a year in a one-room apartment in a brownstone in West 88th Street. The bathroom was shared with I forget how many others on the floor; there must have been a shower of sorts. The apartment was in bad shape; my girlfriend and I spent a week cleaning and painting it. I found the desiccated skeleton of a rat in a ceiling vent. Cockroaches were an ever-present threat. Next door to me, separated by half-inch-thick wallboard (I obtained the telephone number of Citizens Against Wallboard Walls, but never got round to joining), lived a Russian immigrant, about fifty years old. At first, he was friendly, invited me into his tiny room to look at a huge map of China tacked to the wall and ranted about how 500 million Chinese were going to take over the world. He had a job as a night watchman, slept during the day; when he heard me practising he took a day job, which by no means solved the problem entirely. I was practising long and hard for a big competition in Montreal. But he complained only once, when he vocalized— croaked—a bitterly grotesque caricature of the fugue theme of Bach's G minor solo sonata, that he had heard me practising hundreds of times. The crunching chords, repeated endlessly, must have driven him to the end of his tether. I was mortified, but I had to practise. There was no happy solution.

For several weeks, I rehearsed the Brahms Horn Trio with two

Juilliard students. We played it for Felix Galimir at Juilliard. It was intimidating to find myself in the institution that had turned me away five years earlier. Had Galimir been on the jury? I don't remember whether he asked me who my teacher was. At any rate he was thoroughly accommodating. He told me, memorably, that I should play the opening violin melody as if my bow were 'six feet long'. Our performance, at the Liederkranz Foundation cultural centre on East 87th Street, was spoiled by a serious contretemps. The pianist, in what I thought was a surfeit of enthusiasm, took huge liberties with the tempo—rushing, to put it bluntly, beyond anything we had rehearsed. I committed the unforgiveable sin of showing my displeasure during the performance, strenuously and conspicuously trying to pull in the reins, once even stamping my foot. Afterwards we had words. She was furious. I was adamantly unrepentant. I had made a serious mistake; indeed I had acted childishly, not only on the human level, but also on the professional level. It is counterproductive to compromise a performance, as I had done, no matter how justified one feels. Respect for the audience takes precedence over *amour-propre*.

In the spring of 1966, I attended a few informal conducting 'lessons' given by Stokie in his apartment, along with three or four other young hopefuls. He told us to raise questions of conducting technique or interpretation. I remember that I (naively?) asked about the technique of beating time in the second bar of Beethoven's *Egmont* overture and in similar subsequent bars. I was puzzled by the problem of indicating the precise durations, that is the cut-offs, of the minims (half notes), which have staccato dots. It seemed to me, and still does, that when beating three beats to the bar, whether subdivided or not, the task is next to impossible without an absurdly complicated intervention of the left hand between beats (unless the conductor is content to have these notes reduced to crotchets/quarter notes). I don't remember what Stokie said, but the answer became apparent to me not long afterwards: there is no need to indicate precisely these niceties of articulation. The space between the two minims is almost automatically determined if, as is usually done, they are both played with down bows. A reasonably good orchestra will agree on the length of these notes, with a brief verbal prompt by the conductor in the rehearsal (if necessary), who needs only to give the tempo and leave the articulation to the instinct and collective musicianship of the players.

Beethoven: *Egmont* overture, bars 1–4, strings only shown.

Stokie very generously gave each of us in the group twenty minutes of the American Symphony Orchestra's rehearsal time in which to conduct a movement or an excerpt of our choice. I did the last movement, the passacaglia, of Brahms's Fourth Symphony. It was an adventurous choice, full of changes of tempo and metre. I managed to negotiate the technical problems but had little left over to interpret or shape the music.

Villa Cimbrone, May 2015. Due obeisance, though it is Garbo's plaque; Stokie is a mere accessory to her secret happiness.

Leopold Stokowski died in 1977, but I encountered his shade unexpectedly, long afterwards on a visit to the Amalfi coast of Italy. On a wall of the Villa Cimbrone,   perhaps   the   most magnificently situated villa in Italy, near Ravello, on a high promontory overlooking the Gulf of Salerno, there is a marble plaque with the words 'Qui nella primavera del 1938 la divina Greta Garbo, sottraendosi al clamore di Hollywood, conobbe con Leopold Stokowsky ore di segreta felicità' ('Here in the spring of 1938 the divine Greta Garbo, escaping the clamour of Hollywood, experienced with Leopold Stokowski hours of secret happiness').

Intermezzo: sporting life

Our mother taught my brother and me to skate, pushing kitchen chairs around on a small home-made ice rink in our back yard. I love to skate and have always gone out of my way to skate whenever an opportunity presented itself. In my second year at Acadia University, in an intramural hockey game, I collided on the ice with a boy who was holding his stick in such a way (deliberately? Perhaps not—he was a theology student) that the end poked violently into my ribs. Most of us wore no protective gear—no helmet, no pads, nothing at all. The doctor told me that I had probably cracked a rib; he taped it up and sent me home. I was inordinately proud of this battle injury and still am, though all trace of it has gone. But it was the last hockey game I ever played.

As a young man living in New York City, I often went skating in Madison Square Garden, which, though sometimes crowded, at least was big enough for one to get up some speed. I enjoyed being the fastest in the rink, a winged superior being, feeling very smart and athletic in a brilliant cobalt-blue knitted sweater my mother had given me, weaving circles around the mere mortals. More than once, the officials in charge asked me to slow down, but I never bumped into anyone (the reader will understand my efforts to be modest). Years later, on one of my winter trips to Turin to do research in the national archives, seeing to my surprised delight that an ice rink had been set up in the central piazza, just a few yards from the archives, I immediately rented a pair of skates (too effete, too much like figure skates, not nearly enough like my own old hockey skates, but nothing else was on offer). Many years had passed since I had last skated, but, like riding a bicycle and other things learned in childhood, the knack of skating returns quickly, and I did a few turns. That was twenty years ago. I dare say the good burghers of Turin are still talking about it in the bars in the Piazza Castello. It goes without saying that, by Canadian standards, I am a mediocre skater.

Nottingham, about 2010. I leave in my wake a man who has fallen, thunderstruck.

In New York City, I went through a phase of obsession with chess, now thankfully only a distant, uncomfortable memory. I spent too much money and too much time on chess manuals—*Modern Chess Strategy, How to Think Ahead in Chess* and the like. I haunted the Manhattan Chess Club on 42nd Street (the website of the club suggests a different address, but my memory feels secure on this point), then a pretty sleazy part of town. This lasted for one or two years. I would go on the subway after midnight (the place stayed open most of the night) and play with one or two of the chess sharks who lay in wait for easy prey like me. You paid these men a dollar for a game, as I recall, and of course I always lost. I have no talent whatsoever for chess, which I refused to accept. I would come home on the subway at around 3 a.m., dazed and frustrated, aware that it could be dangerous at that hour, but unable to desist. Even after this delirious phase, I maintained for some time an unrequited, sporadic devotion before my passion gradually cooled; I'm not sure why. Perhaps it was because I read in Rousseau's *Confessions* that he too went through an obsessive chess phase, before finally admitting to himself that he had no talent for it. This comforted me. I still occasionally try to solve chess problems in newspapers and magazines; when I succeed (rarely), I swell with pride all out of proportion to the accomplishment, as I did when, as a teenager, I managed to solve a geometry problem in school.

CHAPTER 5

Boston

In the spring of 1966, I decided that I needed either to pursue a doctorate at a university or to get a permanent job, possibly in Europe. I wrote letters of application, filled out forms, gathered recommendations and prepared tape recordings. In March, I wrote to my mother, 'I'm writing to 5 orchestras in London to see if they have openings for next year. … I still haven't heard from the Concertgebouw.' Again, towards the end of the month:

> Still no word from the Concertgebouw. This afternoon I am auditioning for the London Symphony Orchestra which is playing here in NYC this week [I have no recollection of this audition. Was I offered a job?]. I have pretty well decided, though, not to go to Europe next year, tho if nothing comes through satisfactorily re. schools in the USA [I had applied to Eastman, Indiana University and Boston University for a graduate fellowship in their doctoral programmes] I might go, if I get the London job, tho I suppose they will want to know whether I intend to join them before I hear from the schools. It's all very confusing and annoying! But as you say it will all work out for the best.

Sometime in April, I heard from the Concertgebouw Orchestra—they asked for a tape, but by then I had decided on Boston University.

In June, I participated in the Montreal International Musical Competition, which that year was for violinists. I began practising the test pieces well before I knew whether I would even be invited to participate. I entered the competition for the experience, knowing full well that I stood little or no chance of passing even the first round. In fact, I didn't get past the first round, but having to learn so much difficult repertory, including the first movement of Bartók's solo sonata, was a valuable, albeit exhausting, learning experience. The day before I was to play, I received a telephone call telling me what pieces I would be asked to play. I scribbled the information on the inside cover of Wieniawski's *Scherzo Tarantelle*, where it remains: 'Bach [G minor solo sonata] 1st mov complete, 2nd mov stop at beginning of bar 52; Paganini [Caprice] #13 complete; Ysaÿe [*Ballade*] complete; Beethoven F major [*Romance*] stop after the passage in F minor. Come 45 min before calling.' I had never played the Beethoven *Romance* with the accompaniment, and I had never played any of the pieces for an audience, except for the Bach. O innocence! And yet I was twenty-five years old …

The Russian players, with their rigorous selection at an early age, and their state-controlled, extremely thorough preparation, including numerous performances of the competition pieces in Russia, assured their superiority over most of the other participants. I saw and heard the living vindication of Mr Bronstein's opinion. But I do recall an exquisitely poetic rendition of the slow movement of Mozart's Concerto in D major by the American violinist Donald Weilerstein, later the first violinist of the Cleveland Quartet and a distinguished pedagogue.

It was Raphael Bronstein who had suggested that I go to Boston University to study with Roman Totenberg when I told him I wanted to get a doctorate in music, with a view to pursuing an academic career, or at least having an academic career as an option. Once again, I was hedging my bets.

When I returned to NYC from Santa Fe in September 1966, I found that my girlfriend had fallen in love with someone else. I felt very sorry for myself on the train to Boston, and I must have told my mother about it. In two or three of her letters to me she comforted and advised me.

Now Warwick, about J, if you really feel that you want her to marry you do not just let it drop without a more ardent attempt. Maybe she just feels that you are not sufficiently in love with her. Many girls go thru such a stage—I did myself, and if you prove that you are really serious, they can be won. But then maybe you are not completely dedicated to the idea—what she said [in a letter to me] was quite true—you seemed to me to admire her tremendously and to enjoy her friendship, but not to be really in love with her. I should not advise but if you feel strongly enough do not give up on the first refusal. Sometimes the feminine ego simply requires a little more than just a perfunctory proposal. But then, you know the situation better than I do. I just feel sad if you are unhappy about it all.

The voice of experience—Mum surely was remembering Harold Henderson, whom she had refused thirty-four years earlier.

At Boston University, School of Fine and Applied Arts, I had a fellowship as assistant conductor of the orchestra, which involved playing in the orchestra and conducting its rehearsals when Walter Eisenberg, the faculty conductor, was away conducting the Colorado Springs Symphony. I wrote in my pocket agenda on 14 September: 'wrote theory placement exam, didn't finish harmonization question' (my old nemesis—running out of time). On the 15th: 'Met Mr Eisenberg. He calls me "Buddy" already. I'm evidently to be his assistant. I listened to some auditions for the orch. with him.' Since I also carried, unwisely, a full course load including violin lessons (I also played for two seasons in the newly formed Boston Philharmonia), I simply did not have time to prepare for the orchestra rehearsals properly. I became adept at 'winging it' through large portions of the repertory (my agenda: Monday, 10 October 1966: 'W.E. back to Boston. But be prepared to conduct today'), but on the whole it was a glorious opportunity somewhat wasted. It was the first of two occasions when I spread myself too thin as a conductor, and I regret it in both cases, not only for my own development as a musician but also for the students in the orchestra. Mr Eisenberg would often call me on the telephone, usually quite late at night, and talk at great length about nothing in particular. Perhaps he was lonely and simply needed someone to talk to. Not being the chatty type, I'm afraid I was not an ideal conversational partner for him.

Roman Totenberg was the first internationally known soloist with whom I had studied; I felt when he demonstrated a passage that it had stood the test of performance in crowded halls with paying audiences, which lent his comments and suggestions a certain credibility. He was a charming, affable man, always generous with his time. As a teacher, he was perhaps not as demanding as he might have been; on the other hand, he may have seen that I was strapped for time to prepare for my lessons. With him I worked on the Berg Concerto, Beethoven's 'Kreutzer' Sonata, Ravel's *Tzigane* and Saint-Saëns' *Havanaise*. Quite characteristic was his casual, almost absent-minded demonstration during a lesson in which I was struggling with a fiendish (for me) passage of chromatic double-stopped thirds in the *Havanaise*. He said, 'Yes, you could do it that way'—a kind of shimmying glissando up the fingerboard with one pair of fingers—'or you could try it this way', as he played the entire passage with the much more difficult alternating fingering 1/3, 2/4. I nodded in agreement, but I might have said, 'Yes, *you* could.' At least he had demonstrated, however, that the thing was possible.

He asked me to conduct the Mozart Sinfonia Concertante in which he played the solo violin part, a student of his, the viola, the orchestra composed mostly of Boston University students, at a performance in Boston, I forget where. He seemed to enjoy himself enormously with this motley group and to be pleased with the performance. That he belonged to an earlier, courtly generation was brought home to me when I introduced him to my then wife, Barbara (we had married in 1968). As he bowed from the waist, I distinctly heard his heels click together.

It was also Totenberg who told me of the position of conductor of a youth orchestra in an outlying area of Boston. I accepted it, unwisely, as the time and energy required to do justice to the undertaking—eight weekly rehearsals and a concert—was, once again, not justified by the quality of the musical experience. It was a beginners' group, very elementary—I was more of a teacher than a conductor. In my inability to say 'No' I now know that I was in good company: when Gaetano Pugnani travelled to England in 1767, the Torinese foreign minister had written in his letter of introduction carried by Pugnani to the Torinese ambassador in London:

> No doubt, sir, you are already acquainted with Mr Pugnani, and you perhaps are not unaware that along with a great skill in his profession and many other qualities, he has a certain turn of mind that makes him prone to accept engagements easily. It is for this that he will have particular need of your good advice to guide him and to avoid those difficulties which the little acquaintance he has of the country he is entering could bring upon him.

Pugnani, whatever advice he was given, heeded it neither on this occasion (he overstayed his leave of absence from his position as orchestra leader in Turin by more than a year) nor on any other. I cannot say whether, had I been vouchsafed similar 'good advice' in Boston, I would have heeded it.

Kenneth Schermerhorn conducted one of the Boston Philharmonia concerts. I remember, especially, two things about him: that he could sol-fa with incredible facility and that once, in Schubert's Symphony in B-flat major, when we in the violins were having difficulty with a passage in fast sixteenth notes, he said, candidly but sympathetically, 'I'm afraid I can't help you with that; you'll have to work it out for yourselves.' It is odd what one remembers …

Another of our conductors was Michael Tilson Thomas, at the beginning of his career. I remember being impressed with how he dressed: a dark shirt with a subtly contrasting tie—very modern and Californian to my eye. But more important was his stopping the harpist in Webern's Symphony, Op. 21 to ask if a certain note she had played really was, say, F-sharp in her part? This in the context of one of the most rigorously twelve-tone, pointillistic pieces in the repertory. I thought, 'with an ear like that, this man will go places.'

An incident that occurred during a Boston Philharmonia rehearsal left a lasting impression on me. A woman sitting at the second stand of the violas suddenly broke down, sobbing: 'This man [apparently the principal violist] won't stop bullying me. I can't stand it any longer.' The conductor stopped the rehearsal until she calmed down, or absented herself, I can't remember which. I had the distinct impression that this was a conflict that had been some time in the making. It was my first encounter with the stress and personal frictions that can fester and sometimes explode in an orchestra.

In the summer of 1967, I taught violin and chamber music at the Governor's School in Winston-Salem, North Carolina, filling in for my Eastman classmate, Tom Moore. I played first violin in the faculty string quartet, the first time I had done so (the few times I had previously played in string quartets it was always as second violinist). We played Beethoven's Op. 74 at a faculty concert. Learning to play the cadenza at the end of the first movement was a decisive step in the development of both my technique and my self-confidence. That summer was my first sustained encounter with a southern USA accent. The following spring, the director called to ask me back for the next summer. I still remember the surreal, embarrassing experience of not understanding a word of whole tranches of what he said, though the telephone line was perfectly clear, and he spoke with a perfectly clear voice.

I had admired Tom Moore at Eastman—as a violinist and as a person. I got to know him well in my second year when he lived in the Carpenter boarding house. Later, we saw each other briefly at the Montreal violin competition. I was flattered that he had recommended me for the Governor's School job. We then lost touch with each other completely. He became second violinist of the Pro Arte Quartet and a faculty member at the University of Wisconsin, later at the University of Miami, Florida, where he established himself as a leading violin teacher. Early in 2010, after forty-four years, I took it into my head to write to him. He wrote back, told me that he had cancer, and agreed to come to Florence for a visit in May with his wife, Sandra. We talked, reminisced, played duets (including those of Viotti—I had recently finished my book on Viotti); he listened to me play the Schubert Sonata in A major,

D. 574, with a pianist, offered a few suggestions, gave me a bow arm 'lesson' in front of a mirror—he was a born teacher. He was clearly declining physically, his face ravaged and swollen with the side effects of chemotherapy, but I am sure that he enjoyed the week he spent with me. He became fond of one of our cats (Bibi—small, black, affectionate—of all our cats, the one we loved the most; when, ten years later, she died, we put a memorial plaque on our garden wall); once I saw him cup Bibi's head in his hands and plant a gentle, affectionate kiss on her cheek, a sight I will treasure always. Eight months later, Sandra wrote to me of his death, aged seventy-two, mourned by, among others, hundreds of his students.

In February 1968, I conducted the rehearsals and two concerts of the New Brunswick Symphony Orchestra, one in Fredericton and one in Saint John, substituting for the regular conductor, Janis Kalnins, who was ill. A day or two earlier, I spoke to Grammy on the phone. She was pleased with what I was doing and wished me good luck. In the middle of the night after the second concert, Mum and Dad and I, sharing a hotel room, received a phone call from Mum's brother informing her that Grammy had died. I took the early morning bus to Boston after a muted goodbye to my parents at the bus station.

The review in the Saint John *Evening Times-Globe* blazoned the headline 'Symphony Wins Standing Ovation', and was complimentary, except to say that in the Gluck–Wagner overture to *Iphigenia in Aulis*, 'He had at times a tendency to allow the violins to drag a bit behind in tempo while concentrating on the other strings and the woodwinds, but normally the drag was only half to a full beat and quickly rectified.' I am grateful that the drag was no more than that.

In 1968–69, Barbara and I lived in the lovely bucolic village of Hatfield in western Massachusetts. Barbara was in her senior year at Smith College; I wrote my thesis for the DMA [Doctor of Musical Arts] degree, played in the Springfield Symphony Orchestra, and took a course in Baroque Performance Practice at the Hartt School of Music, University of Hartford, to fulfil my Boston University course requirements. I had not done well in my doctoral oral examination; I was ignorant of wide swathes of music history and of the standard repertory. One of the questions put to me was about Mahler's symphonies—what is unusual about them? I was unable to say anything other than that they are long and require a large orchestra. I was also vague in my answer to a question about the origins and early history of the sonata for violin and keyboard. It was only when I came to teach music history fifteen years later that I began to plug these gaping holes in my knowledge.

Once a week, I drove the hundred miles or so to Boston to play second violin in a string quartet that played for the Boston public schools and to teach violin at All Newton Music School on Chestnut Street in West Newton. Playing in the quartet was another taste of what it might be like to play in a serious professional group, but the experience was too brief, too fleeting to do much more than whet my appetite.

By this time, at twenty-eight years old, I was beginning to feel like a professional student. It was time for a change. It seems extraordinary, but as late as the end of April 1969 I still did not know what I would be doing the next season—still casting about, still auditioning. As luck would have it, there were no violin openings in the Concertgebouw Orchestra. I made a tape recording, including a few orchestral excerpts, and sent it to the Netherlands Radio Omroep [Broadcasting] Orchestra.

I went to NYC to audition for Italo Gómez, the cellist and director of the Orchestra Michelangelo di Firenze, then on a tour of the USA. He wrote me a kind letter of recommendation, which I still have and, as I wrote to Mum, 'He more or less offered me a job with them but when I found out they spend a lot of time touring (10 weeks in America, etc.), it seemed senseless for us to go to la bella Italia only to race back here and tour America in a bus.' Also in NYC, I played part of a rehearsal with the English Chamber Orchestra, a kind of try-out, sitting beside the leader, Kenneth Sillito, Daniel Barenboim conducting, with the twenty-year-old Pinchas Zukerman playing Mozart's Concerto No. 4. At one point in the rehearsal, Barenboim made a joke about Zukerman's 'weak tone'. I wish I could remember more about that rehearsal, and I wonder what impression, if any, I made on Sillito, who was less than two years older than I, and had only recently become leader of the English Chamber Orchestra. Apparently, I acquitted myself sufficiently well that I was made an offer, though I do not remember what the offer was, who made it, or how it was made. I told my mother 'I have not yet accepted as I still have a few other things I am inquiring into, e.g. to play in an orchestra in Hilversum, Holland, near Amsterdam, which I think I would prefer over London.' My reason for this preference is now lost on me.

Barbara and I decided to go to the Netherlands (did I write a letter of non-acceptance to the English Chamber Orchestra? I hope it was polite), where I had been hired as assistant principal of the second violins in the Omroep Orchestra. When I told my father I was going to live in Europe, he said, 'Alright, you might as well go and get it out of your system.'

I wrote to my mother:

Boston, Wed. night, 9.30 p.m., Sept. 10, 1969

Hello hello,

Well here it is—on the eve of our departure across the bright blue sea to remote foreign strands. I came into Boston this morning on the bus from Northampton to do a few errands—had a session with my advisor on my thesis—it needs a fair amount of correction and revising, but in general he approves of it—which is something. …

Barbara is staying at a friend's place near Northampton for today and tonight, and tomorrow we meet in New York City at around 12 noon at the Port Authority terminal (39th & 8th Ave.)—(dramatic, eh!), and thence to the pier (at the foot of West 52nd St, on the Hudson River), where the Queen Elizabeth II will be waiting in all its splendid majesty, and at 4.30 p.m. (punctually I'm sure), her great turbines will throb and rumble, with Captain William Warwick issuing crisp nautical orders in a clipped British accent—'All engines astern!', 'Mind that line off the port bow!!' … and we will pull out into New

York harbour, past the Statue of Liberty, with a full array of flags, tug-boats and amidst general hue and cry, on our way to la belle France and so to Hilversum by train. I'm very excited by it all and look forward to a worthwhile and interesting year.

CHAPTER 6

Amsterdam, Northampton

We lived in Amsterdam, and I bicycled to the railway station for the half-hour train commute to Hilversum. The Omroep Orkest (now no longer in existence) was the second orchestra of the Dutch Radio, less grand, in both senses of the word, than the Radio Philharmonic. Barbara and I took Dutch lessons and learned to speak it reasonably well.

In October, I had five days off and we went to Stuttgart to visit one of Barbara's former professors at Smith, Philipp Naegele. His wife, Susie, took us to have tea with an old friend of theirs, a distinguished, gracious lady of about seventy-five. In her sitting room, there was a photograph of a young man in a Wehrmacht officer's uniform, clearly dating from World War II. Our hostess said, 'Das ist mein sohn, aber nicht SS' ['That is my son, but not SS'].

My letter to my mother, 7 November 1969:

Last night our orchestra gave a concert in the big, new, modern concert hall in Rotterdam (about 1 hr train ride from Amsterdam). We had a cello soloist, Paul Tortelier, a marvellous player. It was really a fine concert. He played the Elgar Concerto—a very beautiful piece and he really did some of the finest, most moving playing I have ever heard. Anyway, I feel a bit better about the orchestra—it can play well. Tortelier is French, and he is très agréable—with a beautiful, long, high-cheek-boned face, magnificent patrician nose and leonine white and grey pompadour of hair. He seems about 50ish, but has one of those ageless faces.

As the autumn wore on I became increasingly aware that my violin was not the one that I wanted to play on for the rest of my life. I thought I deserved something better. Most string players go through this stage, sometimes several times. It can be agonizing, both the initial decision and the process of finding a suitable instrument. In Amsterdam, I found a violin by Paolo Testore that I liked very much. I wrote to my mother:

Now, here is something very important: for the last few weeks I have been looking for a good violin. Violins are considerably cheaper in Europe than in the U.S.A. A good violin is a most imp. Factor when one is seeking a performance position of any sort—orchestral, concertmaster, quartet, etc. For one thing, when you audition for an orchestra, they always ask you what kind of violin do you have—it weighs heavily in the balance.

So, after considerable hunting and asking around, I have found what I think is a superb violin. It is a Testore—one of the great makers, only slightly below the rank of Stradivarius and Guarnerius. It is in almost flawless condition, beautiful tone, rich and noble, not overly brilliant or big in sound, but marvellously even throughout its entire range (which is a tremendous virtue)—a dark sonorous, rich G string sound, unusually rich D string sound, fine A string sound, and the E string very sweet but not as brilliant as some violinists might like—but I like it—because I don't want great power & brilliance—enough to fill Yankee Stadium, as is the fashion nowadays—no—I prefer a rounder, less penetrating sound, especially since the bulk of my playing will be chamber music—quartets, vln. & piano sonatas, etc.—not so much concertos with orchestras. Testore lived in the early 18th century— roughly contemporary with Stradivarius.

The price is rather high: 12,000 guilders, which comes to $3,500 in U.S. dollars (1 guilder = 28 American cents). I can't be sure, but I would say this violin would cost around $5,000 in the U.S.A. I think the time is now ripe for me to get a good violin—prices of violins are skyrocketing—they have <u>doubled</u> in the last 10 years, and still rising, so I think I should strike while the iron is hot.

I then go on to ask my mother to cash whatever assets I had (that my parents had invested for me in Canada) to pay for the violin ('of course it will be more than $3,500 [in Canadian funds]'). And I close with, 'I hope you think I'm doing the right thing.' I can only attribute my rather shocking inflation of Paolo Testore's rank to my ignorance, especially since I apparently had not troubled to find out which Testore it was. Or was I knowingly stacking the cards so as to convince my mother, replete with underlining of key words? And what of my unblinking confidence that my career was destined to unfold ('the bulk of my playing') in the higher realms of chamber music? This from a twenty-eight-year-old playing in the second violins of a second-tier radio orchestra.

Two weeks later, I tell my mother that I have received the money.

Thank you very much for looking after it so quickly. However, I am now beginning to think I was perhaps a little rash to jump at this violin. It is by <u>Paolo</u> Testore, the younger son of the family. Neither of the sons are nearly as highly regarded as their father ... So, after thinking <u>very</u> hard about the matter (in fact I'm having a terrible time deciding), I am beginning to think that perhaps $3,500 is a bit too much to pay for this violin, though I do like it. But I think I could find something better for the money. With all that in mind I went to London yesterday—took the night ferry over—and spent the day in London and came back last night. London is a violin-dealers center—perhaps the greatest in the world, so I thought I should go and see what I could find there to compare with the Testore. I went to Hill's and another well-known dealer, Beare's. Hill didn't have anything I especially liked, but Beare's had a lovely violin by Stainer—the greatest of the German makers. It has a <u>beautiful</u> tone (perhaps even more beautiful than the Testore), and for 3 years was played by the concertmaster of the London Symphony, and costs only 1,200 pounds (c. $2,900; £1=$2.40), about $600 less than the Testore.[15]

However, the whole business is frustratingly inconclusive because the room in Beare's in which I played the Stainer had very echoey acoustics—enough to make <u>any</u> violin sound great—and they don't allow you to take instruments out of England on approval, so I have no way of having the Testore and the Stainer in the same place at the same time to compare them. You see it is a tremendous problem. I may just go back to London once more and try and find a room with 'deader' acoustics so I can see how big a sound the Stainer has—I think I can remember pretty well how the Testore sounds—and make my decision. … Another factor with the Stainer is its great antiquity—it has been repaired several times, and is not in as good condition as the Testore, probably not as durable or structurally sound as the Testore, and not as likely to stand up under punishment (such as changing weather conditions) as the Testore. So—quelle dilemma, n'est-ce pas? I'll keep you informed.

A month later:

I am very pleased and relieved to report that, after much deliberation, I bought the Stainer. We went to London on Dec. 26, stayed two nights. I played the Stainer all day in a lecture room in the place we stayed (a hotel run by Quakers—a marvellous place),[16] and in between

---

[15] The present price of a Stainer violin hovers around $90,000. In 2011 one was sold for $331,768. In the early 1970s a Stradivarius violin cost in the region of $50,000 to $100,000. In 1971, one was sold by Sotheby's for $201,000, a record high. The present price is roughly $2 m to $3 m. In 2011 one was sold at Tarisio for $15,821,285.

[16] The Penn Club, in Bedford Place, just off Russell Square, indeed was a marvellous place; it became my home away from home more than 30 years later, on my several trips to London to do research on G. B. Viotti. Virginia Woolf would have approved. I see that it is about to relocate to another part of London (2021).

playing we went to the British Museum. Anyway I finally decided to take it and be done with it. It is really a beautiful violin. I checked very carefully into its condition—perhaps I gave you the wrong idea about it before—it is not in bad condition by any means. Did I tell you, its former owner was the concertmaster of the London Symphony (he still is). I phoned him up and had a <u>long</u> talk with him about it and I am quite satisfied I have not made a mistake. It has a lovely tone—very different from the Testore, but on the whole better, I think. The Testore had a magnificent G & D string, but the E and A lacked character. On the Stainer all 4 strings have a marvellous character—unique, intimate, tender, sweet, not terribly big or powerful, but carrying. This was my chief worry about it at first—that it did not have a <u>big</u> enough tone (this is why Stradivarius violins have become more highly regarded than Stainer—because they have a bigger tone, to meet the demands of modern concert halls and orchestras, but for 100 years or so (until around 1800) Stainer's violins were <u>more</u> highly regarded than Strad's). However, the room I tried it out in in London gave me a pretty good idea of its power, and also the London Symph. Concertmaster told me he played all the big concertmaster's solos on it—in halls all over the world, and he never felt it wasn't big enough. His recording of the violin solo of Rimsky Korsakov's Scheherazade was played on this violin, 2 or 3 years ago.[17] Well, enough—it's a marvellous violin, and I'm glad I've got it. I can hardly wait till you hear it. It was made in 1659.

What I did not make clear to my mother (and which was the deciding factor, for all the rationalizing and financial calculating) was that from the moment I began to play the Stainer in the Beare shop I fell immediately in love with it—its refined, silken tone and its responsiveness, how easy it was to draw the sound from it. I did indeed have a long telephone talk with the Stainer's former owner, John Georgiadis (it now occurs to me that if, in fact, I did audition for the London Symphony Orchestra in NYC in March 1966, he might very

---

[17] In fact, it was recorded in 1968, with Andre Previn conducting.

well have heard me, but, if so, neither of us remembered it), and I did manage (no doubt trying his patience, though he was unfailingly polite) to get him to admit that the reason he sold the Stainer and bought a Guadagnini was the bigger sound of the latter.[18] Again, was I being economical with the truth to reassure my mother on this score, or was it to reassure myself? At any rate, for nine years, the violin proved to be all that I had hoped it would be. It had a magnificent, light golden finish, and the typical Stainer rather high belly. Contrary to my fears, it was robust and resistant to all the hard knocks that an instrument receives on orchestra tours—unceremoniously packed into large cases and stuffed into the holds of aeroplanes and trucked to concert halls, for example. And the longer I played it, the more familiar with it I became, the more I grew attached to it. It was just affordable; at today's prices, it would be unthinkable.

Restless with ambition, I applied in the spring of 1970 for various positions, including that of concertmaster of the Nashville (Tennessee) Symphony. I sent them a tape of my playing and as much supporting material as I could muster. I also auditioned in person for a position in the second violins in the Concertgebouw Orchestra. I received a long-distance call from the manager of the Nashville Symphony, who told me that the conductor, Thor Johnson, wanted me to have the position and asked me what salary I was asking!

In the meantime, I learned that I had been offered the Concertgebouw Orchestra job. I wrote to my mother:

> I have decided to do this instead of the Nashville concertmaster job. It was a tough decision—Nashville wrote me a lovely letter back, agreeing to pay me $10,000, and enclosed a program of the forthcoming season … all very attractive, but I decided that at this point in my career it would be better for me to play in a really good orchestra for a while, and then look for a concertmaster job, when I would be better prepared for it … I have turned down prestige and 'big' money for a better musical experience—noble of me, eh! …

---

[18] Georgiadis confirms this in his *Bow to Baton: A Leader's Life* (2019), p. 395.

I telegrammed Nashville last night, with my regrets, and am sending them a letter tomorrow.

I sometimes wonder how my life and career would have proceeded if I had accepted the Nashville job. But I have no doubt that I made the right decision, and for the right reasons, though it is true that afterwards I never obtained the concertmaster position of a full-time symphony orchestra.

I joined the Concertgebouw Orchestra in August of 1970. A few months later (after another audition), I entered the first violins. The magnificent Concertgebouw ('Concert building'), with its renowned acoustics, was a joy to play in. The orchestra has a distinguished history. Willem Mengelberg, who was its conductor from 1895 to 1945, was the dedicatee of Strauss's *Ein Heldenleben*, and Mahler conducted the orchestra in several of his symphonies. Seated in the orchestra during rehearsals, and, dare I say it, during concerts as well, I could look up at the names of famous composers in cartouches on the boxes all around the theatre (some of the names, such as Sweelinck, are more famous for the Dutch than for others).

With the principal conductor, Bernard Haitink, and the principal guest conductor, Eugen Jochum, the orchestra leaned towards heavier Germanic fare, notably Bruckner and Mahler. The first concerts I played in with the orchestra were four programmes in the BBC Proms in the Royal Albert Hall in early September: Beethoven *Missa Solemnis* (Jochum), Strauss *Don Juan*, Berlioz *Symphonie fantastique*, Mahler No. 9, Tchaikovsky No. 6, leavened by Mozart (the *Serenata Notturna*, K. 239 and Clifford Curzon in the Piano Concerto No. 24) and Mendelssohn (Wallez in the Violin Concerto). After the last concert, as the bus left to take us back to our hotel, we were thronged by a crowd of very young people, shouting compliments, clapping and waving goodbye. I have never, before or since, felt such satisfaction after playing in an orchestral concert. Was it typical of Proms audiences in those days?

From London, we went directly to the Edinburgh Festival: three concerts including *Das Lied von der Erde* with Janet Baker and

Beethoven's Piano Concerto No. 1 with Alfred Brendel. Then, after two concerts in the Beethoven Festival in Bonn (21, 22 September), back to the Concertgebouw, with David Oistrakh playing the Brahms Concerto (7, 8, 11 October), followed by Fischer-Dieskau singing Mahler's *Lieder eines fahrenden Gesellen* (16th) and *Kindertotenlieder* (18th, 19th). All of this within a little over six weeks after joining the orchestra! To be in the company of such illustrious artists was a heady experience.

For recordings, the orchestra was placed in the auditorium of the theatre, the seats removed. Henryk Szeryng, suave, supremely confident, an almost supercilious smile on his face, recorded Brahms's Double Concerto with János Starker, and the two Beethoven *Romances* as if to say, 'Look here; this is how easy it is.' On another occasion, during a recording of Bruckner's Sixth Symphony, a passage with a prominent, sustained, rather high solo horn part needed to be repeated several times. The first horn player, whose name I don't remember, played it over and over again, impeccably—a heroic feat of endurance and professionalism that made a deep impression on me.

In April 1971, the orchestra went on a six-week tour of the USA, Mexico and South America. My mother and father came to New York City to hear us play. I introduced my mother to Haitink while he was having breakfast in the hotel café. Haitink was gracious and polite; my mother was moved to write a letter to him that he received later during the tour. From Mexico City I wrote to her that 'Mr. Haitink appreciated your letter very much—asked me to thank you.' The odd thing is that Haitink later wrote a letter of recommendation for me when I left the Concertgebouw to take up a position in the USA—in which he says that I am a 'good but rather shy musician'. I am at a loss to understand why he had this opinion of me. Surely there was nothing shy about introducing my mother to him. I cannot recall conversing with him at any other time. How in the world did he come to think I was shy? Or did he think my playing was shy? But, again, the only time he heard me play alone was in my audition to enter the orchestra, when I played the first two or three pages of the Sibelius Concerto, which, if I say so myself, I did with a degree of panache.

Four of the major pieces of our programmes were precisely those that we had played seven months earlier in the Proms: Berlioz, Strauss, Tschaikovsky and Mahler, along with Ravel's *Ma Mère l'Oye* and Bartók's Concerto for Orchestra and several other works. We played twice in Carnegie Hall, where I had last played with Stokowski in May of 1966, then twelve concerts on the West Coast, from Seattle to Los Angeles; five in Mexico City; two in Willemstad, the capital city of Curaçao, with its charming Dutch colonial architecture; one in Caracas; five in the huge Teatro Colón in Buenos Aires; two in São Paolo; and one in Rio de Janeiro. Non-musicians are apt to imagine that grand tours of this sort are glamorous and exciting. This may be so early in one's career, but the tedium and fatigue, the repeated cycle of bus, plane, bus, hotel, bus, rehearsal, concert and hotel begins to tell. There are occasional days off, which can be enjoyable. In Buenos Aires, some of us went to a professional tango performance, the first time I had seen this twitchy, nervously erotic dance. But these occasions were rare.

Haitink had begun conducting in England extensively and was beginning his long romance with the British public and critics. As for the Concertgebouw Orchestra, however, older players said that the glory days were in Mengelberg's time, or even van Beinum's, and that the orchestra had slipped in quality ever since. As there was no one in the orchestra from Mengelberg's time, it was hard to verify these assertions. Haitink did not particularly impress me. I know that in this I am flying in the face of the critical and public consensus regarding his performances and recordings. My impression was that he was a solid but uninspired musician. Though he often seemed to be trying to elicit something more impassioned, more personal, his gestures and podium presence rarely rose above the ordinary, at least for me. His relationship with the orchestra was cordial, though I think the fact that a few members of the orchestra had been his classmates in the Amsterdam Conservatory compromised, to an extent, the authority that a conductor ideally exerts over an orchestra. This situation, of course, did not obtain when he conducted foreign orchestras.

Since writing the foregoing paragraph, I saw a television video of Haitink conducting the Vienna Philharmonic in Bruckner's Seventh

Symphony in 2019, when he was ninety years old. I was moved to revise my opinion. He was frail, walked on stage with a cane, his gestures economical and more meaningful than I had remembered them, the score lying unopened on the stand. His eyes, now heavily lidded with age, roamed searchingly, authoritatively, over the entire orchestra, and he elicited from the players what can only be described as an inspired, compelling performance. I tried to recall how I had felt playing this very piece under him in my early thirties, he in his early forties, and I tried to imagine myself playing under him now in this televised performance. Was it Haitink who had matured, gained in musical wisdom, or was it I? Or, I hope, both?

Among the guest conductors were Carlo Maria Giulini, Mario Rossi, David Zinman, Lorin Maazel and Kirill Kondrashin. When Giulini appeared at the first rehearsal, I was taken aback by his coiffure, sumptuously done up in the most extreme Italian style, and by his pained grimace when beginning a piece. But his gracious manner and unassertive musicianship won me over, despite his sometimes-ponderous tempos. Mario Rossi, who had recently stepped down as the conductor of the radio orchestra in Turin, was a pleasant surprise. I had never heard of him. More than once, he enjoined the orchestra to 'sing' when he clearly thought that we weren't. His interpretation of Dallapiccola's *Variazioni per Orchestra* was a revelation—supple, dramatic and, above all, lyrical. The American David Zinman, who then was the second conductor of the Netherlands Chamber Orchestra, conducted us in a memorable performance of Debussy's *La Mer*—his gestural control was masterly. Equally memorable, but for different reasons, was Lorin Maazel. A prodigiously gifted musician, he was acerbic and utterly lacking in warmth. At one point in a rehearsal of Brahms's Symphony No. 2, when a passage was not going as he wished, he said (in English), 'Now you are beginning to irritate me.' This did not sit well with the orchestra. In the opening bar of the Brahms symphony, he asked the cellos to play a slight *crescendo* to the C-sharp in the middle of the bar, then a *diminuendo* away from it; in Strauss's *Don Juan* he was not happy with the concertmaster Jo Juda's *tempo rubato* (actually a slight slowing down) of the first solo, insisting that he play it strictly in tempo. His control over an orchestra, his stick technique, was exemplary, apart from a tendency to over-subdivide beats with miniature flicks of the stick, fluent and visually impressive, but serving no practical purpose for the orchestra that I could see. He played Mozart's Violin Concerto No. 5, quite well, in another concert that he conducted. Kirill Kondrashin was a virtuoso conductor. His *Petrouchka* was an unforgettable tour de force of powerful, compelling intensity. Kondrashin came to our apartment for tea one afternoon, with some orchestra members. When someone asked him (indiscreetly) what he thought of Haitink, he paused and said, 'Well, you can learn from anyone, even from their mistakes.'

One morning, we had begun a rehearsal when the tenor soloist, a young, affable German, came rushing in, flustered and out of breath, and apologized for being late. He had asked for directions to the Concertgebouw but had lost his way—perhaps, he asked, he had misunderstood the directions? Later, a Dutch colleague told me that the Dutch sometimes deliberately give wrong directions to German tourists.

In April 1972, we made a whirlwind tour of Switzerland and Germany: in twelve days we played eleven concerts in ten cities (two in the Philharmonie in Berlin).

I wrote to Mum:

We were in Berlin for 3 days—I went to East Berlin (through 'the wall') twice, and a very strange experience it was. Once, just as I was walking up to a museum [the superb Pergamon Museum], I looked into a side street, and there stood about 50 big mean-looking tanks and a bunch of soldiers standing around with machine guns slung over their shoulders. Also, I ate dinner in a hotel-restaurant one night in East Berlin, and peeked into a sort of side-conference room and saw about a half-dozen Chinese (Communist of course) big brass military men seated at a banquet table with their East German counterparts. It gave me the feeling of being alone in the enemy camp.

I don't know why I chose to eat dinner in an East Berlin hotel—perhaps to use up my East German marks. I have no recollection of it. I am struck by the difference between my memory of these incidents and my description in my letter. Above all, did one of the soldiers unsling his machine gun and menace me with it, so that I retreated very quickly, as I now remember? Did I suppress this detail in order not to alarm my mother? Or have I embroidered the story in my mind with the passing of time? It is clear to me now, as it wasn't then, that the tanks were there at the ready as much to quell any popular disturbance or uprising in the city as to use against Western forces. And it occurs to me that on both occasions I could very well have been arrested (and kept in jail until 1989, or worse?).

In June of 1972, David Oistrakh conducted us in a concert in which he played Mozart's Concerto No. 5 and which included Weber's *Oberon* overture and Wagner excerpts. I remember his modest, soft-spoken manner (he spoke German to us) and his wonderfully pure, natural playing.

In 1970–71, I took fifteen violin lessons from Jo Juda, who in 1930–31 had studied with Carl Flesch in Berlin. I was thirty years old, but still felt the chill wind of technical inadequacy—that I had not yet reached my potential as a violinist. I still have the notebook in which he wrote out each lesson assignment: Flesch scales and double stops; Dont Op. 35 études Nos. 3, 17, 18, 1, 8, 23, 20; Kreutzer nos. 11, 13; Bach D minor Partita: Allemande, Courante, Sarabande, Gigue; Vieuxtemps *Ballade et Polonaise* ('helemaal uit het hoofd'—'entirely from memory').

Afterwards, for about a year and a half, I studied with Isidor Lateiner, a concert violinist, who was demanding and uncompromising—just what I needed. He thought my vibrato was too slow and 'wobbly', as he put it, and with time and effort I learned to play with a faster, narrower vibrato when I felt the music required it. He believed that for every note on the fingerboard, depending on the context, there is an ideal position of the left hand, wrist and arm, all three of which should move in such a way as to support and facilitate finger motion. This is quite opposed to a technique in which the hand is kept relatively stable, the fingers themselves doing the work. He also advocated a kind of symmetrical opposing motion of the bow and the violin: moving the violin (only slightly) to the left on down bows, to the right on upbows. I still find this to be a helpful, tension-reducing habit that facilitates bow changes, obviously not to be followed slavishly nor exaggerated.[19]

I studied the Vieuxtemps Concerto No. 4 and Bach's Solo Partita in B minor with Lateiner, as well as music for a recital in De Suite recital hall and a shared recital in the Kleine Zaal of the Concertgebouw, sponsored by the orchestra, the other half given by a cellist in the orchestra, Lim Kek Beng. (Lim Kek, a charming Chinese-Indonesian, sometimes greeted me before morning orchestra rehearsals with the words, 'Ah, Warwick, this morning I practised for two hours—these stupid skills.') My wife, Barbara, was my pianist. For the Kleine Zaal concert we played Mozart's Sonata in E minor, K. 304; *Three Miniatures* by Penderecki; *Choses Vues à Droite et à Gauche (sans lunettes)* by Satie; and Brahms's A major Sonata. Both concerts were reviewed in the Amsterdam newspapers; it was the first time my playing had been reviewed. Several phrases were useful for my CV,[20] though both reviewers also had reservations about my playing, as well they might have. But the compliment that meant most to me came from the concertmaster of the Concertgebouw Orchestra, Herman Krebbers, who, as I was warming up in my chair just before a rehearsal, put a hand on my shoulder and said a few kind, encouraging words. He had not been to the recital in De Suite, but had heard about it from someone who had. Barbara and I played two or three other recitals in Amsterdam and Haarlem, and three recordings for the Dutch radio, including the Schumann A minor, the Brahms A major and the Strauss sonatas.

Not long after joining the Concertgebouw Orchestra, I was asked to join a string quartet of which the first violinist was a concertmaster of

---

[19] It is, at any rate, far simpler than the tri-partite motion (first the body-swing, then the violin, then the bow change) described by Menuhin in the section 'Sympathetic movement of the body' in his *Violin: Six Lessons with Yehudi Menuhin* (1971), pp. 80–81.

[20] 'Exemplary lyricism in De Suite. Compelling violin-playing' (Het Parool); 'His sound is light and refined; the tone quality pure and elegant … great affinity for Mozart' (De Tijd).

the Netherlands Radio Philharmonic. He was Romanian; his wife, the cellist, Dutch; and the violist a Hungarian who had a tattooed number on his arm from Auschwitz, which he had survived as a boy put to work in the kitchen. We had many rehearsals; the first violinist was keen to have us play in a competition. I remember, in particular, the hard work we put into Beethoven's Op. 130. We asked the pianist Stephen Bishop (thirty years old, not yet Stephen Kovacevich), then in town playing a concerto with the Concertgebouw Orchestra, to listen to us. He was enthusiastic, full of ideas, and he told us how much he enjoyed doing it. Indeed, why should string quartets be advised only by string players? It can be liberating to hear what any good musician has to say.

I was placed in an excruciatingly difficult position when Lateiner told me that he would be unwilling to teach me if I continued with the quartet. I was forced to decide on the one hand between my love of quartet playing and, above all, my commitment to the others in the group, and on the other, my great need to improve my violin playing and to prepare for the recital in the Kleine Zaal. Lateiner said quite candidly that he felt his reputation as a teacher was at stake as, in his opinion, I did not have time enough to do both. It was one of the most agonizing decisions I have ever made. When I told the quartet that I was leaving the group, they were, as I had feared, and as could only be expected, hurt and resentful. It was a betrayal. I have never forgiven myself on the human level, but I am convinced that, from a purely selfish viewpoint, I made the right decision as a musician. I cannot deny that I may have been influenced by my feeling that as an ensemble we were not, and never could be, good enough to have a career as a professional quartet. It was the first in a life-long series of reversals in my relationship with string quartet playing. Not quite a poisoned chalice, but …

One day, I received a letter from Roman Totenberg telling me that he was going to be in Holland for a while and would I like to go with him on a little sightseeing tour? I arranged a rented car, and we went for a long day to various places in North Holland: Hoorn, Edam, Enkhuizen and other places. I wish I could remember more about that trip. Was it just the two of us, or did I bring along a friend? I do remember that Totenberg (and I) enjoyed it immensely. He was good company, very curious about the geography and history of Holland. These proud old Dutch towns are easily reached and splendidly full of character. Hoorn in particular made a lasting impression on me—a windy, salty, once powerful port still redolent of its Dutch Golden Age maritime history. It somehow reminded me of Yarmouth, Nova Scotia.

I decided to take the 1972–73 season off from the orchestra (or nearly off—I continued to play an occasional concert as a substitute) in order to devote myself to practising, raising the level of my playing, learning new repertory and preparing a recital programme for a proposed tour in Canada.

In September I received a call from Joseph Pach, first violinist of the Brunswick String Quartet, in residence at the University of New Brunswick in Fredericton, asking me to join the group, replacing the second violinist, who had left. It was a tempting offer, but I turned it down as I wanted to stick with my original plan. I wrote to my mother, 'I imagine it will be hard to find anyone who is much good at this late date.' In fact, Mr Pach continued it as a trio for the academic year 1972–73 before reconstituting the group as a quartet the following year. What if I had gone to Fredericton? Timing is everything.

In the same letter:

I've been practising violin very hard since Sept. 1—at least 4 hours a day [I had said exactly the same thing in my first year at Eastman, eleven years earlier] and am already beginning to feel (and hear) the difference, I think this is going to be a very productive year—I want to make a really big improvement in my playing, and I think I will. I want to establish a routine of violin practice, reading and outdoor exercise (golf not possible … so will have to do something else) so as to take advantage of all this free time.

A month later, however, I was concerned that 'our plans for next year are still uncertain', meaning the academic year 1973–74. Towards the end of 1972: 'I'm going to apply for some jobs in the USA.' I had problems with a tape recording I wanted to send with the applications, and 'I keep burdening you with a steady barrage of requests. For all these damned applications I'm doing, I need a xerox copy of my Accademia Chigiana diploma (on wall in living room) and a copy of my B.U. doctors [*sic*] degree. Would you be so kind as to have these copied for me?'

In March–April 1973, Barbara and I went on a little recital tour of the Maritime Provinces: Moncton, Saint John, Charlottetown, Acadia University and Halifax, where the performance was recorded by the CBC (Canadian Broadcasting Corporation). My mother had undertaken the huge task of organizing these concerts. She was doing for us what she may very well have wanted to do or have done for herself in the 1930s. My former violin teacher, Mr Kalejs, kindly looked after the Acadia arrangements. The programme, consisting of pieces that we had already played in public, was, I still think, an interesting one, and not as long as it looks: Vivaldi–David Sonata in A major, Op. 2, No. 2; Mozart Sonata in E minor, K. 304; Satie *Choses Vues*; Brahms Sonata in A major, Op. 100; (Intermission) Penderecki *Three Miniatures*; Strauss Sonata in E-flat major. I wrote the programme notes (including a careful explanation—not quite an apology—of the Vivaldi–David piece), which I enjoyed doing; from then on, I wrote the programme notes for most of the chamber music concerts I played in, including those of the Lenox Quartet.

For an academic year, I filled a substitute faculty position at Smith College in Northampton in western Massachusetts, playing the viola in the faculty string quartet and conducting the Smith–Amherst Orchestra. It was through Philipp Naegele of the Smith music faculty that I was offered the position. Philipp combined to an extraordinary degree the qualities of a first-class performing violinist and violist (a fellow chamber musician and pupil of Adolf Busch, six years in the Cleveland Orchestra under Szell, a violinist and violist in the Marlboro School and Festival from its inception, numerous recordings) with those of a scholar (PhD from Princeton, he gave highly regarded courses on Bach and Mozart at Smith). I admired him and no doubt emulated him, or rather attempted to emulate him, whether consciously or not I am not sure. One of my many regrets is that I never asked him about his experiences with

Busch. In retrospect, I think a lack of curiosity was my most serious fault as a young man. It was Philipp who convinced me to teach myself to play the viola for the faculty quartet, to fill in for Ernst Wallfisch, on sabbatical leave. 'It will do you good,' he said, and he was right.

April 30, '73

Dear Warwick and Barbara,

I am glad that you have accepted to come here next term and hope that somehow you can work out your dilemma. One thing is sure: Time moves on: that next September will come and you will find yourselves doing <u>something</u> and some solution, more or less benevolent, will materialize re Amsterdam vs. Northampton, New York studies vs. Boston studies, etc. [Philipp is referring to my uncertainty about the year 1974–75.] All that counts is that one doesn't do anything <u>too</u> stupid and disruptive, and that one doesn't blame anyone for inevitable frustrations.

Vernon [Gotwals, the head of the Smith music department] asked me to write about an instrument for you. Have you asked Giovina? [Giovina Sessions, second violinist in the Smith College String Quartet.] You are in any event welcome to mine, but it is a bit large! If Giovina's is not available let me know and I will try to do something about another Cornelissen [Marten Cornelissen, a luthier resident in Northampton]. I gave the message to the girl now playing on Giovina's. We have a chamber program on November 18th and a chamber orchestra [concert] (only strings) on March 3rd, plus a quartet concert I hope in the Art Museum (brand new and beautiful) in April. Wittig [William Wittig, the conductor of the Smith–Amherst Orchestra for whose sabbatical I was substituting] will arrange orchestra dates.

I will tell Blanche Moyse in Brattleboro that you will be here, and get you into a Bach Festival weekend (on violin) in mid-October at Marlboro College if at all possible (chamber orchestra, St. John Passion).

I would like to do Beethoven Op. 132 and the Bartók Piano Quintet if possible. The Bartók in November if at all feasible. Will Barbara be in Europe then? Would she care to play that? If so I would go about clearing the path for it. Any other suggestions?

To get used to the viola, play the easier DONT and some Sevcik Op. 8 shifting …

The best of good luck,

Philipp N.

This letter gives an idea of how generous and helpful Philipp was to me. He was aware that I had never held a viola in my life; I was flattered and touched that he was confident in my ability to rise to the occasion. In July, I wrote to my mother, 'I've been practising viola very hard on a borrowed viola—gradually getting the hang of it.' I cannot remember whose viola I used that year, and I never played the viola again, but the experience was invaluable for me both as a sometime conductor and as a string quartet violinist. I learned only recently that Philipp himself had done much the same thing in 1951 when he was asked by Busch to substitute for the ailing violist of the Busch Quartet for a concert in Vermont, the last they ever gave.

As it turned out, I did play in that Bach Festival performance of Bach's *St John Passion* at Marlboro College—my first experience of that great work, with its protracted, chromatically agonized melisma on 'und weinte bitterlich' sung by the Evangelist. And as it turned out the quartet played neither Op. 132 nor the Bartók Piano Quintet, the latter presumably because Barbara was too busy in Amsterdam (among other things she was an orchestral pianist for the Concertgebouw Orchestra), the former for reasons that I do not remember. In fact, I cannot recall what we did play in our concerts, except for Webern's *Langsamer Satz*, a hyper-Romantic, wonderfully expressive very early work without opus number, composed in 1905, but published only in 1961.

Philipp was a thoughtful, polished and extremely skilled violinist; as first violinist of the quartet he was collegial and considerate. He had the endearing habit, while playing, of looking heavenwards, as if for inspiration. For some reason, he developed a coolness, an impatience with our cellist, John Sessions, the son of the composer Roger Sessions. Philipp said that he thought John was lazy and content to be a kind of pipe-smoking country squire. This sounded unconvincing to me, as I thought John was a fine cellist and a worthy quartet companion. I suspected that there was some hidden reason. John asked me to intercede; to my everlasting regret, my protestations to Philipp were far too weak, partly because I was slightly in awe of him, and partly because I felt sure there was some underlying bone of contention between them of which I was unaware. Almost certainly, now that I think of it, it was this that was the cause of our giving so few concerts and of our not playing Beethoven's Op. 132.

As for the Smith–Amherst Orchestra, again, it was a difficult learning experience; again, I had spread myself too thin. I seemed to spend half my time on administration of the orchestra, scheduling extra players, planning rehearsals, writing the programme notes, preparing the printed programmes and the like, to the detriment of my musical preparation. I may have learned from my mistakes but didn't have time to profit therefrom. I chose programmes that were ambitious, perhaps too ambitious, including Schumann's Symphony No. 1 and two long movements from Berlioz's *Romeo and Juliet* Symphony. For a performance at Dartmouth College, I played Mendelssohn's early Concerto in D minor. Early in November 1973, Janis Kalejs died, aged sixty-one; I was asked to teach his students until a permanent faculty member could be found. This involved driving to Boston once a week, flying to Halifax and driving a rented car the 100 kilometres to Wolfville, where I gave five or six violin lessons, stayed overnight and returned the next day. I forget how many times I did this. I was glad to do it, indeed honoured, but it effectively took two days out of each of those weeks.

Philipp and one or two others probably saved my life when, towards the end of the academic year, I was taken ill with a weird, vicious virus. One morning, stepping out of the shower, I felt what seemed like a small splinter in the sole of my foot. I could find no splinter and went to a meeting at Smith. During the course of the day, my foot swelled to twice its normal size, the swelling spread to my hands and armpits; I developed a high fever with nightmarish hallucinations—the next night I saw monstrous, orange-coloured scorpion-like creatures, the size of monkeys, crawling on my bedroom walls. Philipp and Vernon Gotwals came in the middle of the night—how did they know how bad my condition was?—and took me to the hospital. I remember hearing the doctors conferring, through a haze of pain and delirium. They had no idea what it was but gave me penicillin intravenously. After two weeks, the swelling went down, but I needed crutches for a month. The doctors could say only that it was a kind of virus and that a considerable amount of cartilage in the metatarsus had been destroyed. My left foot is still sore in the mornings. I have no doubt that, without penicillin, I would have died.

My mother came and looked after me for a few days; we drove together to Ithaca in upstate New York where I had landed a job on the music faculty of Ithaca College. We found a charming apartment at 410 East Seneca Street, upstairs from a small local-history museum, Hinkley House. Then we drove to Parrsboro, where I continued to recuperate. The doctors had given me a packet of pain-killing pills, which I took at night to help go to sleep. I would lie on my back, waiting for the drug to take effect and, in fifteen minutes, with miraculous punctuality, it did. A wave of the most delicious, utterly relaxing well-being crept over my entire body and after a few minutes of this ecstasy I would fall asleep. I had never felt this kind of all-encompassing pleasure before. Hovering on the brink of addiction, I was saved only by reluctantly and uncomfortably reaching the end of the packet.

CHAPTER 7

Ithaca, Berlin

For the next seven years, I was a faculty member of the School of Music at Ithaca College, teaching violin and chamber music as well as music history—an undergraduate survey and a number of graduate period courses. I was not an inspiring teacher. My survey lectures changed very little over the seven years I gave them. I promoted very little class participation. Very occasionally, I played in class to demonstrate an historical or musical point. In some of the period courses, and others such as a course on the symphony and one named 'Masterpieces of Music', I may have been more successful, partly because they were smaller classes. My violin teaching perhaps improved with time. I often found it difficult to assess how much to expect from each student, how demanding to be. This is a critical ability, the hallmark of a successful teacher.

I gave three recitals with piano at Ithaca College and played in many chamber music concerts with other faculty members. Two occasions I remember particularly were Stravinsky's *Histoire du soldat* in which I played the marvellous, challenging violin part, and a tour of a few colleges in New England playing Lou Harrison's Concerto for Violin and Percussion Orchestra with a group led by the percussion teacher at Ithaca College. I was also concertmaster of the Cayuga Chamber Orchestra from its founding in 1976, of which the conductor was the distinguished composer, Karel Husa. Two of the pieces I had the pleasure of playing were the solo violin parts in Bach's Brandenburg Concertos Nos. 4 and 5.

All too rarely, I was able to gratify my persistent itch to mount the conductor's podium. One year, I was asked by some of the students to conduct rehearsals and a concert of a summer chamber string orchestra. It was all organized by the students. The programme: Rossini's String Sonata No. 1; Handel's Concerto Grosso, Op. 6, No. 4; Elgar's Serenade for String Orchestra; and Mozart's Divertimento in B-flat major, K. 137. For the next two summers, the college made it official, and we did two other programmes, with winds added, including Haydn's Symphonies Nos. 93 and 103, Schubert's Symphony No. 3 in D major, and Mendelssohn's D minor Concerto, in which I played the solo part (I had played this work with the Smith–Amherst Orchestra in the spring of 1974, also in Siena at the sanctuary of Santa Caterina in the summer of 1979 with an American student orchestra, and again ten years later in Florence—by that time it had almost become a warhorse of mine). On another occasion at Ithaca College, I conducted a performance of Brahms's Serenade No. 2, Op. 16, for chamber orchestra without violins, a wonderful piece all too rarely performed. For me it was fuel to the fire ...

In the autumn of 1978, Peter Marsh, the first violinist of the Lenox String Quartet, by then disbanded, joined the faculty. With me, violist Patricia McCarty and cellist Einar Holm we became the resurrected Lenox. It was a splendid, exhilarating experience. Peter was a very fine violinist: sensitive, deeply musical, with long experience and profound knowledge of the quartet repertory. I learned a great deal sitting beside him. His playing often took wing with a rhapsodic quality, as if improvised.

Within a few weeks, it became apparent that the sound of my violin, fine as it was, did not blend ideally with the others in the quartet. To be more honest, I was persuaded of this chiefly by Peter. I did not feel confident of my ability to make this kind of judgement myself. In NYC, I happened upon a fine instrument by the Neapolitan luthier Vincenzo Postiglione, dated 1888, whose full, warm tone blended well in the group. I had grown fond of the Stainer. It was not an easy decision, but

'Jacobus Stainer Absam 1659', its magnificent golden varnish only hinted at in this photograph, about 1977. Our days together were numbered. Photo by Jon Crispin.

my wish for the quartet to succeed overcame all my reservations. I gave up the Stainer and took the Postiglione.[21]

We gave our 'debut' in Alice Tully Hall, Lincoln Center, in December: Haydn Op. 74, No. 1; Bartók No. 6; Dvořák No. 7. I felt that it was too soon, but Peter's enthusiasm and vast experience carried us through. The reviews in the New York Times and in Musical America

---

[21] It was a minor case of history repeating itself for the Stainer. John Georgiadis writes that 'although I was very happy and comfortable with the Stainer, when I joined the London Symphony Orchestra in 1966, there were 'mutterings' that it wasn't a suitable instrument for an LSO leader, "being more suited to chamber music than a big orchestra." So I acquiesced to this pressure and bought [a Lorenzo Guadagnini violin]' (*Bow to Baton*, p. 395). From me the Stainer passed to a Baroque specialist who, I believe, had the instrument refitted to its original specifications, which, all considered, may have been for the best. It was not until I moved to Italy that I learned that 'postiglione' is the Italian word for 'postillion'.

were excellent. We were off to a good start.

Lenox Quartet, 1978: Peter Marsh, Warwick Lister, Einar Holm,
Patricia McCarty. Photo by Jon Reis, Ithaca, NY.

With Einar Holm at Lincoln Center, December 1978.

I sent Raphael Bronstein an invitation to this concert. He came
backstage afterwards—he would have been eighty-three years old. He

was kind and gracious and seemed genuinely pleased with my playing and my career. I don't remember what I said, but I hope I conveyed to him how much it meant to me that he had come to hear me, and my gratitude for all that he had done for me. It was the last time I saw him.

A string quartet needs years of preparation to become a first-rate ensemble. Unanimity of sound—vibrato, bowing strokes, the acquiring of repertoire, the slow hammering out of interpretative agreement for each piece—all of this requires many hours of painstaking work, which, frankly, we did not have. Each of us carried almost a full teaching load—only one sixth of our contractual time was allotted to the quartet, if I remember correctly. Through our NYC manager we had engagements in various parts of North America—I remember Baton Rouge, Boston (the Isabella Stewart Gardner Museum), Chapel Hill, Chicago, Nebraska, Florida, Minnesota, Calgary and twice to the USA's west coast. Each time, we had to make up lessons at the college, and I sometimes found it necessary as well to videotape music history lectures if I could not find a colleague to fill in for me. We had teething problems. Patricia, an excellent violist, left after one year to join the Boston Symphony Orchestra. She was replaced by Darrel Barnes, formerly principal in the St Louis Symphony. He too was a fine player, but with a very different style from Patricia's, which, naturally, meant more rehearsal hours. We sometimes collaborated in concerts, both as a group and as individuals, with other Ithaca College performance faculty members. Even so, we knew that a few of them resented our special status: 'We perform in concerts just as you do; why are we not given credit hours?'

I wrote to my mother at the end of spring term, 1980:

Here are some reviews from our California trip and our last program at I.C. All in all it was a very successful tour—good audience reactions, good reviews, etc. It was hectic, but we all felt it had been worth it. We have already been invited back for several concerts in March 1981. ... The quartet will be rehearsing every morning (5 days a week) from 8.30 a.m. (yes!) to 12.30 p.m. starting in 2 or 3 days, for about 7 weeks. It sounds rigorous, but since I will have very little else to do, it will not be hard at all—in fact it will be a welcome schedule as it's something we have not had time to do during the school year— to really rehearse properly and refine ourselves to a sharper edge.

We generally got good reviews. The *San Francisco Chronicle* was particularly complimentary. The one really bad review we got was in Calgary. At a reception after the concert, I had a pleasant conversation with a young man who had gone to Acadia University fifteen or twenty years after my time. As a fellow Maritimer, I felt a certain kinship with him and, my tongue perhaps loosened by a glass or two of wine, I confided in him. I told him how privileged, almost unworthy, I felt to be playing in a well-known quartet. He turned out to be the music critic for the *Calgary Herald*. In his review he excoriated us as opportunists riding on the coat tails of the Lenox name. It was hateful, hurtful, and above all an unconscionable betrayal of a private conversation. Thenceforth, I was careful about what I said at receptions.

Darrel, who seemed to have unlimited technique, suddenly developed a serious problem of rigidity in his bow arm. The opening viola entrance of the fugal finale of Beethoven's Op. 59, No. 3, normally child's play for him, became an insurmountable barrier, his arm locked and immobile. We others tried to suggest ways of coping with this mysterious attack, but it was Darrel himself who slowly worked his way out of it in a few weeks.

Once, on tour, we bumped into (in an airport? Hotel lobby? I don't remember) the members of the Fine Arts Quartet. I believe Peter was already on friendly terms with them. At one point in the conversation, Abram Loft said to me with a twinkle in his eye, 'We second violinists have to stick together.' I was pleased to be included, so amiably, by this distinguished musician in what for me was a new and exalted confraternity.

In my Lenox programme notes, I strove for a personal, informal style, occasionally attempting to be witty:

Anton Webern: Fünf Sätze für Streichquartett, Op. 5

With their uncompromising atonality, their brevity, their fierce insistence on the major 7th and the minor 9th as prime melodic intervals, and their special instrumental effects (playing near the bridge and striking the strings with the wood of the bow), these five pieces still sound startlingly modern. With, however, their swooning melodic gestures, their extreme dynamics, especially those on the soft end of the spectrum, and their highly charged performance directions ('passionately agitated', 'with the tenderest expression', etc.), they evoke a peculiarly Viennese fin-de-siècle atmosphere—hyper-romantic, feverish, overwrought (the reader will forgive the writer of these notes if his prose takes on some of the same qualities). It is as if in these five fleeting, shuddering movements, an entire symphony of Mahler has received its ultimate distillation.

Bedřich Smetana: String Quartet No. 1 in E minor, 'From my Life'

[I quote from Smetana's own description: 'the long note sounding in the finale ... the fatal high-pitched whistling in my ear which in 1874 announced my deafness']

The clinically autobiographical element in this work lies roughly at the historical midpoint of a distinguished pedigree of pathology in chamber music for stringed instruments, which begins modestly in the 'Song of Thanksgiving to the Deity on Recovering From an Illness' movement of Beethoven's String Quartet, Op. 132, gains momentum with the Smetana work and culminates in the heart-attack cum hypodermic-injection music of Schönberg's String Trio of 1946. The present writer looks forward to the day when he will be required to take the Hippocratic oath before performing the latest string quartet.

One warm, sunny afternoon, on tour in California (March 1981), we went on a leisurely drive in a rented car along the wine-growing route in the Napa Valley, a few miles north of San Francisco, dropping in on several wineries to taste some of the excellent wines. Our concert in Fireman's Fund Forum in San Francisco was, I hope, not on the same evening.

Rehearsal break: behind Peter Marsh's house near Ithaca, N.Y., about 1979. Of course I refrained from asking Peter why he had a dinosaur in his backyard.

While in California, we visited Colin Hampton, the former cellist of the Griller Quartet. He had lived in Berkeley since the Griller became the quartet-in-residence at the University of California. The quartet had disbanded about twenty years earlier, but Colin had become the much-respected paterfamilias (his son Ian's word) of the cello-playing community of the Bay area. We played for him some of Beethoven's Op. 132, which was one of our programmed pieces in California. A delightful man, he encouraged and cheered us. Recently I read in his memoir, *A Cellist's Life (String Letter Publishing, 2000),* that Op. 127, 'the epitome of what love should be', and Op. 132, 'incredibly passionate', were his favourite Beethoven quartets. Some of Hampton's other opinions were less benign: critics ('pernicious and useless'), the Suzuki method of violin teaching, the 'terrible German [music] editing and the German way of playing the cello' and 'New York tempi', among other things, are given short shrift in his book.

After three years, we were told that the college would no longer support the Lenox. Academic institutions tend to look at such matters from a purely financial point of view. Our view was that an ensemble such as ours attracted students. In the meantime, I had jumped through the various academic hoops to obtain tenure and an associate professorship in 1981. But the quartet was doomed. Peter left to take another position; I felt that I had had enough of academia and decided to move to Berlin to join my then wife, Anne, who had taken a teaching position. After two weeks at the cottage in Nova Scotia, I returned to Ithaca to pack and to tie up seven years' worth of loose ends. As a fond farewell, I played a short solo, the middle movement, 'Romance', of Wieniawski's Concerto No. 2 with the Cayuga Chamber Orchestra. Four days later, 25 June 1981, I flew to West Berlin.

It seems extraordinary to me now (I have used this phrase before in these pages, for similar reasons) that at the age of forty I was willing to give up a secure position—tenure and a pension—with absolutely no professional prospects in view. In retrospect, I see it as confidence in my ability to find work bordering on foolhardiness.

Early that autumn, I received a telegram from my father saying that Mum was ill. I rushed to Moncton; she died of cancer of the pancreas scarcely three weeks later, just two days after I had gone back to Berlin. One day, about a week before she died, I was busying myself with tucking in the sheets at the foot of her hospital bed—her death bed. I looked up—she had raised her head up from the pillow and was watching me, her eyes full of her love for me. That was the last communication we had. From then on, she was so drugged with morphine that I do not think she recognized me or anyone else.

I now read her letters to me from 1974, when I began at Ithaca College, to about a month before her death, with almost unbearable feelings of self-reproach at how much my visits home meant to her. In many of her letters, she invites me, implores me, to come home. I did whenever I could, usually in the summer, but it was for my own sake, because I loved to be in the family cottage, not to please her.

September 1978:

> It was so good to have you with us, Warwick dear [I had been with my parents for a week or two in August]. You will never have any regrets about your relationship with us—you have given us nothing but great kindness and joy, from your childhood—always.

I must have expressed remorse at my neglect of my parents.
    But, as always, she wrote about music.

October 1978:

> I have been playing your record of the Debussy Sonata, with Isaac Stern and Alexander Zakin. The first movt. has a haunting oriental atmosphere—I never tire of it.

9 January 1981:

> Sunday
>
> My dear Warwick,
>
> We just got back from church. I played (the organ) and the minister wanted 5 (FIVE!) hymns—that and the Prelude and Offertory kept me

jumping. For the Prelude I played the beautiful Beethoven Sonata for Violin—A♭Major—on the organ, not the violin, and it went really beautifully. Such an elegant melody—how I wished you were playing it. Might you come down, for even a few days, or Easter?[22]

How I wish, now forty years later, that I had.

9 February 1981:

Tell me if you got thru Wieniawski OK—Mother.

I played the *Scherzo Tarantelle* in a recital at Ithaca College and must have expressed concern over its difficulties.

20 February 1981:

Well, Mr. Smart-ASS Lister: The composition by Beethoven which I transposed for the magnificent organ in the Treasure Cay All-Denominational Church is the Adagio movement of Sonate pour Violon in A♭Major—at least this Adagio is in A♭Major, and what's more, I'm quite sure that you used to play it. SO, no more foolish questions, but I ought to make clear that I do not play this mov't on the violin.

I must have queried her (rudely) about this movement, clearly the slow movement of the C minor sonata, Op. 30, No. 2. I think she is wrong in saying that I used to play it. She must be remembering the Heifetz–Bay recording that we had had since my childhood.

2 March 1981:

I practise on the organ every morning, after [Ralph] leaves for golf—8.30–9.30. And my fingers are in great shape—I enjoy it immensely.

---

[22] My parents had a cottage in the Bahamas where they wintered for several years.

After I had moved to Berlin, the Lenox, with a new first violin, Paul Kantor, limped along for about a year. I commuted several times to Ithaca, staying with friends, for a week or ten days of rehearsals each time. Nothing could have been more quixotic. We managed to put together one or two programmes for a concert in the Merkin Concert Hall in NYC in October 1982, and a few other concerts. But our unrealistic rehearsal arrangements could not endure. Einar and Darrel had the same time limitations as before, and Paul, at the beginning of a distinguished career as violinist and pedagogue, could not be expected to throw in his lot with a group on such insecure ground. We disbanded.

I had been asked to play a concerto with the Cayuga Chamber Orchestra in Ithaca. On one of my trips from Berlin to rehearse with the Lenox, I played Mozart's Concerto No. 5. The orchestra was conducted by its regular conductor, Karel Husa, with whom I had enjoyed a friendly professional relationship. I was disappointed in my performance. I had managed one playthrough with a pianist for a few friends in Berlin, but this had not sufficiently prepared me. In a way, it is foolhardy for a player such as myself to play a concerto with an orchestra. The big-name soloists who play the standard concertos have done so dozens of times. They are virtuosos, extraordinarily gifted musicians to begin with, and they have the added advantage, almost unfair, of this extremely important backlog of repeated performances, which, ironically, they don't need as much as the one-off performer. In other words, the violinist who has played Mozart's A major concerto many times over a period of several years has a distinct advantage over those of us for whom playing a concerto with an orchestra is a rare, albeit desired event. This may sound like special pleading, but to me it has the inevitability of a self-perpetuating vicious circle.

In Berlin I played for a few months in the second violin section of the orchestra of the Oper Berlin. The pay was good, augmented by the 8 per cent 'Berlin zulag', extra pay, either to compensate for the high cost of living in West Berlin or because living there, isolated as it was, was considered a hardship, or both. Because of the repertory system followed by German opera houses, I played almost all of the performances with no rehearsals—a different opera and an occasional ballet each night. There was usually no time for me to practise the part at home, so it was a crash course in sightreading. Humperdinck's *Hansel and Gretel* was one of the scores that I had not looked at. It is perhaps the most difficult orchestral part I have ever played, let alone sightread. In general, however, other than the time I came blundering in during a silent moment in Strauss's *Electra*, I managed not to embarrass myself. During the intervals of performances, the second violins sat clannishly at a separate table in the theatre canteen, most of them drinking a tankard of beer. They welcomed me into their midst, despite my rudimentary German. The only untoward incident occurred once during a rehearsal when my stand partner fell off his chair, the tip of his bow caroming off my violin, which still bears the scar. I pretended not to notice and said nothing—so like me, not wishing to make a fuss.

There was a kind of hysterical unreality to life in West Berlin before the collapse of the wall: the affluence, the cafés and bright lights of Kurfürstendam, the conspicuous consumption of the top floor of the KaDeWe department store with its international eating counters, the bars where single people congregated and picked each other up, the spectacular Philharmonie concert hall, the Bohemian district of Kreuzberg. That all of this was enclosed by a wall and barbed wire, a mined no man's land and guard towers, was oppressive but, paradoxically, exhilarating—something akin, perhaps, to the atmosphere sometimes described by those who lived through the London blitz.

In the autumn of 1981, Anne and I went to Kraków for a few days with a group of her colleagues, staying with various families in the city. There was a severe scarcity of goods in Poland; we had been asked to bring various items such as detergent, toilet paper, chocolate for our hosts. I can never forget the expression on our hostess's face when we gave these banal things to her—gratitude mixed with pain, sadness, humiliation, or so it seemed to me. She was a teacher, her husband an official of Solidarność. Once, watching General Jaruzelski giving a speech on television, he turned to me and said, 'All lies'. It was scarcely two months later that martial law was declared.

Our group was taken to the historic Wieliczka salt mine, with its cathedral-like underground wooden structure. And we went to the

UNITED STATES OF AMERICA
ÉTATS-UNIS D'AMERIQUE
СОЕДИНЕННЫЕ ШТАТЫ АМЕРИКИ

MOVEMENT ORDERS
LAISSEZ-PASSER
ПУТЕВКА

Name Nom, Prénom Фамилия, Имя	Rank Qualité Чин	Nationality Nationalité Гражданство	Identity Document No. Pièce d'identité No. № удостоверения личности
LISTER WILLIAM W	Civ	American	184392

is / are authorized to travel from   to   and return
est / sont autorisé(s) à se rendre de   à   et retour
уполномочен/уполномочены   **Berlin**   в   **Helmstedt**   и обратно
следовать из

by train or by vehicle No.
par le train ou par voiture No.
поездом или на автомашине №

from (date)   to (date)   inclusive
du (date)   **24 Aug 80**   au (date)   **24 Oct 80**   inclus
от (число)   по (число)   включительно

by
par

The United States Commander, Berlin
Le Commandant Americain à Berlin
Американским Комендантом в Берлине

Signature   *C. C. Bernhardt*
Подпись

Title   **MG US ARMY**
Qualité   **US COMMANDANT**
Звание

Date   **24 Aug 80**
Число

Movement orders, 1980. I could ride on the US Army train from West Berlin to West Germany by virtue of my wife, Anne, being a teacher in the American School in the American sector. It is odd that the East German border officials did not notice that I am Canadian, not American.

Auschwitz death camp. I can only say that no amount of reading and looking at films can prepare one sufficiently for this experience. One of our group, a young German teacher, broke down sobbing on the ride back to Kraków: 'How could we have done this?'

Along with my Lenox commitments, I was able to give two or three recitals—with the pianist Phillip Moll at the Amerika Haus Berlin and with Danielle Sapir at the Château de Ville-d'Avray, at the Château de Breteuil and, later, after I had moved to Italy, at the Canadian Cultural Centre in Paris, then on the Esplanade des Invalides.

With Danielle Sapir at the Château de Ville-d'Avray, December 1981.

By late 1982, my marriage with Anne was dissolving, which was one reason I did not wish to stay in Berlin. By then I was living alone in a one-room apartment in an old villa behind the Einstein Café, near Nollendorfplatz. Forty-two years old, I knew that whatever I decided to do should have at least the possibility of permanence. In 1982, and continuing until well after I left Berlin, I played at least a half-dozen auditions for a concertmaster position in orchestras in Germany, Austria, Switzerland, Luxembourg, France and Italy. I was unsuccessful in all of them.

Looking back, I see that my musical career consisted of periods of relative stability lasting from two to six or seven years, either as a student or as a professional, interspersed with brief, uncertain, often hectic periods of taking stock, considering my options, casting about, applying to educational institutions and orchestras, writing letters, preparing for and playing auditions. This pattern has no doubt always been typical of musicians everywhere, especially young musicians, but what now strikes me is that, between the stable periods, almost invariably I would have no idea of where I would be or what I would be doing in three or four months' time. This was equally as true before the last big change in my life, when I decided to leave Berlin to live in Florence, as it was in the summer of 1957, when I was sixteen.

CHAPTER 8

Florence: orchestra

I had no wish to spend the rest of my professional life playing only operas, sitting in a cramped opera pit. I was attracted by the idea of living in Italy, Florence in particular, and by the variety of musical experience offered by the 'stagione' system in some Italian opera theatres, in which seasons of opera alternate with seasons of symphonic concerts throughout the year. I moved to Italy in March 1983 and for eighteen years played in the Orchestra of the Maggio Musicale Fiorentino. Its name is taken from the yearly May music festival of operas and concerts originating in the 1930s. My audition was extremely informal—three or four senior string players of the orchestra sat down on the stage to listen, and I played for a few minutes—I don't remember what. My contract, after two or three years, included the clause 'con l'obbligo di concertino' ('with the obligation to fill the position of assistant concertmaster [when required]').

For most of my tenure in the orchestra, the chief conductor was Zubin Mehta, a brilliant, charismatic personality whose musicianship and international reputation enhanced the quality and public image of the orchestra. His strengths were in the big Romantic works; he seemed less at ease in the earlier Classical repertory—Haydn and Mozart. I am appalled at the fact that in my eighteen years in the orchestra I played a Haydn symphony only two or three times. Haydn's symphonies should be at the very heart of any serious symphony orchestra's repertory. It will not do to say that they are better off as the exclusive domain of specialist chamber orchestras. In the first place, an orchestra can be reduced to any size; in the second, the orchestra that gave the first performances of Haydn's 'Paris' symphonies, Nos. 82–87, in the Tuileries Palace in 1786, almost certainly comprised some seventy players, and the premieres of his last three symphonies in 1795 in the King's Theatre, London, conducted at the keyboard by Haydn himself, were given by an orchestra of more than sixty players. In any case, the numbers can and should be adjusted to fit the size and acoustics of the hall.

During my time in the Orchestra of the Maggio Musicale Fiorentino, we played in (besides our home base, the Teatro Comunale) the Teatro della Pergola, the Salone dei Cinquecento in the Palazzo Vecchio, several spaces of the Palazzo Pitti, including the Sala Bianca and, in the summer, the Boboli Gardens, and several of the great churches of the city, including the Duomo. The orchestra travelled extensively in Italy, and we went on some fifteen tours abroad, including to such far-flung places as South America, Oman, India, Japan and China, and in Europe to Paris and cities in the south of France, Spain (twice), Turkey, Lisbon, the Edinburgh Festival, Salzburg, Copenhagen, twice to Athens and twice to East Germany, almost always with Zubin Mehta. At the risk of it reading like a travelogue, I give below a few of the more memorable venues and locations.

On a cold and windy March morning in 1985, the orchestra took the ferry from the port of Piombino to the island of Pianosa, not far from Elba, off the Tuscan coast. Since the mid-nineteenth century, Pianosa had been a penal colony and, since 1977, was the site of a maximum-security prison for members of terrorist organizations and of the Mafia. The seas were rough, and almost everyone got seasick. With Maestro Myung-whun Chung among us, we staggered off the boat and made our way to the prison, where we were given a lunch which hardly anyone could stomach. Our concert, intended for the prisoners, was given in a bare, uninviting room and was attended (something of an anticlimax, this) mostly by prison employees and their families. It would have made a better story if I could tell of hardened, cruel-faced criminals in chains being led into the room by heavily armed guards to have their savage breasts soothed by our Prokofiev, but, alas, that was not the case. The prison was closed in 2011.

Closer to home, there was an unforgettable July evening concert in the Piazza del Duomo of the town of Pistoia, near Florence, when a full moon rose up behind the cathedral—beautiful, mesmerizing, as if staged for our performance, or as if it had risen the better to hear the music.

On 20 June 1987, the orchestra played in the Teatro Farnese in Parma for an Italian television programme of operatic and orchestral excerpts, 'Notte della Musica'. There was no live audience; Vittorio Gassman was the master of ceremonies. The concert was broadcast all over the world. The Teatro Farnese, a magnificent, historic space, occupying a room in one of the great palaces of Parma, is in the form of a U-shaped amphitheatre made entirely of wood, facing a monumental stage area. The fourteen steps for the spectators (apparently capable of seating 3,000, though I think it would have been uncomfortable in such numbers) are surmounted by two orders of loggias. The theatre was opened in 1628 with a performance of Monteverdi's dramatic *torneo* (tournament), *Mercurio e Marte*, during which the floor was flooded and a mock naval battle performed (a not uncommon feature of public entertainment in Italy, going back to Roman times). The music for this work is lost, but it is tempting to imagine (albeit difficult with our anachronistic mixed bag of Verdi, Rossini, Dinicu–Heifetz, etc.) that it featured the dramatic string *tremolandi* of Monteverdi's *stile concitato* introduced in his *Combattimento di Tancredi e Clorinda* four years earlier. What could be better for a naval battle?

On two occasions, we played in the Basilica of Sant'Apollinare in Classe, near Ravenna, consecrated in the year 549, one of the great early Christian churches. In the superb sixth-century mosaics of the apse, the solemn, hierarchical Byzantine figure of Saint Apollinaris is depicted preaching in a charming green meadow with plants, flowers, trees and birds; twelve lambs are listening attentively. They would have been hard-pressed to hear this saintly sermon during the great orchestral and choral outbursts of Beethoven's Symphony No. 9, conducted by Carlo Maria Giulini. Outside the church, tents had been set up for us as changing rooms. The wet, muddy ground made getting in and out of our concert dress and shoes something of a feat.

The 'Three Tenors' concert (José Carreras, Plácido Domingo and Luciano Pavarotti) in the ruins of the Baths of Caracalla in Rome, 7 July 1990, was by far the most publicized performance in the history of the orchestra up to that time. We joined forces with the orchestra of the Rome Opera, sharing stands in the string sections. Maestro Mehta revelled in this kind of gala event. I am usually averse to such spectacles, but I must admit that at the rehearsals and even in the concert, despite the televised showbiz ballyhoo, there was a genuine atmosphere of spontaneous, joyous music-making. The hulking ruins of the *caldarium*, as if in brooding disapproval, loomed shadowy and sombre behind us in the festive night air.

We had at least one orchestra meeting in the weeks before the concert to decide whether to take royalties or a lump sum. Some of the younger members of the orchestra urged for royalties, but older heads prevailed—the majority vote was for a lump sum. The recording of the concert became the best-selling classical record (DVD) of all time. I presume we would all still be collecting royalties.

In Barcelona, on a tour of Spain, we played in the Palau de la Música Catalana, built between 1905 and 1908. The interior is a brilliant example of Catalan Art Nouveau, gleaming white statues of the muses, flowers, palms, fruits thrusting out in exuberant profusion from the proscenium arch. In any city other than the Barcelona of Gaudi, it would seem an exaggerated architectural folly. Seated onstage, some of us felt threatened by the sheer weight of the statuary looming above us.

In the oil-rich sultanate of Oman, our hotel, the Al Bustan Palace, was easily the most sumptuous I have ever experienced. I cannot improve on the description that my friend and quartet colleague, the cellist Roger Low, sent to his father:

> an enormous wedding cake of a hotel by the sea with a long white beachfront, tennis courts, an Olympic-sized swimming pool and an adjoining concert hall. The lobby looked as if the atrium of a Hyatt Regency had been conceived by the husband of Scheherazade:

Moorish arches laden with exotic geometric designs and gilt, in all colors of the rainbow, and bubbling pools and fountains surrounded by richly cushioned armchairs. Indian porters stood by the entrance and the elevators in spotless white outfits and helped settle us into our rooms. These were like the anteroom to a Sultan's harem, with geometric tiling in blue and white.

In the second of the two concerts we gave in Oman, there was a near-disaster in Ravel's *Daphnis et Chloé*. About halfway through, a wind player came in early on an important entrance. Chaos ensued. Some players followed the errant colleague, others went their own way. Mehta struggled to bring us back on track. I have never seen him so distressed. After what seemed an eternity, we somehow got back together to finish the piece. Afterwards, we all agreed that probably no one in the audience had noticed.

In Bombay, we were feted like conquering heroes: at the airport; at the hotel,[23] where rose petals were strewn at our feet and hostesses in saris anointed our foreheads with the traditional red dot, the *bindi*, as we arrived; and at various receptions. This, of course, was thanks to Mehta, who is revered in India. The lad who showed me to my hotel room said, 'I am very much looking forward to your concerts.' I can't imagine this occurring anywhere else. But nothing could have prepared me for the poverty. Coming into the city in the bus from the airport, we passed mile after mile of harrowingly wretched slums, a vast, heart-sickening scene of abject squalor—hell upon earth. On the streets in the city, skeletal men in rags begged, pointing with bony fingers at their mouths. At one of the receptions, in the torch-lit gardens of a magnificent villa, with a tame elephant and sumptuously garnished dining tables, there were starving beggars lying on the ground just outside the gates. At another reception, after the meal there was a kind of scrum by the waiters, begging for a tip and scavenging the left-over food, which presumably was part of their compensation. I must confess that I did very little

---

[23] The Oberoi, one of several sites in Mumbai (so-called since 1995) attacked by Islamic terrorists in November 2008, in which hundreds were killed and wounded.

sightseeing in Bombay; I stayed sequestered in my hotel room for hours, too depressed to venture out.

At our departure at the airport, I realized that I had left my passport in my concert tails, which had been packed in the hold of the aeroplane. One of the orchestra administrators (or was it an Indian immigration official?) told me that the plane would have to leave without me, that I would be left alone in Bombay to make my way to New Delhi (how?) to get another Canadian passport. For a few minutes I was desperate and—I do not deny it—was reduced to tears. But two *dei ex machina* in the persons of Mehta and Emilio Pucci, who was travelling with us, apparently managed, with their combined influence, to convince Indian immigration to allow me to leave. When we landed at Pisa, Pucci literally took me by the hand and whisked me through Italian immigration, saying, 'This man is travelling with me; I take responsibility for him.' He was instantly recognized and due obeisance paid. When, as a city councillor, Mr Pucci married Susan and me in the Palazzo Vecchio in Florence the following year, he did not remember me, and I was still too embarrassed by the incident to tell him.

One stop in the orchestra's South American tour of 1991 was Manaus, in the depths of the Brazilian rain forest. The relatively small but opulent opera house, after decades of neglect, had been refurbished and reopened the year before, partly as a delayed result of the interest aroused by the 1982 film *Fitzcarraldo*. This jewel of a structure, with its daringly curved galleries and extravagant painted interior decoration and ceiling, sat uneasily in the oppressively humid and rather rundown city, which had fallen on hard times since the collapse of the rubber trade before WWII. We orchestra members were taken on an unforgettable boat ride on the blue-grey Amazon at the point where it is joined by the mud-coloured Rio Negro, the two rivers running side by side for about six kilometres without mixing. Afterwards, I thought, what if the boat had capsized? Were there piranhas? I think so.

It was backstage in the Manaus opera house, I believe, in a cramped, cluttered 'dressing room', where a few of us were waiting for a performance to begin, that one of our violinists, a Pole, began to play some Slavic folk music to while away the time. He played softly, more

On the Amazon near Manaus, 1991. Astern are the brown waters of the Rio
Negro beside the blue of the Amazon.

for himself than for us. After a few minutes, our principal violist, a
Ukrainian, joined in with an improvised accompaniment. It was one of
the most memorable musical performances I have ever heard. They
inspired each other; it was as if the great oceanic distance that separated
them from their lands of birth had opened the gates to their shared
cultural heritage.

In September of 1998, the Maggio orchestra and chorus participated
in eight performances of Puccini's *Turandot* in the Forbidden City,
Beijing. It was a feather in the cap of the Florentine theatre to be the first
to perform the work in a place traditionally so difficult of access and so
closely corresponding to the locations of several scenes in the opera.
The opulent production, much publicized, involved hundreds of
Chinese extras, including soldiers from the People's Liberation Army,
dancers from the Beijing dance school, and drummers, all dressed in
Ming dynasty costumes. The raised terrace fronting the Hall of Supreme
Harmony provided the immense stage, with the orchestra below and the

audience seated in the courtyard between the orchestra and the Gate of Supreme Harmony. There were three different casts for three of the main roles. Zubin Mehta, very much in his element, conducted the large orchestra, including an onstage brass band. The director of the sumptuous staging was the film director Zhang Yimou. An elaborate sound system was installed with fifty-two microphones for the orchestra alone. We were told that the total budget was almost US$15 million. It did not escape some of us that we were committing a sacrilege of sorts, profaning an ancient civilization with a garish simulacrum, with all the trappings of a Hollywood extravaganza.

The day before the first dress rehearsal, a pall was cast over the members of the company by the death of an English soprano in the chorus, a much-loved friend of many of us. She had succumbed to a sudden flare-up of a chronic condition.

We also gave two performances of Verdi's Requiem in Beijing—these, with jet lag, rehearsals and the eight *Turandot* performances, left little time for sightseeing in our eighteen days in Beijing, though on one day off we were taken to see the Great Wall on the outskirts of the city.

One day, in Tokyo, I took the hour-long train ride to the town of Kamakura to see the annual enactment of an ancient samurai horseback archery contest called *Yabusame*. In the large crowd of onlookers, as we stood for two hours in a wooded area waiting for the spectacle to begin, I was the only non-Japanese person. It was a rather hot day; a middle-aged couple beside me smiled sweetly and the wife took out a prettily decorated fan and fanned me for several minutes after I had let them stand in front of me. I was touched and grateful, but slightly embarrassed. Was it a cultural thing—Japanese courtesy towards a foreigner, or a spur-of-the-moment, strictly personal gesture? Finally, the horsemen, dressed in magnificent samurai costumes, paraded in. Then, each in turn, riding at full tilt, drew three arrows from his quiver and shot them at a succession of three targets as he thundered past—a thrilling display of pomp and skill. Afterwards, I strolled around this lovely town, looking at the splendid shrines and temples. I was back in Tokyo for the dress rehearsal of *Lucia di Lammermoor* at 6 p.m.—from twelfth-century samurai to sixteenth-century Scotland.

For my first two or three years in Florence, I would go into a different church almost every day, seeking out the works of art mentioned by Berenson, and Alta MacAdam's *Blue Guide*. Now I am surprised at such zeal, and I'm not sure how much of it was genuine desire, how much a sense that it was what I ought to be doing. Ghirlandaio's frescoes in Santa Maria Novella gave me pleasure. But Berenson excoriates them: Ghirlandaio 'had not a spark of genius', the frescoes are mere 'genre illustration', lacking in 'higher significance'. I was mortified, but not sufficiently to cease enjoying the frescoes. It was exhilarating to know that I could break free from Berenson and form my own aesthetic judgements.

So true was this, that as the years went by, my taste in Florentine art, while not entirely abandoning Berenson's 'life-enhancing' 'tactile values' and the new-fangled vanishing-point perspective, gradually, perhaps reluctantly, receded to the fourteenth century, in particular its frescoes. I was attracted to Maso di Banco's frescoes of the *Life of Saint Sylvester* in Santa Croce dating from the 1330s, especially that of Sylvester quelling the dragon. Most of all (perhaps because it was nearer to where I lived), I found myself returning time and time again to Lorenzo Monaco's scenes from the *Life of the Virgin* in a chapel in Santa Trinita, especially the fresco of the suitors. These, though coming almost a century after Maso's in Santa Croce, appealed to me for similar reasons, which I am unable to explain. I felt a different kind of emotion, but equally powerful, in the presence of the detached fresco, dating from about 1390, of Spinello Aretino's *The Mystic Marriage of Saint Catherine* in the neighbouring chapel. This had been found in 1961 beneath Lorenzo's frescoes next door; along with its sinopia, it was detached and moved, disfigured by hammer marks—gouged out portions of the fresco to permit the attachment of Lorenzo's new intonaco. The cruel vagaries of taste: Spinello's style had already gone out of fashion by 1420, when Lorenzo began work; his fresco ignominiously painted over and forgotten until 1961.[24]

---

[24] To be fair, perhaps the gouged-out fragments represent an (unsuccessful) attempt on the part of Lorenzo and his patrons to salvage parts of Spinello's fresco, as has been suggested.

Turning more willingly to sinuousness of line; gracefulness, rather than weight, volume or monumentality, I began to prefer Sienese to Florentine art. Simone Martini's *Annunciation* in the Uffizi gallery moved me despite the milling crowds on their way to the Botticelli paintings. Over the years, I pilgrimaged not only to Siena for the panels of Duccio's *Maestà*, and Lorenzetti's frescoes (perhaps to atone for my neglect in the summer of 1965?), but also to Assisi for Martini's *Saint Martin Renouncing the Sword* in the Lower Church of San Francesco; to San Galgano, not far from Siena, for the sinopia of Ambrogio Lorenzetti's *Annunciation*, the Virgin shrinking back and clinging fearfully to a column; to San Gimignano for Barna da Siena's great fresco cycle, especially The *Crucifixion*, the most '*sonorous*' image known to me: the tumult of the onlookers, the brutal shouts of the soldiers on horseback, the lamentations of the women and the keening of the hovering angels; and, inspired by Pope-Hennessy's book on Sienese quattrocento painting, to the Musée Condé in Chantilly for the exquisite *Marriage of Saint Francis to Lady Poverty* by Sassetta. But I never completely shook off Berenson's influence: his glittering description and the illustration of a detail in his *Italian Painters of the Renaissance*, of Lorenzo da Viterbo's fresco of the *Marriage of the Virgin* in the church of Santa Maria della Verità in that town, was more than I could resist—I went, I saw and I was life-enhanced.

The architectural beauties of Florence—the masterpieces of Brunelleschi—have always given me intense pleasure, though Alberti's façade of the Palazzo Rucellai was and still is my favourite piece of architecture in Florence.

One tiresome feature of life in the orchestra was the frequent and interminable orchestra meetings. There was not one, but several musicians' unions, all politically affiliated, with varying degrees of explicitness: the CISL (Confederazione Italiana Sindacati Lavoratori—Christian Democrat), UIL (Unione Italiana del Lavoro—Social Democrat), CGIL (Confederazione Generale Italiana del Lavoro—Communist), and the CISAL (Confederazione Italiana Sindacati Autonomi Lavoratori), ostensibly non-political but, in reality, the right-wing union. Most of the orchestra members, but not all, belonged to the Autonomi. In my early years, I was scarcely able to understand what was being discussed at the meetings, but I soon became aware that it was usually a matter of whether or not to go on strike over contractual terms and salaries. In fact, the orchestra often did go on strike, on one highly publicized occasion causing the cancellation of the opening performance of Verdi's *Ballo in Maschera*, scheduled for 31 October 1985, with Luciano Pavarotti.

As a foreigner, I had the regularly occurring problem of renewing my *permesso di soggiorno* (residency permit). In November 1985, perhaps because of my tardiness in doing the paperwork, I was told that I would have to leave the country and then re-enter—a kind of bureaucratic sleight of hand to resolve a bureaucratic problem. And so it was that I found myself on the train to Chiasso, just over the border in Switzerland, departing Florence at 12.27 a.m., arriving at 6 a.m., and making my way to the Italian Consulate at 9 a.m., then again at 11 a.m. to collect my *visto di ingresso* (entrance visa). The consular official was clearly disgruntled and gave me to understand that this procedure was highly irregular. My protestations that I had been instructed by the Florence Questura fell on deaf ears. I arrived back in Florence late that evening feeling that I had escaped serious consequences by the skin of my teeth.

Besides myself, there were twelve or fifteen foreigners in the orchestra—Americans, Hungarians, Romanians, Israelis, a Ukrainian, a Frenchman and an Austrian. We became dissatisfied with our contracts, by which we were 'aggiunti', literally 'added' or deputy players, with annual contracts (eleven months), renewable at the end of each season, with no pension plan. More than one player was told in June or July that their contract would not be renewed for the next season, beginning in September. It was an intolerable working situation, blatantly inferior to the Italian players' contracts. We hired lawyers and took our case to court. I see in my yearly agendas from January 1988 to September 1994 that I attended fourteen meetings with one of our lawyers. We lost this case and a second one because, according to some, our lawyers and the theatre administrators were fellow Masons.

Only by obtaining Italian citizenship could we become eligible for the same contract as that of the Italians. It was a long bureaucratic process: endless forms to fill out, birth certificates, documentation of all our previous residences and police records, all of which needed to be officially translated, trips to the Prefettura and the Questura, the latter an extremely depressing place, utterly unable to cope with the crowds of 'extracomunitari' who stood for hours in long lines waiting to have their papers processed. One day, I wrote in my pocket diary, '6.30 a.m. to Questura, waited in line on sidewalk til 10.30, left'. Clearly, there was no hope on that day of getting into an office to be seen and interviewed. We were also required to obtain *equipollenza* (equivalence) of our foreign advanced education—that is, we had to go through the complicated process of getting our degrees and diplomas officially translated and legally recognized.

Meanwhile, we foreigners were required by the theatre to take two further auditions, one in 1990, which was invalidated, on the grounds that we did not have Italian citizenship(!), and another in 1993. By this time, the auditions had been brought up to European standards—there were applicants from several European countries competing with us for positions that we had held for years—in my case ten years. All of us who had taken out the lawsuit passed. Finally, on 19 January 1994, at 8.30 a.m., I attended the swearing-in ceremony for my Italian citizenship, in the Palazzo Vecchio, Sala Rosa, with two Italian friends as witnesses. Duly noted in my agenda: 15,000 lire for *carta di bolla*, the official document with special stamps.

There is no doubt that there was a degree of xenophobia among a few of the Italians in the orchestra. A few of the less qualified players felt threatened by some of the foreigners who were more skilled. In other cases, it was perhaps simply a sense that the orchestra was losing any national identity it may once have had. One of the unions, thankfully not the most powerful one, seemed to be openly against the presence of foreigners; many Italian players presented a façade of welcoming openness, but one sensed an undercurrent of discomfort, if not resentment. Once, a Romanian who was to audition for the position of principal cellist, the position he was already filling in practice but not in name, was prevented from auditioning because one or two Italian jury members refused to participate. The cellist thereupon threatened one of them with a knife and was restrained only with difficulty. Even allowing for a certain instability of character, this incident gives an idea of the stress that many of us felt at the time.

Twenty years earlier, in the Concertgebouw Orchestra, there had been far fewer foreigners, and I never felt unwelcome, though once, I was told candidly by my stand partner there was a feeling that the presence of foreigners was diluting the 'Dutchness' of the orchestra, not only from the players' point of view, but also for the Concertgebouw Orchestra as an ambassador of Dutch culture.

Rather more unpleasant was an incident that occurred within a few days of my joining the Ithaca College music faculty in 1974. I had just walked into the faculty room. A few faculty members were standing or sitting around, chatting. Suddenly one of the trumpet professors spoke to me loudly across the room; everyone else stopped talking. 'I'm told you are Canadian,' he said, in a distinctly unfriendly tone. 'Well, let me tell you how I was treated by the Canadians.' And he proceeded to harangue me about the bad experience he had had on the faculty of a Canadian university—that he had been made to feel unwelcome and eventually was more or less forced to leave. I was unable to respond properly, muttered 'I'm sorry,' and he left the room. There was indeed a 'Canadianization Movement' in several Canadian universities in the 1960s and 70s. It was felt that Americans were filling the important professorships; that a kind of American 'old boy' system was in place, by which an American would become the chairman of a department and then proceed to bring in classmates or, at any rate, graduates of USA universities to fill vacant positions. Canadianization was the reaction, or overreaction, and my American colleague at Ithaca College had been one of its victims. He never again expressed his resentment to me, for which I was grateful, though his outburst had come close to the bone. In my wilder moments pondering the question of an orchestra's 'identity', I sometimes think that, for example, even if every single chair in the Toronto Symphony were occupied by an American, or by a Chinese musician, then so be it, assuming that they have all been hired by rigorously fair and impartial criteria. Let the Canadians raise their standards to the required level. Restrictive quotas are detrimental to quality, as has been made clear in the field of higher education in several countries.

One winter's day late in 1983, to prepare for an audition in Bonn, I played Mozart's Concerto No. 5 and the Sibelius concerto at the Dutch Institute in Florence for a festivity at 5 p.m. I had a hot bath, walked with my violin and music stand up Costa di San Giorgio from my tiny apartment on the top floor at no. 79, along Via di San Leonardo, across the very short Via Schiaparelli to Viale Machiavelli, up to Viale Torricelli and the Institute, about a three-quarters-of-an-hour walk, most of it up hill. At the brief pre-concert rehearsal with my pianist-friend I became extremely nervous—almost having a panic attack, but then calmed down and was able to get through the two pieces without major mishap or memory slip. That evening at 8 p.m. I had a rehearsal (the 'anti-generale', or pre-dress rehearsal) of the ballet *La Sylphide*. I was (relatively) young then. Now it makes me tired just thinking about that day.

In my hotel in Bonn, six days later, I got up early for the morning audition. At around 8 a.m. I started to warm up in my room; almost immediately, there was angry knocking on the wall from the next room. As a result, I began the audition completely cold—not a recipe for success. This was the last, or nearly the last, audition I did. I gave up trying to get a concertmaster post.

In February 1984, I saw an advertisement in the trade magazine *das Orchester* in which a string trio in Zurich was looking for a violinist to form a string quartet. I answered it, giving my qualifications with emphasis on my chamber music experience. I received a reply politely informing me that they were impressed with my credentials but that they were looking for someone younger than I, since they were planning to compete in chamber music competitions. It was something of a shock, as until then I had never thought of myself as being too old for anything (I was forty-three), at least not in the music profession. From then on, I was acutely aware of my age, my declining saleability on the job market. It made me distinctly uncomfortable. I remember being outraged by the advertisements in *das Orchester* for positions in the Munich Philharmonic, conducted by Sergiu Celibidache, in which the upper age limit was thirty-five. I thought, and still do think, that this was a blatantly discriminatory policy, undoubtedly imposed by Celibidache himself, who, I was convinced, wished to have an orchestra of young people who would be more easily moulded, less likely to chafe at his authority. I made a point of referring in conversation to the orchestra as 'the Munich Youth Orchestra', which gave me some satisfaction. At any rate, the young Zurich trio did find a violinist, becoming the Carmina String Quartet, which has enjoyed a long and distinguished career, two of the founding members, the first violinist (who had written to me) and the violist, still performing in it.

A few months after joining the orchestra, I experienced what might be described as a baptism of fire. It was a concert of contemporary music in the lovely Teatro della Pergola, one of the most distinguished theatres in Italy, its history going back to the mid-seventeenth century. At one of the rehearsals, the prominent Italian composer Luigi Nono, two of whose works were on the programme, gave a brief talk to the orchestra, in which he intimated that we were not up to the task of playing contemporary music. All hell broke loose. One of the double bass players, roaring insults, came charging through the orchestra towards Nono, kicking over music stands. Nono fled; the rehearsal broke up in utter pandemonium. I don't remember the outcome; there must have been a reconciliation of sorts and the concert given. The episode invites comparison with certain scenes in Fellini's film *Prova d'orchestra*, premiered only four years earlier. But I am by no means convinced that it was a case of Life imitating Art, quite the contrary.

The opening spectacle of the Maggio of 1984, *Rigoletto*, became a cause célèbre days before opening night when word got out of the provocative staging by the Russian director Yuri Lyubimov. Among other things, Edita Gruberová, playing Gilda, was held aloft on a swing for her first-act aria 'Caro nome'. A veritable Guerre des Bouffons ensued in the press in the week before the opening; the baritone playing

Rigoletto resigned, as did two successive conductors. At the opening, the audience was at a fever pitch of opposed camps, whistling, shouting and clapping. But the performance, with another baritone and a third conductor, proceeded without serious interruption, thanks to the superlative singing of Gruberová, who, though she had complained during rehearsals, did as she was instructed and was roundly applauded.

Gianandrea Gavazzeni often conducted us. He was an elder statesman of Italian musical life, a grand old man, much respected by the orchestra. He had courtly manners and a distinctly old-fashioned way of expressing himself. When he was annoyed, he would mutter the imprecation 'Ostia!', the word for the host, as in the Eucharistic host, or wafer.

Bruno Bartoletti, who for several years was the Artistic Director of the Teatro, and who conducted us a number of times, had the worst stick technique of any professional conductor I have ever witnessed. His upbeat for *Allegro furioso* was indistinguishable from that for *Adagio mesto*, a quivering, claw-like scratching motion devoid of a tempo or rhythmic pulse, and he was incapable of maintaining the normal conducting patterns. But he knew the opera repertory—under his 'conducting', among many other performances, a witty and polished version of *Gianni Schicchi* was produced, as well as a solid performance of *Wozzeck*; I could never quite understand how.

Wolfgang Sawallisch was one of the finest conductors I ever played under—benign *kappellmeister* discipline of the old school combined with highly refined, deeply prepared interpretive insight. He came several times to conduct us; it was always a memorable experience. Once, in a rehearsal, he showed us how he wanted us to play a melody from Schumann's *Scenes from Goethe's Faust* (I believe it was the magnificent passage introducing the first scene of Part II (Sunrise)). He sang the melody with an exquisite, cantabile beauty of phrasing; we could but do our best to attain the ideal he had set forth for us.

Carlos Kleiber conducted an inspiring *La Traviata*. He exuded a kind of nervous excitement that galvanized the orchestra and, I am sure, the singers. Perhaps more than any other conductor, he could convey to the orchestra the essence of a passage with wonderfully fluid, swinging

In costume, preparing for the tavern scene in Wozzeck, June 1998.

gestures. Sometimes, however, he seemed to exist on the podium in a kind of self-absorbed, other-worldly trance, as if he were communing not so much with us as with the composer. He was scheduled to conduct *La Bohème* in 1987, but he cancelled, giving reasons of health, something he had become notorious for. I wish we could have done with him *Der Rosenkavalier*, widely regarded as his signature piece.

One of the most depressing orchestral debacles I ever experienced was an ill-fated performance of Beethoven's Ninth, conducted by Georg Solti. It was a summer concert (July 1986) in the central courtyard of the Palazzo Pitti, a magnificent, historic space, but unsuited to music. We had had too few rehearsals, and apparently Solti hadn't been told that the concert was to be outdoors (it was originally scheduled for the Teatro Comunale). The conditions were atrocious: appalling acoustics, a swirling wind and a noisy audience, including curious tourists milling about. The orchestra was far from its best. It was an insult to Solti, though he soldiered on through the performance, great professional that he was. We were told that he was furious and that he vowed never to return. In fact, he never did.

In March 1987, Antal Doráti, aged nearly eighty-two, included Beethoven's 'Eroica' Symphony in one of two concerts he conducted. In the Adagio, there is a problematic passage (bb. 139–140) in which the third horn, in unison with the clarinets, suddenly drops out, because the notes in question were available only as poor-sounding stopped notes on the horn in Beethoven's time, and is replaced by the violas. After one of the rehearsals, I knocked on the door of Doráti's dressing room. He invited me in, and I asked him why he didn't adjust this passage, as many conductors do, continuing the horn up to the (concert pitch) C with the clarinets. His reply, quite simply and humbly, was, 'Because I don't dare change what Beethoven wrote.' In the first performance, when we came to this passage, I glanced over towards the horns, then looked back at Doráti. Our eyes met; he was looking straight at me, seated in the depths of the first violins, as if to say, 'Yes, that's the way I do it.' I remain puzzled by his unwonted conservatism in this passage, since he has gone on record with a more pragmatic opinion: 'In the Beethoven symphonies I accept the minor amendments of orchestration. … I think Beethoven has to be helped in his fight with his material. Beethoven suffered, for example, when he wanted notes from the horns they didn't have and wrote all kinds of things instead.'[25] At any rate, I

---

[25] Richard Chlupaty, *Antal Doráti and the Joy of Making Music* (n.p., The Antal Dorati Centenary Society, 2006), p. 403.

was impressed by Doráti's quiet control in rehearsals and his thoughtful, deeply musical interpretation of this work. Musicians of the stature of Yehudi Menuhin, Gunther Schuller (who is the sternest of critics) and András Schiff are unstinting in their admiration for Doráti's musicianship. I have since read that he had been known for tantrums with orchestras and with ballet dancers. He himself admits in his autobiography to having had a 'regrettably short temper' that 'I have only mastered quite late in life.'[26] By 1987 he most certainly had. He died in November 1988. I am glad to have had the privilege of playing under his baton.

My father outlived my mother by nine years. When she died, the house in Moncton was sold, and he moved into an apartment with Harold, on whom he increasingly depended. Dad's letters became more frequent. He sometimes complained about Harold's neglectfulness, other times, praised him for being so helpful. I now know that Harold was unfailingly kind to Dad. Their relationship was sometimes stormy, but Dad recognized, if reluctantly, how well Harold looked after him. I spent part of several summers in Parrsboro with the two of them. Once, when Dad saw me off at the airport for my return to Italy, there were tears in his eyes. It was the first time I had experienced such a display of his affection for me.

In 1990, I went to Parrsboro for the August holiday, partly to spell Harold. It had been a bad summer. Dad was showing his eighty-two years (exactly my age as I write)—emphysema (oxygen mask), lame in one leg (Zimmer frame), medicines, pills, side effects, medicines for the side effects. He would get depressed: 'I feel useless,' he would say as he limped around the cottage, his voice muffled by the mask. On a hot day, I drove him to the golf course; we sat in the car, looking out over the course to the bay—the course we had played together so many times. The water, at high tide, ruffled by a light breeze, shimmered brilliantly in the sun, an unforgettably beautiful sight. We stopped at a little shop

---

[26] Antal Doráti, *Notes of Seven Decades* (Detroit: Wayne State University Press, 1981), p. 223.

on the Two Islands road, I went in, leaving him in the car for too long in the sun. When I returned, he complained—he had been uncomfortable, and his lameness prevented him from joining me.

One day, I cut his toenails for him; he could not do it himself. They had become yellowed and fibrous. Once, he insisted that he be taken to a hospital. I drove him the eighty miles to Moncton, but the doctor said, 'Ralph, there's nothing wrong with you that you need to be here.' Dad was disappointed. He wanted to be looked after, which neither my brother nor I could do properly. Then, towards the end of the summer, we made the agonized decision to sell the cottage—the much-loved cottage our mother designed and had built—the cottage in which all of us had spent the happiest years of our lives, the cottage that my mother wouldn't have wanted us to sell. Dad said he didn't feel able to spend another summer there, my brother didn't want the responsibility, and I thought it impossible to maintain a place in Nova Scotia while living in Italy. So we sold the cottage, to be occupied as soon as my father left. As it turned out, he left early in September with the colder weather and, shortly thereafter, *was* admitted to the hospital. By then I had returned to Italy. We talked on the phone two or three times, he in his hospital bed. He said once, in his usual matter-of-fact way, 'I won't be getting out of here alive.' But his voice was strong, and I said, 'Dad, for heaven's sake …' He died a week later. I managed to get back to Moncton for the funeral and to Parrsboro for the burial, on a miserably cold, windy, rainy day. Six or eight of us huddled around the grave for the brief service, then to refreshments kindly given by the undertaker in his home. I cried in the car on the way; tears that I had not shed for my mother I shed for both of them, now together again.

In May 1992, Myung-whun Chung conducted us in two performances of Berlioz's *Romeo and Juliet* Symphony. Always impressive as a musician and technician, he was our principal guest conductor for a few years. But he appeared to be learning this piece as he went along. He seemed unaware of a crucial E major pizzicato chord in the strings that launches the brief adumbration of the Fête music in the Prologue, a characteristic Berliozian stroke of inspired orchestration. Since Chung didn't conduct it, no one played it (at least no one among the violins; the concertmaster should have mentioned it to Chung). I became increasingly frustrated, and in the dress rehearsal, seated at the third stand of the first violins, I played it, alone, *fortissimo* (it is marked *forte*). The violinist sitting directly in front of me nearly jumped out of his seat, but Chung didn't seem to notice. I don't remember if I had the courage to do the same in the concerts. On another occasion, just before a rehearsal of Beethoven's Ninth Symphony, I spoke to Chung about the transition in the last movement from Maestoso to Prestissimo on the words 'Götterfunken'. I wanted to know if he agreed with Leinsdorf's opinion in his book, *The Composer's Advocate* (1981, pp. 135–137), of the rhythmic and metric relationship between the two sections. He didn't seem very interested. In retrospect, I quite understand why he might not have been especially receptive to unsolicited musical information from an orchestra member. Conductors of his repute have acquired the habit of dispensing it, not receiving it. Lest it be supposed that I was a kind of celebrity-chasing gadfly, constantly pestering famous conductors, I hasten to add that this and the conversation with Doráti were the only times I ventured to beard these lions in their dens.

Anthony Pappano came to conduct us quite early in his career. At one point in a rehearsal, he turned to the violas and cellos and made the well-known Italian hand gesture, the fingers of one hand extended upwards and gathered together to form a pine cone. It is one of those gestures whose meaning, depending on the context, ranges from the completely inoffensive ('Whatever does this mean? I don't understand') to the quite rude. ('What the devil are you talking about? Are you serious?'). I am sure that Pappano did not intend to be offensive. A first-stand violist, however, was offended, and took Pappano very severely to task, as if giving a lesson in manners to a misbehaving child. Pappano, to his credit, listened quietly, did not reply and continued with the rehearsal. My impression was that he had probably seen his Italian parents use this gesture since childhood and had not considered it offensive. I thought, 'Quite apart from his talent, this young man has what it takes—the confidence and the sang-froid to take the hard knocks.'

Seiji Ozawa, who led us in Mahler's Symphony No. 2, had probably the most fluent and masterly manual control of any conductor alive, with or without a baton. His repertoire of gestures was inexhaustible, but perhaps more than any other conductor that I can remember, he conducted with his eyes. His presence on the podium ran the gamut from elfin whimsy to guru-like spirituality.

The great German tenor Peter Schreier came twice in the 1990s to conduct and simultaneously sing the role of the Evangelist in Bach's *Saint Matthew Passion*. It was a technical tour de force. He stood behind the orchestra, facing the audience, singing and conducting (without baton) the entire work from memory, his gestures a model of economy of means. But, above all, his interpretation of the Evangelist was the most moving I have ever experienced.

Roger Norrington was always interesting. He revealed an unexpectedly *spiritoso* side in one of his rehearsals. My stand partner was a notorious talker. She was in the habit of giving a running commentary, often negative, throughout rehearsals, about the music, the conductor, in fact almost anything, in a voice loud enough to be heard by the conductor. Norrington put up with this for several minutes before finally saying to her, in English, with unforgettably English aplomb, 'Why don't you just shut up?' as if he were asking, 'Why don't you just sit down and have a cup of tea?' My stand partner seemed not to understand, and the incident passed un-noticed. But she continued to talk; Norrington turned to her again and said, 'You know, Madam, you are a real pain in the arse.' And he immediately began to rehearse another section of the orchestra, as if nothing had happened, so that the culprit didn't have a chance to react. Brilliant!

Once, Norrington appeared, unannounced, on the podium to conduct a performance of *Rigoletto*. We in the orchestra had not been told, but clearly, he had been called in at the last moment as a substitute. I and most of my colleagues thought of him as a (controversial) 'historically informed performance' specialist, forgetting, or not knowing that he had conducted the standard operatic repertory for many years. Only a musician of high competence can step in to conduct a work, especially an opera, even a well-known one, without rehearsals. There are dozens of places where an ambiguous gesture, a missing cue, can spell disaster. Norrington took us through the work with crystal-clear ease and assurance; we had not the slightest difficulty following him. The *enfant terrible* of classical music had more than one string to his bow.

One of the last concerts I played in before I retired from the orchestra (the retirement age was sixty for orchestral musicians in Italy) was a performance of Bach's B minor Mass conducted by Ivor Bolton, on 22 November 2000, in the Teatro dei Rinnovati in the Palazzo Pubblico in Siena, where I had conducted Mahler's Adagietto thirty-five years earlier.

CHAPTER 9

Florence: chamber music

For six or seven years in the 1990s, I gave a lecture on Renaissance music and one on Baroque music, ten or twelve times a year, at the British Institute of Florence. These were part of the month-long art history courses attended chiefly by foreign students, most of them English. Armed with my experience at Ithaca College, I was determined to make these lectures as interesting as possible for young people who were not especially interested in music. For both periods it was possible to relate developments in music to those in the visual arts. Several times I was asked to give two lectures on Renaissance music, so I divided the material into sacred and secular music. Similarly, when there was a call for it, I divided the Baroque material into vocal and instrumental music. In the Baroque lectures, I was able to demonstrate with the violin such things as changes in the structure of the violin, the development of violin technique, ornamentation, cadenzas and the like. I had hoped to have the services of one of my keyboardist friends to help demonstrate the realization of a figured bass, but scheduling difficulties never allowed it. The whole experience was extremely rewarding.

Not long after joining the Orchestra of the Maggio Musicale Fiorentino, I was invited to Richard and Anne Maury's house for supper and string quartets. They were both artists, both Americans who had lived in Florence since 1960: she painted plants and flowers beautifully for clients such as the Florence Botanical Garden; he was a freelance painter. They were enthusiastic chamber music players. We met once every six weeks or so for more than twenty years. I played first violin; Richard, second; another member of the orchestra, viola; and Anne, cello. We played mostly Haydn's quartets, occasionally one by Mozart. Richard was an intense, sometimes prickly person; his facial expression, his gaze, reminded me of Van Gogh. He painted in his own personal version of realism—powerfully expressive faces, stark but beautiful nudes, sometimes placed in mysteriously arranged interiors with enigmatic reflected images. Richard had a spikey, ironic sense of humour that immediately attracted me. Occasionally, in our quartet sessions he would become so frustrated, so enraged at his inability to play a passage that we had to stop and wait until he calmed down. Anne was always sweet and serene. They and their four children lived frugally for years in a large apartment on Costa di San Giorgio, until Richard was taken up by a gallery in New York City and began to acquire a reputation and to earn more money. He died a few years ago. I miss him.

Quartet session with Richard Maury and violist Claudia Wolvington, about 1995.
The cellist is a guest, not Anne Maury.

It was at the Maury home, sometime in the 1990s that, after thirty years, I again met my old Siena mathematician friend, George Wilson. By coincidence, he was also a friend of Richard and Anne and regularly came to Florence in the summers and practised on their piano. For several summers, we happily read through works of the violin and piano repertory, including the Elgar Sonata, which I had never played before. It was a providential, extremely pleasant reunion.

Merritt Cootes, a retired US Consul General in Florence and his wife, Jean, a pianist and enthusiastic chamber music player, occasionally had musical soirées, followed by dinner, in their country house a few miles from Florence. Several Maggio Musicale Fiorentino players and others would join these gatherings. Once, Harold Acton was the guest of honour. He would have been in his mid-eighties, dressed impeccably in a double-breasted pin-stripe suit. After we had played, waiting for dinner, we musicians sat with Acton. I remember, with infinite regret, having this distinguished man in our midst, this link with Oxford of the 1920s, this splendidly elegant, cultured author, scholar and aesthete (the British Institute library in Florence, with its superb English language collection, was named after him in 1989), that none of us was able to ask him an intelligent question—not so much, I fear, because we were too awestruck, as because we were too ignorant. I don't remember precisely what he said to us, only that he was charming and not in the slightest condescending.

Jean Cootes was not one to mince words. Once, she kindly drove Susan (this was very early in our courtship) to a concert of the Orchestra of the Maggio Musicale Fiorentino in a very large conference hall. As they were looking for a seat in the vast space, Susan timidly asked if they could sit a little closer to the orchestra (she wanted to be able to see me, of course). Said Jean: 'Wadda ya' want—to sit on his lap?' Years later, after she and Merritt had returned to the USA, Susan and I happened to be in the bookshop of the National Portrait Gallery in London, and there she was! We chatted—she was all sweetness and light—we said our goodbyes and went our separate ways. I never saw her again. She died in 2004.

For nine years, Susan and I lived on Via Piana in Bellosguardo, on a hill on the southern edge of Florence. Our next-door neighbour was Joan Haslip, whose biographies of royal personages (Catherine the Great, Marie Antoinette, Elizabeth of Austria and others) enjoyed considerable success. We hardly ever saw her—she was of an older generation, and her circle of friends included the cultural and intellectual elite of Florence. One night, close to midnight, we heard two men shouting goodbye to Ms Haslip, their dinner hostess, and rollicking down the road, chatting in louder-than-usual voices, no doubt wine-induced. We looked out the window and saw that it was Harold Acton and John Pope-Hennessy, old friends of hers, both knights of the realm.

On the morning of 19 February 1994, I played the Siciliano from Bach's G minor unaccompanied violin sonata at a funeral in the Lutheran church on the Lungarno Torrigiani in Florence. I had been asked on the telephone by someone unknown to me, and I had no idea who the deceased was. The shortness of notice had overcome any qualms I might have had about the suitability of such a piece on such an occasion—it was the only unaccompanied piece I felt prepared to play. At the ceremony, most of the people spoke German, and it didn't seem appropriate to ask questions, so I played and went home. It was a strange, dream-like experience. But the thing nagged at some part of my consciousness, and more than twenty years later, in 2015, I mustered the courage and the energy (so late, so slow!) to call the church and got the name of the deceased, a certain Frau L. Z., born in Hamburg, resident in Florence. I had had some vague notion that the deceased (I hadn't known whether a man or a woman) was a violinist—someone must have told me this. I obtained from the church the name of a daughter of Frau L. Z. in Florence, Signora C. I called her, and she told me that her mother was not a musician but that her (Frau L. Z.'s) father had been a professional violinist in Hamburg. And that was why they had asked for a violinist to play at his daughter's funeral. I sometimes wonder about him. What was he like? What did he think of his daughter going to live in Florence? And above all, would he have been pleased at her being sent off with my rendition of Bach?

Intermezzo: sporting life

I began playing tennis, took my first tennis lessons when I was forty years old. Within a few months, I conceived the perverse, utterly hopeless ambition, which I still harbour at the age of eighty-two, to become a good player. Looking over my pocket diaries from the 1980s and 1990s, I am dismayed at the time and energy I put into tennis that might have been better spent. I played almost every day of the week, often twice, even three times a day, sometimes alone practising serves, sometimes having two lessons in one day in different clubs.

My first tennis teacher was a German in his sixties from whom I took ten lessons in Berlin in 1981. He was very strict, not at all sympathetic. I guessed that he resented having to teach tennis to American military personnel at the US Army base in the American sector—he would have been in his twenties in 1945, but perhaps I am over-interpreting. He spoke German in the lessons, so among other things it was a way of picking up some of the language, most of which I have now, unfortunately, forgotten.

My first tennis *maestro* in Italy was W. P., a very thin, wiry man who dyed his hair blonde and drank himself to death. He had once been a good player but, when I came to him, was well past his prime. He used to irritate me in lessons during the winter by saying, 'You can never improve in the winter; just be satisfied with maintaining your level.' I didn't want to hear that.

Over the years in Florence, I have had several tennis *maestri*. I became quite close to one of them, whom I followed as he switched to three different clubs over a period of about eight years. At my last lesson with him, on a hot August day in 1993, before he and his wife moved to France, I gave him a bottle of champagne, duly recorded in my pocket diary.

For several years, I had a lesson at seven o'clock in the morning, which meant getting up at five-thirty, eating a bowl of muesli (doing without my normal coffee), and making the three-quarters-of-an-hour drive on my motor scooter, in complete darkness in the cold winter months, to a club on the outskirts of the far side of the city. It was an obsession. Now I am no longer capable of such heroism.

I attended, doggedly and compulsively, numerous summer tennis camp sessions in Austria, Italy and the USA. I acquired and studied a whole shelf of tennis manuals. I bought a ball-throwing machine, an appalling extravagance, and used it for two or three years, but it eventually became unusable because of clay getting into its works.

I often scheduled my tennis appointments alarmingly close to the time of orchestra rehearsals or concerts. Morning rehearsals were normally from ten to one; in the afternoon from four to seven; quite often, I would squeeze in an hour of tennis between them, from two to three. On one March day in 1989, after a ten-to-one rehearsal, I played tennis from three to four, then from five-thirty to seven-thirty with another player at another tennis club, followed by a quick shower, a motor scooter drive to the Teatro Comunale, a change into my tails, and a concert at eight-thirty (Beethoven Nos. 6, 5 conducted by Gustav Kuhn). This was an extreme case, it is true, but I now find this behaviour insouciant to the point of recklessness.

For ten or twelve years, I faithfully recorded in my diary the scores of all the matches I played, often with comments. The sheer, numbing, discouraging frequency of these entries is only partly conveyed by the following, more or less random sampling, long as it is (the uninterested reader is invited to skip it):

with Fantecchi, 7–8, bad, couldn't serve into the sun, very hot day, sluggish

with Simone [maestro], bad. Palleggio [rally] was OK but then we played games, he hitting the ball hard and moving me around—my strokes fell apart

with Susan, then lost a set (5–7) to a very bad player

with Gordon, 6–1, 6–1!! But he was playing very badly, seemed distracted although he denied this, said it was his legs—wasn't moving well. He made <u>many</u> mistakes, shots into the net or out. Now I know what I'm like to play against!

with Tilli, 6–8, I was listless, moving badly, 2 dbl faults

with Candela, 3–6, but close

with Gordon, 7–8, hard fought, some good tennis

with Gordon, 7–5, I was ahead 5–1 then lost my edge partially

with Tacchi, 5–7, bad tennis

with Pernigotti, 4–6, he hits the ball hard

with Stefano, 1–6, he's still too strong for me

with Tacchi, 2–6, 4–3, he was playing very well in 1st set. I made too many mistakes, esp in approach shots, return of serve. A little better in 2nd set

with Zucchelli, 4–6, 0–6, I was OK but then got terrible—all balls too long

with Gordon, 1–6, 1–5, then rain. I was good when we played points, but then bad in sets. He kept me on the defensive, attacked my 2nd serve. I couldn't return his serve.

with Zucchelli, 6–3, I was fair, had trouble with 1. his sliced serve far to my right, 2. his low sliced backhand to my forehand

with Frosecchi, 6–4, 0–3, struggled to win 1st set facing sun, then collapsed completely

with Stefano, 2–6, massacre

with Nicky, 6–4, but bad tennis

with Nicky, 1–6, unbelievably bad

hit backhands with machine

with Nicky 0–6, 1–6, 0–6 disaster, wild flailing at ball

with Patrizio, 6–6, I was determined

[31 August 1994] with Gordon, using Western grip—will give myself
till end of Sept to decide whether to use it or no

In December 1988, I took part in a six-day tennis *stage*, ten to twelve-
thirty each day at one of the Florence tennis clubs. On the 27th (my
forty-eighth birthday), at the end of a typically mournful entry, there is
a solitary happy note:

groundstrokes, lots of running: 1 forehand then 1 backhand—
exhausting. Then videotape—appalling. I shuffle about the court like
an old man—grimly apposite in view of the date ... then ½ hour of
volleys. Susan gave me two lovely gifts, was waiting for me with a
lovely lunch of scrambled eggs & salmon, and a yellow rose in a vase.

By 1996, I was still recording scores, but the dreary litany of comments
is petering out. I am not especially athletic, my hand–eye, or rather more
crucially for tennis, my foot–eye coordination is, if anything, below
normal, yet still I persist with two lessons a week, and still, after forty
years, become frustrated at the slowness of my progress and at the
knowledge that I will never be more than a mediocre player. My father
was an athlete, good at several sports. I suppose I want to be like him,
and I will go to the grave trying. I excuse my obsession on the grounds
that playing tennis is good for my health, but I know perfectly well that
it is only an excuse. Now that I am in my eighties, my physical decline,
my lumbering, varicose-veined legs, slower reflexes, weaker eyes

exacerbate my frustration without mitigating my ambition. I am unable
to shake off this form of self-mortification.

In action on the tennis court, Florence, about 1995. It took years
of practice to reach this level.

I must say, however, that I've met a few interesting people on the tennis
court, in some cases because the game, especially in competition,
reveals certain character traits. One person I used to play with was Padre

S. (the courts at my club were owned and operated by the Church). He was a charming man and very light of foot. His specialty was his sliced backhand which involved an elegant pirouette on the follow-through, coming around full circle to face his opponent again, who would be mesmerized by this balletic display. He would occasionally make a dubious call of an opponent's shot, which somehow endeared him to me—that a priest, after all, was human. But, over the years, I have been less amused by other players, not all of them Italian, who habitually called their opponent's ball out when it was in.

Padre S. stopped playing after a few years, perhaps because the Church sold the courts to a private owner. Years afterwards, I bumped into him on the street. He had changed, was no longer his jovial self, spoke in a strangely distant, detached manner. Later, reflecting on it, I thought he might have been trying to tell me something and that I should have read between the lines. But what?

One man who would rather have died than make a bad call was Gordon Moran, who became a good friend. When I met him in 1983, he had acquired a certain notoriety as one of two American art historians who maintained, very publicly, that the *Equestrian Portrait of Guidoriccio da Fogliano*, the famous fresco of a condottiere in the Palazzo Pubblico in Siena, was not by the great fourteenth-century Sienese artist Simone Martini as commonly thought, but a much later work, from as late as the eighteenth century. Gordon marshalled a vast amount of evidence—documentary, iconographic, stylistic and physical—to support his claim. I was completely convinced that he was right and still am. The fresco had become a much-loved, indeed revered, Sienese symbol, emblazoned on everything from tea towels to jewellery boxes.

The furore rumbled on, stoked and revived almost gleefully by Gordon for thirty years, right up to the year of his death (2014). Gordon clearly enjoyed his role as a muckraker, a whistle blower. He had a pugnacious side to his character, which, allied to his terrier-like conviction that he was in the right, made him a difficult adversary. He became persona non grata in certain Sienese circles, though he maintained a close and affectionate relationship with one of the

Equestrian Portrait of Guidoriccio da Fogliano, probably not by Simone Martini, Palazzo Pubblico, Siena. (Photo: Alinari Archives)

contrade. He was effectively banned from attending certain art-historical conferences in Siena. His art-historical enemies, however, were not only Sienese.

I was present on one occasion, in 1983 or 1984, at a lecture given by the Swiss art historian Max Seidel to a sedate audience at the Villa I Tatti, the former home of Bernard Berenson, near Florence, occupied by Harvard University as a study centre. Suddenly, Gordon stood up and interrupted: 'Why haven't you quoted the second half of that sentence in the document?'

Seidel (visibly shaken): 'Well, I can't very well quote the entire document, and anyway I may have omitted the phrase through an oversight.'

'No, you have deliberately suppressed crucial data that casts irrefutable doubt on your claims.' An embarrassed silence blanketed the room. Gordon kept hammering away with his accusations. Eventually Seidel managed to finish his lecture, and a few years later he got his revenge. The Kunsthistorisches Institut in Florence, of which Seidel became the director, somehow contrived to obscure for some time all bibliographic references to the writings of Gordon Moran in the catalogue of its (renowned) art history library.

Such was Gordon's dedication to the truth that he would make a ritual on the tennis court of examining, with infinite care, the mark made by the ball in the clay if it had landed near the line, before calling it in or out. I respected him for that—it was utterly characteristic of him. He was a better player than I—not his strokes, but he was more astute, and his left-handed serve always confounded me, although the last few times that we played, he had gained too much weight and was visibly weaker. Gordon often had a ribald story to regale me with as we walked onto the tennis court. He very much enjoyed watching the annual international junior tennis championship in Florence, especially the girls' tennis, and it wasn't just to study their backhands. He was an aficionado of bel canto opera and told me that when he sang Donizetti's arias (he had a terrible singing voice) to the olive trees on his wife Lucia's family property near Montepulciano, the harvest invariably benefitted dramatically. I miss him.

One day, the director of my tennis club, a very fine player from whom I had taken lessons for several years, asked me to be his partner in a doubles match with George Soros and another player. He made it clear to me that Soros did not like to lose and that we might perhaps win one set but see to it that Soros and his partner won the match. Soros and his friend arrived without fanfare in an unostentatious car; we were introduced—I was only vaguely aware of Soros's fame and indeed notoriety. He was an enthusiastic but mediocre player, perhaps even more mediocre than I (he would have been about seventy-five years old at the time). During breaks, the four of us chatted amicably about nothing in particular. The match went according to plan. The score, as I recall: Soros/partner vs Billi/Lister: 3–6, 6–4, 7–5. It was a very pleasant two hours.

The similarities between training for tennis (almost any sport, I suppose) and practising the violin (any instrument?) are perfectly obvious, but not at all superficial:

Staying in shape: regular, consistent practice;
Warming up: stretching, preliminary calisthenics = scales and other warming-up routines;
Just two basic strokes: forehand, backhand = just two basic strokes: downbow, upbow;

BUT variety of shots (top spin, backspin, fast shots, delicate drop shots, etc.) = variety of bow strokes (martelé, spiccato, flautato, varying bow speeds, etc.);

The principle of repetition of movements, but not blind repetition;

The principle of breaking down large movements to their smaller components, then putting them together: e.g. practising only the backswing = practising a shift by playing the 'passing' note;

The principle of economy of motion: abbreviated backswing for the return of serve = minimal vertical motion for smooth string crossings;

The principle of finishing one movement before beginning the next, especially critical when there is little time between the two: e.g. following through on a stroke in a baseline corner before returning to a more central position = finishing a note immediately before a big shift of position;

Strategy/tactics: planning the point: serve to the outside line, if possible walk around my backhand to hit a forehand to the open court, come to the net, volley = begin the first phrase *mezzo piano*, build to the fifth bar of a six-bar phrase, *diminuendo* to the end of the phrase, ever-so-slight delay before beginning the second phrase, slight *accelerando* to the third bar, agogic accent on the downbeat;

Last split-second adjustment of a stroke because of a bad bounce = last split-second adjustment of a finger up or down for a slightly out-of-tune note;

Endurance, mental and physical, maintaining concentration: in a long match = in a long piece of music or a recital.

CHAPTER 10

G. B. Viotti

As if it had been planned for my retirement, at almost the same time that I left the Orchestra of the Maggio Musicale Fiorentino, I became interested in the great Italian violinist-composer Giovanni Battista Viotti (1755–1824) and ended up writing a biography. It began in the spring of 2000. I had just given a violin lesson to a student who was working on Viotti's Concerto No. 22 and I was depressed about how the lesson had gone. It occurred to me that I knew absolutely nothing about Viotti—I had only the vaguest idea of when he lived. I looked him up in a dictionary of music and was struck by the drama of his life and career. I began to look into other sources ('research' would be too strong a word), without any thought other than to learn a little more about him. One thing led to another. I found various gaps and discrepancies in the Viotti literature, wrote a few articles in scholarly journals and began to think that it might be possible to write a biography.

In the meantime, I made the epistolary acquaintance of another Viotti researcher, the Australian Denise Yim, who had written her thesis on the Chinnery Family Papers, the huge collection that she had uncovered of the correspondence of Viotti's closest friends in England. When I saw her thesis, which was exhaustive, I experienced a moment of extreme doubt and discouragement: was there anything left for me to say? Then Denise published an excellent book, *Viotti and the Chinnerys: A Relationship Charted Through Letters,* in 2004, which redoubled my fears. I toyed with the idea of writing a half-biography treating the first part of Viotti's life, before he moved to England and met the Chinnerys. But the impracticality of this idea soon became apparent. Eventually, I decided that I had discovered enough new material to justify a full biography. In the meantime, Denise had become a valued friend and comrade-in-arms whose generosity and expertise were valuable beyond measure.

For eight years it was a labour of love. I made three visits to Fontanetto Po (Viotti's birthplace): the parochial archive; fourteen or fifteen to Turin (Viotti's early career): various archives; four or five to Biella: the archive of the Dal Pozzo family, Viotti's patrons in Turin; shorter visits to other Italian archives; seven or eight to Paris (Viotti lived in Paris for ten years): various archives; nine or ten to London: mostly the British Library; and one (two weeks) to Sydney, Australia, where the Chinnery Family Papers collection is housed in the Powerhouse Museum and in the University of Sydney library. I spent more money than I dare think about on trains, planes and hotels. It became (another) obsession, but they were also some of the happiest and most rewarding times of my life. When I found a document that no one else had noticed, my hands trembled with excitement.

At night, in my hotel room, in the various cities I visited (usually for stays of from two or three to ten days), I would spread out on my bed the copies of documents I had acquired and the notes I had taken that day, look them over and try to map out the next day's plan of attack. Undoubtedly, I wasted hours, through inexperience, searching the archives (especially the *Archives nationales* in Paris, which are of a Byzantine complexity), taking proper notes and performing similar routine scholarly duties. Dr Johnson was never nearer the mark than when he wrote, 'A man will turn over half a library to make one book.' Only a fraction of what I read or took notes on entered my book. On the other hand, one thing I learned from writing the book was the importance of reading as widely as possible, not only specifically about one's subject, but more broadly. Through reading Jeremy Black's *The Grand Tour in the Eighteenth Century* (1992), for example, I was able to find, indirectly and almost accidentally, in an archive whose existence

I had been completely unaware of, what turned out to be an important letter written by an Englishman who heard Viotti play in Geneva early in his career.

I was lucky not only in that Viotti was of the highest importance in the history of violin playing and composition for the violin but also in that he led an extremely interesting life, brilliant but chequered, and in some ways, tragic. It was a story that could almost have told itself, considered against the social and political backdrop of the French Revolution and its aftermath, the change from courtly and aristocratic patronage of the *ancien régime* to the increasingly commercial, box office-centred institutions of the nineteenth century. Luckier still, there had been no biography in English other than Denise Yim's, which, indeed, presented difficulties since it was well written, and I was anxious not to duplicate it. I decided almost at the outset that my book would be a Life, not a Life and Works. To treat the works in detail in a separate section would have made the book far too long.

I soon became aware that the only full-scale biography of Viotti written in the twentieth century, by an Italian author, is blemished by numerous blatant fabrications—wholly invented 'archive files', 'documents', 'newspaper articles', 'events' and even one 'person'. I came to resent the mischief this book had created in the Viotti literature and the time I was forced to waste tracking down illusory sources and fictitious citations. Unfortunately, despite my efforts and those of others to alert the scholarly community, it was, and still is, a commonly cited source.[27] It was a bracing lesson in the fragility of the historical record, only partly assuaged by the hope that my book had helped to set the record straight. I was disinclined to be charitable towards this author since he is unrestrained in his denigration of the writings of others on Viotti. I compiled a list, some eight single-spaced pages in length, of the

---

[27] For example, H. C. Robbins Landon, *Haydn in England, 1791–1795* (London: Thames and Hudson, 1976), p. 234, n.1: 'See the excellent full-length study … with a very useful and accurate thematic catalogue.' I am at a loss to understand how the distinguished American musicologist arrived at this judgement, so spectacularly wrong.

fabrications (not mistakes, mind you) that I found in the book. There are probably many more.

On the other hand, I was pleasantly surprised by the spirit of scholarly cooperation and generosity in musicological circles. Musicologists of repute, such as Clive Brown, Simon McVeigh and Neil Zaslaw invariably responded to my questions and shared information with me, an unknown new arrival, with complete openness, though they had nothing to gain from it. I also found most librarians and archivists to be courteous and helpful. Indeed, were it not for the timely suggestions volunteered by two alert Italian archivists, I would probably have remained ignorant of two crucially important sources: the Royal House of Savoy accounts (*Recapiti*) in the Biblioteca Reale in Turin, and the Dal Pozzo family papers in the Archivio di Stato in Biella. I had never heard of Biella, let alone the archive.

In Turin, I always stayed in the Hotel Dogana Vecchia, in bygone days the Osteria della Dogana Nova, in which, in January 1771, Leopold Mozart and his son stayed for a week, the latter celebrating his fifteenth birthday in Turin. In my book, I regretfully point out that in his travel diary Leopold mentions making the acquaintance of Viotti's celebrated teacher, Gaetano Pugnani, as well as of his patroness, the Marchesa di Voghera of the Dal Pozzo family, but does not mention Viotti, who was only a few months older than Wolfgang. Surely the two teenagers were introduced to each other, and surely they played together at an *accademia* in the home of the Marchesa! Alas, there is no proof ...

Once, in the National Library of Florence, my request for a nineteenth-century book came back with the single word 'alluvionato' (literally 'flooded') written on the request slip. After my initial shock, I realized that it meant that the book had been rendered unusable by the overflowing of the Arno in 1966.

I was at first thoroughly intimidated by the Bibliothèque François-Mitterand (Tolbiac), one of the sites of the Bibliothèque nationale in Paris—its sprawling, forbidding exterior, with its four glass, book-shaped skyscrapers and its vast plank deck, like that of an aircraft carrier. Descending into the bunker-like interior, surrounded by massive chain-mail curtains (against aerial bombing attacks?) I felt that I was entering a prison. But, once inside, miraculously, the light comes pouring in from a kind of forested nature reserve in the central atrium. There could be no greater contrast than with the nineteenth-century domed wooden Oval Room of the old Bibliotheque nationale, Site Richelieu library, with its individual green lamp shades and the little white enamel number plates. This magnificent space was no longer in use except once, when it was occupied temporarily by the *Archives nationales* during the refurbishment against asbestos of the normal site of the Archives in the Hôtel de Soubise. The huge new site of the *Archives* at Pierrefitte-sur-Seine in the northern suburbs had not yet been built.

In the Palermo national archive, a man (another researcher?) took me aside without introducing himself and warned me, sotto voce, about vague threats to my research—persons who might try to steal my discoveries if I were not careful. He must have overheard me talking to the librarians about my interests. He seemed genuinely concerned. Occurring as it did in the land of the Mafia, I was alarmed but not surprised, and nothing came of it.

I append a sampling of entries in my pocket agenda from those years, in the hope that it gives an idea of what researching a book can entail. For the present volume, a few words of explanation are enclosed in square brackets. The importance I attached to my stomach will not escape the reader.

2001

24 April, Tuesday: 7.30 a.m. to Gatwick [**London**, first visit] arr. c.9.30, train to King's Cross, taxi to Penn Club. Terrible cup of soup from a machine. 14.00–20.00 at U. of London Library, Music Room mostly, photocopied excerpts from Brenet, Baillot, McVeigh diss. Phoned Susan several times, no answer.

Wednesday: To **Oxford** arr. c.9.15. The quadrangles of Christ Church. Library. Into a cramped basement—G. Chinnery's letters—14 vols. 2

huge vols of Denise Yim's thesis *Chinnery Papers*. Discouragement, bad headache. Could only skim thesis, glance at one vol of letters, ordered c.300 pp photocopies from thesis. Train back [to **London**]. British Library, got temp Reader's Card. 19.30 phoned Susan—she is sad. Greek restaurant.

Thursday: To ULL [U. of London Library]. Looked at maps, got 5 photocopies: London + Gilwell. Back to Penn Club. Taxi to King's Cross. Sunny. 45 minutes to Chingford. Heavy wind, rain, lunch in café, walked to **Gilwell** [the Chinnery home], very rainy then stopped. About 1.5 miles, past golf course. Gilwell House in the sun. Walked around, saw C[aroline]'s column, W[alter]'s urn, poked around in the house, no one saw me, took photos, but ran out of film before staircase. Train + U back to King's Cross. Ind. restaurant.

Friday: 9.30 to 17.00 in British Library, 20 m. for lunch. Frustrating— learning the system, getting wrong books, 15-book limit. Back to Penn Club.

Saturday: 9.30–17.00 BL. I was more efficient this time. Copied by hand, photocopied. Supper at very good Indian restaurant.

Sunday: 10.30 a.m. walked around Mayfair: Curzon St, Half Moon St, Shepherd Market, Berkely Sq. Lunch with Gilly [a friend] at Zen Garden Rest. To Royal Acad. exhibit of Botticelli's Dante drawings— crowded, to Gilly's for tea. Supper—sandwich from Saintsbury's [*sic*] at Penn Club.

Monday: 9 a.m.–4 p.m. Royal College of Music Library. Made an inventory of V. collection for myself. Looked at an interesting opera libretto—V. co-author [*sic*]—1 act—'Corinne au capitole' Ind. restaurant.

Tuesday: To **Gilwell**. Photocopied a few docs. Huge modern wing tacked onto Gilwell House. Mrs T. took me around old house. Took photos. Last walk around grounds—photos. c.15.00 to Guildhall, photocopied Harwood[?], looked at old wine book [regarding Viotti's wine business?].

Wednesday: 9.30–15.30 BL, some time in Map Room, ordered photocopy of 1782 Paris map (excerpt).

Walked to Thames Link etc. 17.30 lv Gatwick.

2002

17 February, Sunday: left Fl 13.13 train, changed at Bologna, arr. **Torino** 17.50 [first visit]. Taxi to hotel Dogana Vecchia, €83. Walked to Sezione Riunite [a division of the Archivio di Stato], Via Piave 21. Found trattoria via S. Tommaso 10, good. Skating in pza Castello.

Monday: breakfast downstairs—old (historic?) room. 8.45–14.00 at Sezione Riunite. Very modern. Nice librarian helped. *Conti Camerale* and *Insinuazioni*. 3 p.m.–6.30 p.m. Bib[lioteca] Reale, photocopied DeGregori + Feb 1774 Carnevale booklet. Dinner in hotel—bad. Went skating 9–10 p.m., shaky at first, got better, called Susan.

Tuesday: breakfast downstairs. 8.30–16.30 at Archivio Storico [della Città] di Torino [A.S.C.T.], via Barbaroux with 45 minutes for panino at nearby bar. Conti of Teatro Regio: *Ordinati and Carte Sciolte*. To Archivio di Stato [Prima sezione], c.5.00–6.30 p.m. Finally found, ordered for Thursday: *Lettere di Ministri* (Prussia: Fontana, 5 mazzi: 1778–83?) done for me on computer—computer system looks <u>very</u> difficult. Supper at same place as Sun. Tired, to bed—phoned S., she wasn't very nice.

Wednesday: Couldn't sleep. Up at 7 a.m., to station, rent car, to **Salussola**—nice hill(!) town. Nothing in basement archive—nice secretary + elderly man helped me. She photocopied map on wall, glass and all. Was about to leave, elderly man (geometra) [told me of] another archive (catastale) upstairs. But I found nothing. Drove out towards Borriana, home—via Corso G. Cesare thru centre. Car to station—drug addict [in the car park]. c.4 p.m. into bib. in Palazzo [Dal Pozzo della] Cisterna, but no time. To Arch. di Stato—looked at *Lettere Ministri*. Skated 19–19.30.

Thursday: A.S.C.T.: 8.30 to finish (c.2 hrs). To Bib. Reale, looked at one reel (April–July 1773) of microfilm of Recapiti. To Arch. di Stato—*Lettere Ministri*, c.14.00–18.30. Panic: I've left agenda, money at giornalaio [newsstand]. Phoned S.—her email virus, to bed.

Friday: 6.30 a.m. to giornalaio—he had agenda. To bib. In Pal Cisterna, 8.15–c.12.30. Nice librarian gave me book on Dal Pozzo, photocopied pp. of another book. Sandwich, taxi to Bib. Della Corte, took notes on Laborde, Scanarelli. Bus to Pza Statuto, walked to hotel for bag, taxi to station. Train to Milano, changed for Florence, arr. c.10 p.m.

26 March, Tuesday: 13.13 lv. Fl., 17.58 arr. **Biella** [second visit].

Wednesday: Archivio di Stato 8.30 a.m. to 6.30 p.m. non-stop except for a pee. No lunch. Back to hotel for bag, taxi to station, terrible sandwich in terrible station bar. Change at Santhia, arr. Torino 9.02 p.m. Taxi to hotel, phoned S. Ate at usual place.

Thursday: 8.35 lv. Torino, arr. **Genoa** c.10.20. Taxi to Archivio di Stato, archivists couldn't find letter [cited in the previously mentioned twentieth-century Viotti biography]. Train 11.50 back to **Torino**, to Archivio di Stato: *Lettere Ministri*: Genova; *Matrimoni* (2 mazzi).

Friday: Up at 5 a.m., couldn't sleep. Train 6.50 to **Biella**. Again to Arch. di Stato: *Famiglia dal Pozzo, Beni Diversi*, m. 27, etc.—several photocopies. Train 12.30 back to **Torino**—slow (3 hours).

Saturday: 9 a.m. to Palazzo Cisterna, guided tour—nice lady guide but disappointing, I learned almost nothing, saw 1st floor (only) west wing. To Bib. Reale: *Recapiti* 1st. reel of 1774 (in part—to May 1774). 14.07 lv. Tor., 16.00 lv. Milano, home by 19.00.

2004

27 October, Wednesday: arr. **Torino** c.13.00 [tenth visit]. Sandwich in bar. Archivio di Stato, Sezione Riunite: *Cariche and Cariche di Corte*, looking for 1786 dimissione of Viotti. No luck. c.8 p.m. train to **Trino** [birthplace of Viotti's stepmother]—carabinieri took me from station to hotel!

Thursday: staying at Massimo, v. Ferrari. To S. Bartolomeo. Don Natalino was at first *very* off-putting—'un altro momento', then c.30 minutes later had softened, was all apologies. Found 1763 matrimonio doc. of Felice V. [Viotti's father]. Train to **Fontanetto**. Archivio comunale: nothing (almost). Lunch at Orso.

Friday: Fontanetto [returned to Florence in afternoon].

2005

2 April, Saturday: 15.25 Air France arr. CDG [Charles de Gaulle Airport, **Paris**] 17.15 [sixth visit].

Sunday: Splurge brunch at Le Castiglione, r. St. Honoré nr. Vendôme. Scrambled eggs and bacon! To Cité de la Musique—V's blue eyes [portrait], took notes. Bookstore, looked at new Conservatoire. Back to hotel.

Monday: Archives nationales until 3 p.m. Delay, got renewed card. Mystery of André's [Viotti's brother] Légion d'honneur birthdate.

Sandwich walking to Metro. To Richelieu, got renewed card. To Louvois [Bibliothèque nationale Music Dept.] til 6 p.m.—nothing.

Tuesday: Tolbiac, 9 a.m. to 8 p.m. Journal de Paris (most seemed wrong—no announcements of spectacles? [this refers to fictitious newspaper announcements]); *Mercure; A[ffiches] a[nnonces] [et] a[vis] d[ivers]*, etc. Nothing. 3 mfiches: *Livre rouge*, Pougin: Rode, Viotti.

Wednesday: Tolbiac 9 a.m.–7.45 p.m. Ate at Stella.

Thursday: 9 a.m. A.n. André's Légion d'honneur photocopied. Looked at mfilm of O1617 De La Ferté's Opéra correspondence—nothing. c.12.00 Richelieu, looked at 1788 Soc. Olympique directory, lunch at café. Mfilm of [Masonic] *Contrat Social* membership. c.3 p.m. to Louvois: Viotti mss etc., Concerto No. 28. Supper Moroccan.

Friday: Tolbiac till 7.30 p.m. Ate at L'Incroyable.

Saturday: 9 a.m.–12.30 Louvois. Lunch r. St Anne, across from hotel. 18.45 lv CDG, arr. Fl 20.40.

14 September, Wednesday: lv Fl 8.14, arr. **Torino** 13.10 [c. tenth visit]. A.S.C.T.: *Collezione IX, Conti*, vols 59, 48, 56. *Ordinati*, vol 9. Left archive 16.15. Train 17.10 arr Fl 22.15 via Genoa, Pisa. Had only sandwich for lunch & supper but then carrot & avocado + ice cream(!) home.

In 2003, I got wind of a collection of Viotti research materials in the music history department of the Freie Universität Berlin. I went to Berlin, was led into the basement of the library and was shown several shelves crammed with folders and binders. I ended up staying a week looking through this extensive collection compiled in the 1980s and 1990s by a German graduate student whose uncompleted dissertation was on Viotti's chamber music. He seems to have decided in midstream to begin work on a critical edition of the complete works of Viotti—an extremely ambitious undertaking, indeed impossible for one person. As I sifted through the copious notes, photocopies of music manuscripts and other documents, following him, as it were, on his trips to various Italian archives, I began to feel a certain empathy for his struggles with the research, struggles that I was experiencing myself at the time. I had not learned of the reason for his abandoning the project. Then I found two or three extremely intimate photographs that he had presumably left by accident among the papers. I removed them, wrote up a summary description of the collection and gave it, along with the photographs, to the musicologist in charge, who subsequently told me that the young researcher had died. He was clearly at the beginning of a distinguished career, having already contributed several review articles to the prestigious journal *Die Musikforschung*. A pity.

My efforts to leave no stone unturned were not always rewarded:

25 February 2005

Dear Venetia Murray,

I take the liberty of writing to you concerning two references in your excellent book, *High Society in the Regency Period 1788–1830*. For the last several years I have been researching the life of G. B. Viotti, the late eighteenth-century violinist-composer who lived in England from 1792. You twice make mention of Viotti's daughter (pp. 121 and 125), which puzzles me, since Viotti did not marry and is not known to have left issue. This is the first time I have seen a reference to Viotti having a daughter. Would you be so kind as to inform me as to what your sources are for these references?

I am sorry to trouble you with this. I should be most grateful for your help.

With best wishes,

Warwick Lister

27th May 2005

Dear Mr Lister,

I've seen your letter that you sent on 25th February to Venetia Murray, about some puzzling references. Sadly, Venetia Murray died late last year, and so I'm afraid nobody can help you on this.

Yours sincerely …

Editorial Director

The reviews of my book, *Amico, the Life of Giovanni Battista Viotti*, were generally favourable—especially the one in the *Times Literary Supplement*—but not ecstatic, and one, in *Notes*, the music librarians' journal, was hostile. My book has its defects. Perhaps the most noticeable is a stylistic infelicity—overuse of the first-person plural, the authorial 'we': 'we cannot be sure that …', 'we may well suppose that …', etc., *ad infinitum*. I am at a loss to understand why I did not notice this annoying linguistic tic. The book perhaps also suffers from an overabundance of detail. This, however, I think is justified, at least to an extent, by my desire, stated in the Preface, to tell all that is known about the life and career of Viotti. A common criticism of biographies, including mine, is that the author indulges in too much speculation, too many scenarios involving 'might very well have happened'. Reviewers should be careful when making this criticism. For my part, I think it would be a dereliction of duty for a biographer *not* to speculate in this manner. It is a question of how frequent, how relevant and how plausible these speculations are; how important the occasion or event is that is being so treated; and how much the speculation contributes to the reader's understanding or (dare I say it?) enjoyment. I leave it to the reader of my book to decide whether my speculations meet these criteria.

One area in which I chose not to speculate was the nature of Viotti's relationship with Margaret Chinnery, though I did go so far as to assert that 'It is very likely that they were lovers.' Since there is no concrete evidence one way or the other, I preferred to let readers decide for themselves on the basis of the numerous letters that Viotti wrote to Mrs Chinnery, several of which I cite.

I have made a point of playing the sonatas, quartets and other chamber music of Viotti in recitals and concerts whenever possible. All of his concertos and a great deal of his chamber music has been recorded, but he remains an unjustly neglected composer. Since his concertos were used in the Paris Conservatoire as imposed examination pieces from the beginning of the nineteenth century and are still given to students before they go on to study the concertos of Mendelssohn, Bruch, Brahms and the other standards of the present concert repertory, there is now a tendency, including on the part of those who should know better, to regard them as 'student concertos'. Nothing could be more wrong-headed. Eugène Ysaÿe, Fritz Kreisler, Yehudi Menuhin and Isaac Stern were pleased to play Concerto No. 22, the most popular of Viotti's concertos since receiving Brahms's praise, in many of their performances, not only with orchestra, but also in recitals with piano accompaniment.

I have also had the pleasure of giving, in Florence and elsewhere, several lectures and lecture recitals on various aspects of Viotti's life and music. His life cannot but arouse interest and sympathy. As for his music, as Viotti himself wrote to a friend about his recently completed last three string quartets in 1812, 'If I were not the composer, I would say that they are really charming—even more than that, but the modesty of your Jean Baptiste must impose silence upon him.' This is not the place to preach a sermon about Viotti. Suffice it to say that I have met many people who tell me what a revelation for them it was to discover his music.

There have been a few spin-offs from my book: I wrote the bibliographic article on Viotti for the online *Oxford Bibliographies*, and I was asked to revise the article on Viotti for the online *New Grove Dictionary of Music and Musicians*. The latter was a delicate task as the original article, by Chappell White, dating from 1980, is excellent. I changed as little as possible—just sufficient to accommodate recent research. I also wrote the article on Viotti for the *Italian Dictionary of National Biography* (*Dizionario Biografico degli Italiani*). In the earlier volumes (the 100-volume project was begun in 1960), the authors were treated rather too generously as to the length allowed for their articles. At some point, it was decided that this was unsustainable, and much more stringent word-count restrictions were introduced. As a result, the article on Corelli, for example, in the volume issued in 1983 (the volumes were issued in alphabetical order of the articles), is more than five times longer than mine on Viotti (Vol. 99, 2020) who, after all, is a comparably significant figure. For me, it was a severe lesson in compression; the discrepancy between the earlier and the later volumes is regrettable.

My most recent musicological undertaking, and the most onerous, was a critical edition, for the Italian Musicological Society (Società Editrice di Musicologia), of Viotti's last three string quartets, WII: 13–15, composed in 1812. Most non-musicians, and perhaps even some musicians, are unaware, or at least not sure, of what distinguishes critical editions from traditional editions, namely that in the former, all editorial interventions—additions, omissions, corrections, amendments—are accounted for, or should be, so that you know what was put in the score by the composer (so far as that can be determined) and what was put there by the editor. Normally, a critical edition also investigates all the known sources of the works, manuscript and printed, attempts to discover any relationships among them, and offers an opinion as to their comparative reliability. In the preface to my edition of these quartets, I also devote several paragraphs to performance practice—such things as tempos, improvisation, cadenzas, bowing techniques, fingerings and vibrato, in particular as they apply to what is known of Viotti's style.

Perhaps the most difficult task was to reconcile the many ambiguities and discrepancies—chiefly of dynamics and articulation—within and among the four individual parts that are to be found in the early printed editions of these works. The sheer number of these difficulties in printed music of the period might indeed surprise many listeners and players. (I should add that until well into the nineteenth century, chamber works, and for that matter, symphonies, were invariably published only as separate parts, not as scores).[28] In several cases, when I could see no obvious solution, or none clearly superior, I thought it best to inform the players of the discrepancies in the Notes, perhaps suggest a possible solution, but leave the final decision up to the players. Indeed, one result of this experience was to disabuse me of the notion that a critical edition can be, or should be, an attempt to pin the composer's text down like a butterfly on a board (as Raymond Leppard aptly put it), to create a kind of sacred tablet—*the* authentic text, the *Urtext*, which, frankly, is something of a chimera. It is the performers who thaw the notes frozen on the page. And, indeed, the editor in his ivory tower does well to extend to them a certain freedom of manoeuvre, which I hope I have done.

One (I hope, final) unpleasant experience to do with Viotti was coming to terms with the writings of an Italian violinist, whom I shall not name. This man was building his career partly on performances and recordings of Viotti's works. He was an excellent violinist but, like a nightmarish reincarnation of a previously mentioned Italian author, had constructed, chiefly in his publicity and CD sleeve notes, a whole edifice of falsehoods and concocted stories—new concertos and other music by Viotti that he claimed to have discovered, a letter written by Viotti and the like, all of it sheer fantasy. I began to see that much of what he was saying was taken seriously, and so, in 2015, I wrote an article in the music journal Ad Parnassum refuting, point by point, all of these fabrications. To tell the truth, I am not sure whether the article had any effect beyond musicological circles. Such weeds, once they gain a foothold, are hard to eradicate. But at least in writing the article I had cleared my conscience. Viotti, I am sure, will survive and flourish despite the weeds.

One day, in 2016, I received a letter from an art and antique dealer in Modena who had acquired the long lost (since 1913) portrait of Viotti

---

[28] Although now considered indispensable by chamber musicians and conductors, scores, too, are not immune to human error. It is not unknown, even in modern 'urtext' editions, to find discrepancies between the score and the parts.

painted by Élisabeth Vigée Le Brun, probably completed in 1815. I had included a reproduction of the painting in *Amico*, with the rueful caption 'From a reproduction in the *Connoisseur*, November 1911. The present location of this painting, if it has survived, is unknown.' As soon as I could, I went to Modena and had a look. The painting was in bad condition: dirty, with a small tear in the canvas under Viotti's right eye, but I was overwhelmed by the sight of it. It is a superb portrait—the painter and the musician had been friends since the early 1780s in Paris, and there is no doubt in my mind that she captures vividly and faithfully Viotti's strong personality. The painting has been restored and is now owned by a private collector in Italy.[29] I hope it will not be 'lost' again, though frankly, experience tells us that that is what could very well happen.

My interest in Viotti was kindled not by his music but by his life, which may seem strange for a musician. Though I had studied one of his concertos and taught the same work more than once, his music held no special interest for me. It was only when I had read about his life, as I describe above, that I was drawn into the orbit of his music and began to study it, play it and appreciate it. The relationship between a composer's life and his works is far too vexed and complicated a subject to consider here. But I am bound to say that I hear very little trace of Viotti's sometimes turbulent life in his music. Quite the opposite is true for my appreciation of the music of Berlioz, who will appear later in these pages. It was his *Symphonie fantastique*, which of course has autobiographical elements, that first aroused my interest in Berlioz the man and *his* turbulent life, and from then on, I listened to as much of his music as I could and at the same time read as much as I could about him, and, above all, by him. I sometimes wonder what Viotti would have

---

[29] Those wishing to learn of the fascinating circumstances surrounding the painting, its background, history and disappearance, and of Le Brun's musical connections, may read Denise Yim's excellent 'The portrait of Giovanni Battista Viotti by Élisabeth Vigée Le Brun' in *Musique-Images-Instruments: Revue Française d'Organologie et d'Iconographie* (Paris: CNRS Éditions, No. 18, 2021), pp. 242–253.

thought of the *Symphonie fantastique*, composed only six years after the
Italian's death.

Giovanni Battista Viotti, portrait by Elisabeth Vigée Le Brun, oil on canvas,
1805–c.1815, rediscovered in 2016, collection Sig. Giovanni Accornero,
Casale Monferrato.

CHAPTER 11

Florence: quartet

One of the great pleasures, indeed honours, of being a musician in the Florence area is the unrivalled beauty and historic interest of many of its performing venues. As a chamber musician and recitalist with piano, I have played, in some cases several times, in such magnificent spaces as the Palazzo Capponi, the Palazzo Davanzati, the Palazzo Tornabuoni, the Palazzo Rucellai, the Salone Brunelleschi in the Palagio di Parte Guelfa, the Saloncino delle Statue and the Cappella Palatina in the Palazzo Pitti, the cortile of the Casa Buonarroti, the Salone Martino V in the Ospedale di Santa Maria Nuova, the Sala della Musica in the Palazzo Gianfigliazzi Bonaparte, the Museo Marino Marini, the frescoed Sala Vanni in the convent of the Carmine church, the British Institute (in both the Palazzo Spini-Feroni and the Harold Acton Library in the Palazzo Lanfredini), as well as several churches and private homes. In a recent chamber concert in the splendid Ognissanti church, we used as a greenroom a chapel in the right transept across from the chapel containing Botticelli's tomb. During the concert, looking up the nave, we could see on the wall to our left Botticelli's fresco of St Augustine at his desk, and on the opposite wall, Ghirlandaio's of St Jerome at his.

Not long after finishing my book on Viotti, I persuaded three former orchestra colleagues to work on the late Beethoven quartets with me. We had played together many times previously in various chamber music

Refectory of the Badia di Passignano, near Florence: a chamber group led by
Eduard Melkus, 31 May 1991. Ghirlandaio's fresco, *Last Supper*, on the
wall behind.

combinations, in *ad hoc* concerts, but this felt different. We were
motivated by a strong collective dedication, unlinked to any
professional commitment, and we had more time to rehearse than we
ever could have when in the orchestra. As first violinist, I tried, not
always consistently, to plan each rehearsal based on my notes on what
hadn't gone well in the previous rehearsal. Sometimes, I would
forewarn my colleagues by email, occasionally adopting an ironically
formal or mock-hectoring tone. Anyone who has played in a string
quartet for any length of time knows that, to overcome the strains and
stresses that inevitably arise, a certain *esprit de corps* usually develops,
indeed *must* develop if the enterprise is to get off the ground.

05.07.2012

Dear colleagues,

On Tuesday could we please work on op. 131? I have a list …

26 July 1794: Robespierre menaces the Convention: 'I have a list of delegates who have committed treason.' Murmurs of fear amongst the members, turning gradually to outraged protest: 'Give us the list! The list!' Two days later Robespierre is guillotined.

… of passages in op. 131 that I would like to go over.

You will be checked at the door for weapons.

Warwick

Practise the Scherzo with the metronome. That's an order.

Recital with Natascha Majek in the Palazzo Rucellai, 29 June 2023.
Note the redness of Postiglione's varnish.

28.05.2013

Cari colleghi,

If you have a moment and if it is not imposing upon you, would you be so kind as to try the scherzo of Op. 135 with the metronome at 116 to the bar? Yes I know, very fast, but exhilarating, and in a way less difficult for the spiccato. ... A domani.

Quartetto Musica Ricercata just before an informal house concert, about 2016: Warwick Lister, Claudia Wolvington, Michael Stüve, Roger Low.

We decided, after several months and several house concerts, that we could venture to play in public. Our second violinist, Michael Stüve, a remarkable musician and an able organizer, arranged for us to play in the Casa Buonarroti, a museum dedicated to Michelangelo in the house owned by the sculptor's family. Summer concerts are given in the open courtyard. Under the aegis of the concert organization Musica Ricercata, of which Michael is the director, we played the five late quartets in three concerts over a period of three summers. The middle concert consisted of Op. 130 with the *Grosse Fuge* as the finale, then a

MARTEDÌ 1 LUGLIO 2014, ore 21.00

Ludwig van Beethoven
(1770 - 1827)
I quartetti della maturità

Ludwig van Beethoven
Quartetto in si bemolle maggiore op. 130
con il finale originale (La Grande Fuga op. 133)

Adagio, ma non troppo - Allegro
Presto - L'istesso tempo
Andante con moto, ma non troppo
Alla danza tedesca. Allegro assai
Cavatina. Adagio molto espressivo
Grand Fugue

Joseph Boulogne Chevalier de Saint-George
(1745-1799)
Quartetto in sol minore op. 16 n. 4

Sine nomine
Allegro

Ludwig van Beethoven
Dal quartetto in si bemolle maggiore op. 130

Cavatina. Adagio molto espressivo
Finale (seconda versione). Allegro

Warwick Lister, violino primo
Michael Stüve, violino secondo
Claudia Wolvington, viola
Roger Low, violoncello

MARTEDÌ 15 LUGLIO 2014, ore 21.00

Ludwig van Beethoven
(1770 – 1827)
I quartetti della maturità

Quartetto in la minore op. 132
Assai sostenuto - Allegro
Allegro ma non tanto
Canzona di ringraziamento offerta alla divinità da un
guarito, in modo lidico. Molto adagio. Sentendo nuova
forza. Andante
Alla marcia, assai vivace - Più allegro
Allegro appassionato

Quartetto in fa maggiore op. 135
Allegretto
Vivace
Lento assai, cantante e tranquillo
Grave. Allegro

Warwick Lister, violino primo
Michael Stüve, violino secondo
Claudia Wolvington, viola
Roger Low, violoncello

Programmes, Quartetto Musica Ricercata, 1, 15 July 2014. The photograph
shows the courtyard of the Casa Buonarroti.

quartet by Saint-Georges, then we repeated the Cavatina of Op. 130
followed by the other finale. This procedure, though perhaps not ideal,
at least gives the audience an idea of the problem posed by the two
finales. For one of the concerts, one of us took seriously ill at the last
moment; the remaining three had to throw together a programme of
string trios (Beethoven and Schubert) with only about twenty-four hours
at our disposal. The performance was not flawless, but it was too late to

cancel; we had salvaged an emergency situation.

I sometimes felt, and sometimes still do feel, that as a newly formed group, our having undertaken to play publicly these monumental works was presumptuous. We had not put in the years of intensive preparation, described earlier in these pages, that the established quartets devote to them. On the other hand, it is arguable that if only the established groups played these works, far fewer people would have the opportunity of hearing them in live performances. And I do feel that, though our performances were not comparable to those of the 'name' groups, we did have something to say.

And what a privilege it is to study, rehearse and play these works! I will take just one passage as an example: the second theme of the last movement of Op. 131—the indescribably exalted effect it had on me (infinitely more than when simply listening to it). It is, after all, just a descending scale followed, however, by that striving, yearning upward leap of a minor thirteenth, still wider on its repetition, then becoming the *ultima Thule* of an octave plus a diminished fifth. Not until Mahler do we have such rapturous expressivity, replete with *ritardando* hesitations and gasping crescendos, but all in a soft dynamic—rapture, yes, but hushed, repressed. John Dalley, the superb second violinist of the Guarneri Quartet, said about this finale, 'You want to bark like a dog',[30] which, now that I have played it, strikes me as not at all an odd thing to say.

The Quartetto Musica Ricercata managed to rehearse amicably despite some rather pointed differences in personality, with only an occasional eruption of the tensions that accumulate in any string quartet. One such took on a seriousness that went far beyond its banal cause, a difference of opinion about our dress for a concert. Since the concert was to be outdoors in July, our cellist wished to have the option of wearing a short-sleeved shirt, an idea strenuously opposed by our second violinist, who

---

[30] The Guarneri Quartet and David Blum, *The Art of Quartet Playing: The Guarneri Quartet in Conversation with David Blum* (Ithaca, NY: Cornell University Press, 1986), p. 230.

Beethoven: Op. 131, last movement, bars 56–72.

thought our appearance on stage should be more formal. He argued the impropriety of 'beach-concert dress' against the cellist's position that in the hot weather he was uncomfortable in long sleeves. The discussion became acrimonious and took up so much precious rehearsal time that I feared for our concert preparedness. The violist and I stayed out of the argument. I now see that, as first violinist, I should have at least attempted to reconcile my two colleagues with some kind of compromise, though an easy solution does not spring to mind. In the event, the evening of the concert was relatively cool for July in Florence, and our cellist wore long sleeves. It might be thought, 'Such a storm in a teacup!' But as is almost always the case, more fundamental rifts lay beneath the surface.

Buoyed by the success of the Casa Buonarroti concerts, we continued to play in various venues in Florence—several Haydn and Mozart quartets, Schubert's *Quartettsatz*, Beethoven's Op. 59, No. 1, and Op. 74, Viotti's splendid Quartet in F major, WII:13, and other works.

More emails:

27.01.2015:

> Beethoven [Op. 74] mov 3: I noticed several times [we had recorded a rehearsal] a big swell in bars 5–6—very strange. Did we REALLY do that?

Beethoven: Op. 74, third movement, bars 1–8.

Michael, upbeat to b. 19 and upbeat to b. 27, and parallel places, your last eighth note is the same note as my quarter note (F) and it sounds as though I am entering too early or you are too late with that note. But in fact I think we are playing it accurately and it just sounds sloppy. Did Beethoven really want that?

Beethoven: Op. 74, third movement, bars 16–19.

Last mov. Some funny intonation beginning of 4th variation approx. bar 80, and bars 129–130 and 132–133.

Beethoven: Op. 74, last movement, bars 81–84.

27.10.2015:

Bartók No. 5, first mov., letter J. Suggestion: to rehearse the 6 bars starting at b. 178 by playing only the first 3 notes of each of our entrances, exaggerating the accent, all very soft at first. Perhaps under tempo at first but then up to tempo with metronome, then without.

Bartók: String Quartet No. 5, first movement, bars 178–182.

Last 2 bars: 'Poco allar[gando]' which implies a ritardando, no? But he gives a metronome marking (130), which implies that these 6 notes are to be in that one tempo, without a ritard (???)

Bartók: String Quartet No. 5, first movement, bars 216–218.

Roger, our cellist, replies:

> There's probably no time to do a ritardando, even if you'd like to. The general effect is of a door slamming in your face, or a rider pulling the emergency cord to get the hell off the train.

24.12.2015

> Not very festive, I know, but I am plagued, tormented, anguished by two or three bars in the *Allegretto vivace e sempre scherzando* [of Beethoven's Op. 59, No. 1]:

> Bar 60. Are we absolutely SURE that Violin II has a *sf* on the third beat, and not on the second beat with the rest of us? … If I were Beethoven, I would have put this third-beat *sf* in b. 296 [when this passage reappears in another key, without the *sf* in the second violin part on the third beat] rather than b. 60. It seems anticlimactic to do it the first time, but not the second time. Could it not have been a space problem: not enough room to write the *cresc.* and the *sf*, so it all got

[Allegretto vivace e sempre scherzando]

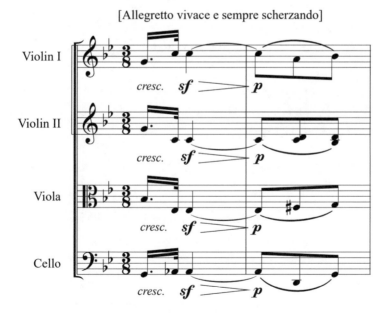

Beethoven: Op. 59, No. 1, second movement, bars 60–61, Henle Urtext edition.
In earlier editions the *sf* in Violin II in bar 60 is indeed placed on the second beat
with the others, not on the third beat.

[Allegretto vivace e sempre scherzando]

Beethoven: Op. 59, No. 1, second movement, bars 296–297, Henle
Urtext edition.

Beethoven: Op. 59, No. 1, second movement, bars 183–185, Henle Urtext edition. In earlier editions there is no diminuendo in any of the instruments in bar 184.

pushed to the right in Beethoven's ms, and the copyist misread it?[31]

Also, does the *cresc.* in b. 183 go all the way to b. 185 as written? Surely it should go only to Michael's *sf* on the downbeat of 184, then diminuendo to b. 185 with Michael.

---

[31] We were using the Henle 'Urtext' parts. In the holograph in the Berlin Staatsbibliothek, this bar (b. 60) appears to have caused Beethoven problems, or at least second thoughts. The second violin part is crossed out after the first note and a corrected version (notated with what appears to be coloured pencil) is placed ('Vide') in the margin, which unequivocally reads as given in the Henle edition. So my anguish and my conjecture, both no doubt fuelled by my Capricorn craving for consistency—an innate discomfort with discrepancies between expositions and recapitulations—were unjustified.

27.12.2015 [Roger replies]

I am quite sure the second violin's little outburst in bar 60 is intentional. ... The addition of your G this time only adds to the Neapolitan tension that Uncle Ludwig was clearly seeking to cultivate with the second violin's momentary doubling of my Eb, and leads one to speculate that perhaps by the second time the harmonies are less shocking [because already heard] and need less rhythmic [spiciness]. At any rate, I don't think Michael's sforzando note is a coffee or soup stain. ... Coming down with Michael in b. 184 seems a good idea.

16.04.2016

I'm having second thoughts about doing all the repeats in the Haydn [Op. 20, No. 4]. It makes for 32 minutes which I think is a bit too much with the Brahms, for that audience. What about doing only the first repeats in the first and last movements? I think that's enough Haydn for these folks, if you know what I mean ...

In the last movement, the section beginning at the double bar (bb. 50–67) seems aimless the way we play it. [We had recorded a rehearsal]. ... Following the pitch levels of Roger's five entrances [starting at b. 56], how about 56–57 loud, 58–59 soft, 60–61 loud, 62–63 soft, 64 loud, then diminuendo 65 down to 66. Or is that too much echoing? One must observe a certain economy of echoes?

I am ashamed of my condescending reference to our audience, and my cavalier dismissal of the repeats now strikes me as presumptuous, especially since, in both cases, there is different music in the first and second endings.

We were in the midst of preparing Beethoven's Op. 59, No. 2, Schubert's 'Death and the Maiden' and Bartók's Quartet No. 5 when, in April 2018, something happened that all quartets dread: an irremediable falling out between two members of the group. This had been brewing for some time, but we had found it convenient to ignore it. It seems futile

Haydn: Op. 20, No. 4, last movement, bars 56–67.

to try now to distinguish whether it was a clash of personality or a fundamental difference of musical approach—the two are sometimes inextricable. Attempts at reconciliation were in vain; we disbanded, after six and a half years together. For the third time, I was forced to admit that my love of playing string quartets was star-crossed, if not unrequited. Now, when I hear a string quartet my enjoyment is suffused with nostalgia and regret.

*

In 2011, I had the very pleasant experience of meeting the late distinguished English pianist, Hamish Milne. His daughter, Sara, was then the Director of the British Institute in Florence, where Susan was head of the History of Art Department. Hamish was a leading interpreter of the music of Nicolai Medtner. I boldly asked him if he would play through the first movement of Medtner's Sonata No. 1, Op. 21, with me, which he kindly did, twice, one afternoon in September, in the British Institute. I had practised the piece, which is quite complicated, but it was chiefly thanks to Hamish's skill and his knowledge of the score that we got through it without mishap. It was a lovely, memorable hour with a splendid musician, for which I am grateful. I have since read his sensitive and perceptive biography of Bartók.

CHAPTER 12

Literary matters

For almost as long as I can remember, I have had the habit of annotating the books I read, often copiously. Sometimes I have so much to say that I am forced to continue my comments on a separate sheet of paper. When, after a few years, I happen upon these productions, I am sometimes embarrassed, but by no means always. They are expressions of my critical impulse—fault-finding, to put it plainly—and of the curmudgeonly side of my character, reacting to what I see as authorial negligence or a cavalier attitude towards the facts. I have already mentioned my vivisection of a biography of Viotti. Gabriel Banat's *The Chevalier de Saint-Georges: Virtuoso of the Sword and the Bow* (2006) provoked a similar reaction, similarly unpublished until now:

> One hesitates to criticize this book, because of Mr Banat's reputation as an expert on Saint-Georges (he is the author of the article on Saint-Georges in the *New Grove Dictionary*, second edition, 2000), but in my opinion the book is seriously compromised by many errors of fact, unsubstantiated assumptions and hypotheses, sometimes presented as fact, the omission, misattribution, misquotation or fanciful interpretation of sources, and garbling of information.

And I go on for six pages of itemizing. I did not write the above words lightly. I was aware that Banat had a distinguished career as a violinist and editor of music. One of the things that irritated me most in the book was Banat's serene, unquestioning assumption that it was Saint-Georges who led the Olympique orchestra in the first performance of Haydn's 'Paris' symphonies, Nos. 82–87 in Paris in 1787. There is not a shred of evidence that Saint-Georges had anything to do with the Concert Olympique, let alone that he led these performances. I had written on the much-vexed question of who the leader was for these concerts in an article of 2004, two years before Banat's book. He clearly had not seen it.

I am equally unforgiving, equally waspish with Edward Lockspeiser's *Music and Painting: A Study in Comparative Ideas from Turner to Schoenberg* (1973)—its vague, meandering prose, rife with non sequiturs, irritated me, and still does; with Toby Faber's book on Stradivarius (2004)—the chapter 'Viotti and his Strad' is strewn with my corrections and objections ('No!'); and with the chapter on Viotti in Margaret Campbell's *The Great Violinists* (2004): 'This chapter gets wrong almost everything there is to get wrong about Viotti's life.'

Following is an example of my annotating at its most priggish, on the title page of Ronald Blythe's *Akenfield: Portrait of an English Village* (1969):

This book is beautifully, poetically written (indeed the second monologue, that of the horseman's widow, is one of the most touching few pages of prose that I have read in a very long time), but that's just the trouble with it. All of the persons in the book ostensibly are speaking with their own voices, but are they really? Did Blythe tape-record these people and faithfully transcribe the recordings word for word? Obviously not. To what extent did he edit them? Did he take poetic liberties? Or did he use the original words only as a point of departure? Blythe gives us no clue as to any of this, which in my opinion is a failure of editorial candour and scholarly responsibility. To put it bluntly, in a work purporting to be a study in social history, it is dishonest. W.W.L., Nov 2, 1998, Florence.

Yes, priggish and self-righteous, but do I not have a point?

I perhaps reached the culmination of this tendency in my copy of an execrable, near-illiterate history of the symphony by an author who shall remain nameless, in which I wrote what amounts to a mock-serious, ironically complimentary review, that I confess I think is quite witty, and since I have no intention of showing it to anyone, no harm is done. But as almost every book I own is full of these pencilled (or often penned) lucubrations, I suppose it will be the better part of good sense, before I enter that Great Symphony in the Sky (will I have to audition? Could it not be a celestial string quartet?), to have them all destroyed (though I feel no urgency in this regard).

While in this critical frame of mind, I feel bound to protest against the outrageously arbitrary, high-handed assertions in Tully Potter's chapter entitled 'The concert explosion and the age of recording' in *The Cambridge Companion to the String Quartet*[32] (2003). A few examples: 'Since 1995 [the Takács Quartet] has consisted of two Hungarians and two Englishmen, a most unsatisfactory mixture.' Dogmatic, illogical. What evidence can Mr Potter bring forward for this? How is it unsatisfactory? Three pages later, we are told that another quartet, consisting of a Frenchman, a Dutchman and two Romanians, is 'already ... of world class'. 'Lukas Hagen [first violin of the Hagen Quartet] is one of the few leaders to play consistently in tune.' Who are the others, so that we will know which leaders do not play consistently in tune? 'Its [the Quartetto Italiano] Achilles heel was rhythm.' Really? How so? Dotted rhythms not dotted enough? Syncopations not together? Was it a group Achilles heel or individuals' heels? '[The] founder leader [of the Borodin Quartet] Rostislav Dubinsky, a preening, narcissistic player'. Is this a visual observation? Or auditory? How does a violinist sound preening, narcissistic? Too much rubato? Too many portamenti? 'The Juilliard Quartet ... never came near an authentic Beethoven style.' Aha, so there is an authentic Beethoven style. In what way did the Juilliard not come near it? 'The Guarneri Quartet ... has

---

[32] Tully Potter, 'The Concert Explosion and the Age of Recording' in *The Cambridge Companion to the String Quartet*, Robin Stowell, ed. (Cambridge: Cambridge University Press, 2003), pp. 68–90 *passim*.

even had a book written about it, and one wishes its members played as profoundly as they talk.' Spiteful, gratuitously offensive. 'The Emerson Quartet ... has consistently failed to find the right style or even the right sound for Beethoven.' The *right* style, the *right* sound for Beethoven? It beggars belief that anyone in the twenty-first century can write something so silly. What a pity that the Juilliard and the Emerson were unable to find the right style for Beethoven—they had only to ask—Mr Potter could have revealed it to them.

Not all of my marginalia are hostile. I sometimes manage to scribble a few words of praise. In the margin beside the fifth paragraph of Johnson's *Preface to Shakespeare*, I see I have written 'superb paragraph'. My copy of Charles Rosen's *The Classical Style: Haydn, Mozart, Beethoven* is peppered with exclamation marks in the margins, registering what, for me, were brilliant insights, as is my copy of De Quincey's 'On the Knocking at the Gate in *Macbeth*', in my opinion the finest essay in the English language. The first sentence of Lorna Sage's *Bad Blood* is similarly marked—indeed I consider it to be one of the most memorable openings of any book I have read, along with that of Gibbon's *The History of the Decline and Fall of the Roman Empire*, that of Melville's *Moby Dick*, that of Orwell's *The Lion and the Unicorn: Socialism and the English Genius* and that of Michael Baxandall's *Painting and Experience in Fifteenth-Century Italy*.

I have before me a well-thumbed paperback copy of Mary McCarthy's *The Stones of Florence*. Tucked inside the front cover are three pages of a meticulously hand-written index of the artists mentioned in the book, compiled by me not long after I bought the book a few days after arriving in Florence in March 1983. I am perversely proud of this curious artefact. It is all too characteristic of the Capricorn side of my personality, which I detest—linear, clerical, persistent, pedantic, plodding. Anyone who has compiled an index will know what a painstaking job it is—of course I had no computer. It must have required several hours and several drafts before I could carefully print out a final copy. I don't remember using it very much at all, but an inner need was satisfied—my Capricorn syndrome.

Now that I have suggested how well-read I am, I am bound to admit that, with very few exceptions, my reading habits have always been unsystematic, anything but catholic and, so to speak, opportunistic, increasingly leaning towards non-fiction. I have very few memories of children's books. I remember a book containing a version of the Grimm Brothers' 'The Brave Little Tailor: Seven at One Blow', but only that part remains with me, not the other stories. I read one or two of the *Bomba the Jungle Boy* series (now considered racist), but they don't seem to have made much of an impression on me, except for one of Bomba's hair's-breadth escapes—from falling off a narrow ledge into a pit of deadly snakes. There was also a book about explorers—the fate of Scott and his comrades touched me deeply. Much later, I was outraged by Roland Huntford's hatchet job on Scott in *Scott and Amundsen* (1993). Suffice it to glance at the section in the index on Scott's characteristics—a grotesque travesty. I wrote on the front matter pages:

Note to the Reader: Historical fiction has long held a special place in the affections of English readers. Of course, Shakespeare's historical plays are not consulted by historians of republican Rome, of late Ptolomaic Egypt, or of the English monarchy of the 15th and 16th centuries, nor is Dickens for the French Revolution. But the English persist in their fondness for the genre, and this book will no doubt find a wide and enthusiastic public.

The eponymous chief characters, based loosely on two historical figures, Captain Robert F. Scott and Roald Amundsen, the Antarctic explorers, are expertly delineated and the author tells his tale with a deft sense of suspense and pacing, culminating in the doom of one man and the triumph of the other. Particularly praiseworthy is Huntford's seamless interweaving of fact and fiction as the story builds to its denouement with the inexorableness of a Greek tragedy. The character named Scott in the book fairly leaps from the page, so vivid are the author's powers of psychological realism and dramatic characterisation. All in all, a jolly good read. For those readers who, stimulated by this exciting book, wish to find out what actually happened regarding the events and persons upon which the book is based, I would recommend any one of several available historical accounts, as well as the published diaries and other documents.

I also wrote, or rather began to write, a list (again!) of falsehoods and unsubstantiated defamatory assertions in the book about Scott but gave up in frustration because I lacked the knowledge and time to pursue each point. I was comforted about ten years later by Sir Ranulph Fiennes's *Race to the Pole: Tragedy, Heroism and Scott's Antarctic Quest* (2004), which undertakes to set the record straight.[33]

To return to my boyhood, when I was twelve or thirteen, a school friend told me about the Hornblower books by C. S. Forester. I immediately got three or four of them from the city library. A year or two later, I bought Wilfred Funk's *Six Weeks to Words of Power*, published in 1955, and studied it on my own from cover to cover, faithfully doing the vocabulary exercises at the end of each chapter. This was an exception to the general haphazardness with which books came into my hands. Even later, in my twenties, many of the books I read were ones that happened to be in my parents' house: André Maurois's *Prometheus: The Life of Balzac*, and Émile Zola's *Nana*, both in English translation, and Abram Chasin's *Speaking of Pianists* (1961).

My mother persuaded me to read Albert Schweitzer's *Out of my Life and Thought*. She admired Schweitzer. From her descriptions of him I had the impression of a saintly, super-human polymath and musician.

---

[33] Fiennes's compilation of Huntford's falsehoods is by no means exhaustive. One, particularly blatant, is the assertion (p. 465), offered as an example of Scott's incompetence, that he put only two depots between the Beardmore Glacier and One Ton Depot, when in fact there was another, Mount Hooper or Lower Barrier Depot, which is brazenly omitted from Huntford's map (p. 511) showing the depots. Unfortunately, Fiennes himself slightly muddies the water by referring to the Upper Barrier Depot as the Lower Barrier Depot (p. 311), and in the index twice confusing the Lower Barrier Depot with the Lower Glacier Depot (pp. 455, 456: 'Lower Glacier/Mount Hooper Depot').

She told me how he had decided, at the age of thirty, to dedicate himself to medical healing in Africa, getting a medical degree and opening a hospital in Gabon. She was not explicit, but I felt that she would have been proud of me if I were to undertake something similar.

Once, when I was about fourteen years old, I casually took Orwell's *1984* off the bookshelf and asked my mother what it was about. She said 'Oh, you shouldn't read that, it's a terrible book.' Of course, I immediately read it. At around the same time, I asked her about *Lady Chatterley's Lover*, having seen it on her bedside table. She said it was about a man and woman who fall in love, an explanation so anodyne that I was not at all curious to read it.

My letter to Mum, spring 1962:

> Have you read the Alexandrian [*sic*] Quartet by Lawrence Durrell? It is four novels and they are wonderful—perhaps the very best fiction of the 20th century. I have read the first two novels, starting the third. Really faaabulous. First book is Justine, then Balthazar, Mountolive, Clea.

As a literary critic I was nothing if not confident. *The Alexandria Quartet* was all the rage in the early 1960s in the USA. I read *Justine* in order to impress a young woman I was interested in, but flagged before finishing the second volume, contrary to what I told my mother.

But it is now clear to me that my mother and I had a relationship, obviously musical, but also intellectual (if that is not too pretentious a word) that she did not have with Dad or anyone else. In 1978, three years before she died, she wrote to me while reading Mann's *The Magic Mountain*:

> I think Mann's portrayal of the long vacuous speeches of this fellow [Peeperkorn] are masterful. Then the endless arguments between Ludovico Settembrini and Naphta, the Jesuit Jew, are priceless. They walk and walk and talk & talk and fight—poor little Hans tries to enter into the intellectual duel—to be swept aside by Settembrini—a marvellous character—lovable and brilliant—with a great kind heart.

I have not yet come to the part that you told me about on our visit to
the old San outside Amherst—because I started at the end of the book,
then went to the beginning, so I must be getting there soon. I am
reading two other books so am not making great headway.

My mother refers to a visit we made—it must have been four or five
years earlier, when I lived near Amherst, Massachusetts—to an
abandoned sanatorium in the hills not far away.

A few days later:

I finished MAGIC MOUNTAIN!! Oh Warwick—it broke my heart—
those two wonderful, sensible, serious, honorable, humorless young
German boys—the cousin Joachim dying at the sanatorium, and
realizing it so well, then adorable, dull Hans Castorp marching across
the field of mud and dead and dying, singing some military song, into
the smoke-filled no-where. I wept bitterly as I finished it, and my heart
was heavy for days. Still, Mann has a wondrous light, gay touch of
humour and satire too—altogether a great man. Thank you dear, for
remembering to bring it to me—sorry I nagged so much—I could have
<u>bought</u> a copy for heaven's sake, but we all do odd things occasionally.

In the same letter, she writes about Menuhin's autobiography.

I am finishing the Yehudi Menuhin book … a wonderful, kindly
outlook on life and his fellow humans—quite noble—not a good
writer, I think—but he gives a fine picture of <u>his</u> whole life and style—
have you read it?

I did not read Menuhin's autobiography *Unfinished Journey* (1976) until
only a few months ago, prompted by a rereading of this letter from my
mother, forty-five years after she wrote it. I must say that I think he *is* a
good writer. The two paragraphs, for example, on the decline and death
of his revered master and friend Georges Enesco reveal a depth of
feeling and an eloquence that match his violin playing. Menuhin's
almost worshipful admiration for his second wife, Diana, however,

seems excessive, the more so in the light of their elder son Gerard's shockingly hostile portrait of her in his autobiography *Lived It Wrong: An Autobiography* (2020).

I have been especially drawn to autobiographies, memoirs and diaries, literally dozens of them (partly, I admit, to prepare myself for the present volume, just as I consumed books for chess and tennis): from Cellini, Pepys, Rousseau, Boswell, Goethe (*Italian Journey*), Parson Woodforde, Élisabeth Vigée Le Brun, Chateaubriand and Francis Kilvert (the most charming) to Virginia Woolf, Goebbels, Vincent Massey (the dullest), Vladimir Nabokov (the most brilliant, most masterly stylistically), Charles Ritchie, Iris Origo (the most poetic), Kenneth Clark, James Lees-Milne (the most entertaining and, along with Boswell, Clark and Ritchie, the most sharply observant of themselves and others), Lorna Sage, the most merciless (about her grandfather), as is John Pope-Hennessy (chiefly, but not only, about other art historians, though he is unstinting in his praise of those whom he respects)—he is also the most musically literate of all the non-musician autobiographers, Diana Athill (by far the frankest about sex and old age, possibly excepting Rousseau), Alan Bennett (the wittiest) and, most recently, Rod Madocks, to name only a few.

As for musicians, Alfred Brendel once wrote that he would never write his autobiography: 'I am too fond of the truth for that.'[34] He does reveal something of himself, with wit and elegance, however, in his *The Veil of Order: Conversations with Martin Meyer* (2002) and *The Lady from Arezzo* (2019); as does András Schiff in his *Music Comes Out of Silence* (2020). Of all the musicians' memoirs, Berlioz's has pride of place; we are swept along by the hurricane force of his personality. From the twentieth century, Robert Craft's *Stravinsky: Chronicle of a Friendship* (1994) is as much, if not more, about the author than about Stravinsky, and is a masterpiece, pure and simple. Arthur Rubenstein's two-volume autobiography is gossipy, self-indulgent and far too long.

---

[34] Alfred Brendel, *The Lady from Arezzo: My Musical Life and Other Matters* (London: Faber & Faber, 2019), p. 91.

Stephen Hough's scintillating *Enough: Scenes from Childhood* (2023) is the most brilliantly written recent memoir by a musician that I know of. And like the previously mentioned memoir of William Aide, it is moving, nostalgic but not maudlin, razor-sharp in its insights. Both authors are pianists. Could it be that, presiding over not only the melodies, but also the harmonies, the counterpoint, just about everything, and that having the other players' parts in their score in a piece of chamber music, lord of all they survey (whereas we lowly string players grope blindly with only our own parts, reduced to scribbling cues in the music: 'with vla', 'follow pno', etc.), pianists have a more all-encompassing grasp, a larger view of life itself? Perhaps. But I think of Arnold Steinhardt's poetic *Violin Dreams* ...

Speaking of pianists, Susan Tomes's *Beyond the Notes* (2004) is partly a memoir of her early career with the chamber group Domus and, later, the piano trio Florestan. The section on Domus, from her diary kept at the time, is a sensitive, powerfully evocative, utterly candid daily chronicle of the sorrows, the difficulties—practical, musical, personal—and the joys and triumphs of a touring chamber group.

Belonging to a similar category is Abram Loft's *How to Succeed in an Ensemble: Reflections on a Life in Chamber Music (2003)*. When he hints—more than hints—at friction between him and the first violinist of the Fine Arts Quartet, Leonard Sorkin, and other personal discords within the group, I wish he could have told us more. Are such disharmonies purely a matter of personality or, at least partly, a result of musical differences, or can the two be separated? Loft, in his book, enters these dangerous waters gingerly (as indeed I have in these pages), no doubt out of respect and a desire not to cause offence.

On the other hand, in *A Quartet for Life* (2018), by the cellist Valentin Berlinsky of the Borodin Quartet, the exchange of letters between him and Mikhail Kopelman, the first violinist, when the latter left the quartet in 1996, are suffused with a barely concealed, searing bitterness. Berlinsky considered Kopelman's defection a 'betrayal' and said so. The fanatic dedication of this group, especially in its early days, almost defies belief.

Of the violinists,[35] Spohr is breathtakingly sure of himself. Albert Spalding's *Rise to Follow* (1943) is the most polished, the most self-consciously literary of the musicians' autobiographies I have read, for all that not the most interesting, though his account of his encounter, aged seventeen, with Saint-Saëns, is a vignette of irresistible charm. Szigeti's insistence, in his *With Strings Attached: Reminiscences and Reflections* (1949), that being chronologically exact or complete in a book of reminiscences is 'positively unseemly', seems perverse to me, and I primly say so in the margin: 'In my opinion, it is unseemly to be vague and sloppy about chronology.' But this niggling matter aside, Szigeti's is the most rewarding of all the violinists' autobiographies I have read, though Menuhin's and Henri Temianka's come a close second. Carl Flesch's memoirs centre on detailed, highly analytical dissections of most of the prominent musicians of his time. Not content to describe a violinist's playing and career, he must minutely examine the causes—physical, psychological, pedagogical, social, national and racial, often rendered *de haut en bas*. On Szigeti: 'I have always regretted that he did not spend two years of his youth under my supervision. I could have normalized his bowing within the shortest space of time … and taught him methods of study that would have reduced his excessive working time to a minimum.' To be fair, one cannot deny that Flesch might very well have been able to do just that. And, to be fair, Flesch pays homage to Szigeti's 'high artistic level'.[36]

---

[35] There are more violinists' autobiographies and memoirs than the unwary reader might suppose. An incomplete list, in addition to those mentioned in the text: Franz Benda (1763), Charles Dancla (1893/98), Leopold Auer (1923), Ida Haendel (1970), Nathan Milstein (1990), Isaac Stern (1999, the photographs in the Da Capo Press paperback edition are of a stupefyingly poor quality), Steven Staryk (2000), Emanuel Hurwitz (2006), Anshel Brusilov (2015), John Georgiadis (2019), Kenneth Sillito (2019), György Pauk (2021).

[36] Carl Flesch, *Memoirs*, p. 331. Carl F. Flesch's *And Do You Also Play the Violin?* (1990) provides much additional important information, unavailable elsewhere, about his father's life, times and contemporaries, including excerpts from his diaries and correspondence.

Since it is part of the *raison d'être* of a memoir to reveal the author's personality, warts and all, I now wish to get a few things off my chest. For years, I have been increasingly intolerant of what I consider to be assaults on the English language—vogue words and usages which scream ignorance and arrogance equally, some of the worst listed below.

'Like' and 'you know' constantly interjected. A symptom of Tourette's Syndrome. The sufferer is to be pitied.

'I was' to mean 'I said', often in tandem with 'like': 'I was, like, "are you kidding me?" ' Bad enough in the mouths of teenagers; adults who say it should be taken out behind the barn and reprimanded.

The habit of beginning almost every sentence with 'So'. To defend myself against perpetrators of this meaningless idiocy, I reply, when I feel brave enough, by beginning my sentences with 'Crochet'. It's a more interesting word than 'Sew', that is, the word itself, but also its meaning—crocheting is a more artistic activity than sewing, if you must begin a sentence with a meaningless idiocy.

'Gay' to mean 'homosexual'. Why? Utterly stupid and offensive. 'Gay' was a perfectly serviceable word until it was appropriated in this way; 'homosexual' is a perfectly accurate, neutral, innocuous word that should offend no one.

'Date of expiry' referring to a credit card. This is an extremely irritating abuse of language. On most credit cards, the phrase 'expires end' or 'valid dates' is followed by a month or months and year(s) (for example '03/25' or '07/20 [and] 09/23'). Apart from the fact that a month and a year do not constitute a date, these indications show the period of validity of the card, not the date of expiry, which, of course, is the first day of the *next* month. Therefore, the dates of expiry for the two examples given above are respectively 1 April 2025 and 1 October 2023, and it is quite wrong to expect people to say or write otherwise.

'Awesome' to mean 'good' or 'enjoyable' or a half-dozen other things. Perhaps the most common, and the most egregious example of abject slovenliness in the English language known to me.

More recently, we have such outrages as 'social media'. This is a ridiculously meaningless phrase. Telephones and newspapers are social media, as much as any of the electronic media.

'Double down'. Now very much in vogue. What's wrong with 'insist'? It can be argued, it is true, that we have 'double back' and 'double up', so why not 'double down'? Yes, yes, but still it irritates me.

'Multiple' to mean 'many'. They do not mean the same thing, but 'multiple' is preferred by those who think it sounds more intellectual or sophisticated.

'Ramp up' to mean 'increase' or 'augment' or 'intensify'. Silly, pretentious, infantile, ignorant.

'Kick off' to mean 'begin' or 'start' or 'initiate'. Silly, pretentious, infantile, ignorant.

'Reach out', meaning to send a message or to communicate with someone: 'Thank you for reaching out'. Cloying, numbingly silly.

'Ahead of' to mean 'before'—exactly the opposite of what it really means or should mean. If you refer to an event taking place, say, in 2021, and then to another event taking place in 2022, you are going forward, that is, *ahead* in time. So, when one event is ahead of another, it is further ahead in time, that is, it comes after, not before the first. Television announcers are especially guilty of this solecism, now become universal. Similarly, to bring an event 'forward' correctly means to postpone it, that is, to push it forward in time, or ahead chronologically, not to anticipate it, which is to bring it back in time, that is, earlier.

'Boots on the ground', or simply 'on the ground'. Again, a meaningless, infantile, smart-alecky expression that television announcers think is more arresting than a simple statement.

'Icon/iconic' and 'legend': 'Sid Pelvis, the rock/football icon/legend'. People who say this don't know an icon or a legend from their elbow. *The Concise Oxford Dictionary*, 1975 edition, with weak-kneed permissiveness, labels the use of 'legend' in this sense as colloquial; in my opinion it is semi-illiterate and 'icon', illiterate.

'Issue' to mean 'problem', which it doesn't. The word 'issue' has a variety of precise, distinct meanings; none of them can remotely be construed to mean 'problem'.

'Fast-track' to mean 'hasten' or 'accelerate'. Again, mindless seeking after novelty to express something that is perfectly expressed by ordinary language. Oops, hold on a minute: perhaps, after all, I am willing to accept 'fast-track'. Perhaps it connotes something not connoted by 'hasten' or 'accelerate', that is, the idea of choosing a faster means from a variety of possibilities—the faster of several tracks. Oh, alright then. Harrumph.

The insanely proliferating pestilence of acronyms. In my opinion, they all should be abolished, every single one of them, even including UN, USA, UK and NATO, and, more recently, CEO.[37] The use of these hieroglyphs amounts to a kind of secret, condescending, backstage language: 'I know what it means because I'm in the know, whereas you, in your ignorance, don't know.' It is also laziness: how much longer does it take to say 'United States' than to say 'US'? To tell the truth, I am also irritated by the modern mania for abbreviations, many of them spawned by the advent of the computer—abominations such as 'app', which, if anything, should stand for 'appointment', as indeed it did until a few years ago. I derive peculiar satisfaction from using 'app' to mean 'appointment' in conversation and in my personal correspondence.

I am perfectly aware that all of the above may seem petty and pedantic or, worse, the futile rantings of an old man against anything new, and that well-intentioned but misguided persons have for centuries railed against the perceived corruption of the English language and have been mocked for it. Yes, language evolves, yes, words and usages that once seemed indefensible were eventually accepted. But I suggest to the mockers that they read Johnson's Preface to his Dictionary.[38] No one has improved on it. I hold fast to what he says. The attentive reader will have noticed, however, that I myself am guilty in these pages of more than one of these transgressions. My hypocrisy surprises me.

---

[37] I recently learned, involuntarily and unwillingly, that it stands for 'Chief Executive Officer', an inflated, redundant, pretentious phrase—'Director', 'President' or 'Manager' should do perfectly well.

[38] Of the many books on the subject of the degradation of the English language, John Simon's *Paradigms Lost: Essays on Literacy and Its Decline* (Penguin, 1981), is perhaps the most convincing, certainly the most provocative. Steven Pinker's criticism of Simon in *The Language Instinct: How the Mind Creates Language* (Penguin, 1994), p. 385, is unfair and unsubstantiated.

CHAPTER 13

Musical afterthoughts

My favourite composers are Haydn and Berlioz. I do not say that they are the greatest composers, but they are my favourites. Much of Monteverdi's and Bach's music, Mozart's operas and Beethoven's late works tower above all, but I am attracted to Haydn and Berlioz. To have played Haydn's string quartets and symphonies (not enough of them!) has given me unalloyed pleasure, as does, for example, his piano sonata in E-flat major, Hob. XVI/49, especially as played by Alfred Brendel. I admit that there are *longueurs* in some of Haydn's symphonies, in *Les Troyens*, in *L'Enfance du Christ* and in the final Friar Laurence scene of the *Romeo and Juliet* Symphony and elsewhere in Berlioz's works, but so there are in *The Ring* and even, dare I say it, in the ceremonial scenes of *The Magic Flute*. And I admit that the passage of chromatic scales tediously up and down in the first movement of the *Symphonie fantastique* (bb. 200–220) are vulgar and completely without musical or programmatic justification. But certain scenes in *Les Troyens* and the song 'Absence' move me deeply, and I would trade much of Wagner, Verdi and Puccini for the climax of the tomb scene in the *Romeo and Juliet* Symphony. Berlioz's early works composed for the Prix de Rome are unjustly neglected, particularly the cantata *Cléopâtre*, which is a wonderful, thrilling piece, erupting with Berlioz's volcanic genius. But I am inconstant—I recently rushed into Schumann's arms, bewitched by his *Three Romances* (originally for oboe and piano), that I came upon a

CHAPTER 13   231

few months ago and learned.

A personal, highly selective list of recorded performance moments that, over the past seventy years, have left the greatest imprint on my musical landscape, in no particular order: Cortot's playing of the opening bars of the Schubert B-flat piano trio: swaggering élan, irresistible *schwung*; Brendel's 'Diabelli' Variations: the waltz theme, incomparable Viennese lilt (in comparison, Serkin's version seems to me heavy handed and lacking in charm, though I hasten to add that here I am speaking only of the theme and that I consider Serkin to be one of the great pianists of the twentieth century); Kreisler playing his cadenza for the first movement of Beethoven's concerto—a tour de force of elegance and purity of intonation, especially the double-stop fourths; Harnoncourt's *Le Quattro Stagioni* of Vivaldi (1977), in particular the barking dog in the Summer movement and the galloping hunt music at the beginning of Autumn—both audaciously, dangerously literal, with snapping whipped bow strokes—a ground-breaking revelation; Oistrakh's playing of the cadenza at the end of the third movement of the Shostakovich Violin Concerto No. 1 in a video of a concert with the Staatskapelle Berlin—five minutes of inimitably pure, ringing tone but at the same time of unremitting, bleak intensity—the grim (1967) East Berlin greyness contributes to the desolate effect; the Amadeus Quartet's first violinist Norbert Brainin's heavenly playing of the first variation in the slow movement of Schubert's 'Death and the Maiden' quartet: exquisitely subtle rubato and agogic accent; the tenor Julius Patzak singing the first movement of Mahler's *Das Lied von der Erde* with Bruno Walter and the Vienna Philharmonic in 1952: unmatched emotional power; Janet Baker's rendition of Berlioz's song 'Absence' from *Les nuits d'été*, the greatest song of the nineteenth century after Schubert, sung with indescribable longing; Heifetz in the last eight bars of Beethoven's Romance in F major: how to explain the extraordinary, valedictory effect of his playing, his alone, of these few bars, the heart-wrenching sadness of the grace notes? As a boy, I listened to this recording over and over, waiting for this ending, hating for it to end; four unsurpassable examples of intimate song-like melody-spinning: Kreisler playing his *Liebesleid*; Szigeti playing his arrangement of

Elgar's *Serenade* (already mentioned in these pages); Gidon Kremer in the opening twenty-eight bars of Schubert's Sonata in A major, D574 (the sensitive playing of the pianist, Valery Afanassiev, makes no small contribution), and Ida Haendel playing the opening phrases of the first movement of the D major Nardini–David sonata (YouTube video, I am the Violin, beginning of Part Four); and finally, an admittedly eccentric choice: Szymon Goldberg's first note, the upbeat 'A' to the theme at the beginning of the theme and variations movement in Schubert's 'Trout' Quintet: extraordinary that a single note can carry so much musicality, an upbeat, so much promise!

As it is for many who play and listen to stringed instruments, for me it is the tone, the sheer sound that makes the first impression: the silvery, shimmering tone of Heifetz, Temianka and Perlman; the golden, luscious tone of Elman, Francescatti and Zukerman. But there are others: the virile, ringing, heavy-grained tone of Gidon Kremer; the incomparably sweet tone of Norbert Brainin; and the speaking, human tone of Szigeti and Sándor Végh. Beyond the sheer physical sound itself, however, it is the ability to give the violin a declaiming, sometimes lamenting eloquence that is the supreme quality, given to very few—indeed all too rare in this age of constant hyper-intense vibrato ('éternelle effervescence', as Lucien Capet complained). It is more likely to be heard in a string quartet performance than in a concerto. If there is any place where you will hear it, where the first violinist, somehow, must achieve it, it is in such places as the sublime embroidery of the theme in the first variation of the slow movement of Schubert's 'Death and the Maiden' quartet, or the recitative preceding the last movement of Beethoven's Op. 132, or in certain (very brief) passages in Webern's *Fünf Sätze*, Op. 5, or (perhaps most of all) the *Beklemmt* section of the Cavatina in Beethoven's Op. 130. Or (not to imply that only the violin can do it!) the opening viola solo of Bartók's Sixth String Quartet, the Sarabande of Bach's Fifth Suite for unaccompanied cello, or certain passages in Elgar's Cello Concerto.

I never learned to play the piano and I do not have a highly developed harmonic sense, which is one of the reasons, perhaps the main one, why I could not have become a really competent orchestra conductor. On the other hand, I am sensitive to the effects of harmony. In Mendelssohn's Violin Concerto, the entrance of the orchestra strings in the tenth bar of the *Allegretto non troppo* just before the last movement always thrilled me, though I could not have told you why, nor that it is, in fact, a simple dominant ninth chord with the 'A' of the solo violin. This knowledge, however, neither increases nor diminishes its effect on me in the slightest.

Mendelssohn: Violin Concerto, Op. 64, *Allegretto* non troppo, bars 9–11.

When, in my mid-twenties, I played for the first time in a performance of Bach's *St Matthew Passion*, the shout of the chorus, 'Barrabam!', on a ferocious diminished chord almost knocked me out of my chair.

And, in the seventeenth bar of the Prelude to Wagner's *Tristan und Isolde*, I dare say the famous fortissimo dissonant *appoggiatura* 'B' in the violins against the F major harmony casts its spell on me as much as it does on anyone who has listened to it or played it (or conducted it).

At the other end of the dynamic spectrum, near the end of the Adagio of Mahler's Tenth Symphony, the slow, soft, descending minor ninth in the cellos, F sharp to E sharp, resolving first into B major, then E-flat major harmony is, for me, perhaps the most powerful passage in all his

Bach: *St Matthew Passion*, the chorus answering Pilate.

Wagner: *Tristan und Isolde*, Prelude, bars 16–17 (only the string parts shown).

works. I still remember, during a recording session, looking across at the principal cellist of the Concertgebouw Orchestra, Tibor de Machula, and thinking, 'How wonderful it must be to be a cellist at this moment!'

The sense of occasion in a performance: presence, charisma. Oddly enough, as an orchestral player, I have almost never felt this in a conductor, perhaps on account of (or despite?) the 'psychic bondage' an orchestra conductor exerts over the players, described by Carl Flesch. (This phenomenon is perhaps less true for the wind players, who by definition are soloists, having their own individual parts, whereas a violinist is one of a dozen or more players all playing the same notes.) But I felt it palpably when Yehudi Menuhin and Wilhelm Kempff walked magisterially onto the stage for a recital in Carnegie Hall,

Mahler Symphony No. 10: bars 241–244 (only the string parts shown).

sometime in the mid-1960s. When Menuhin raised his violin to his shoulder to begin (was it the Brahms D minor sonata?), you sensed that a significant event was about to take place.

The performer's duty. How well I remember a performance in the Casa Buonarotti a few years ago: my lacklustre playing of the second theme of the first movement of a string quartet by Saint-Georges. Our second violinist, Michael Stüve, then played the same theme with infinitely more verve. My rendering sounded grey and limp by comparison. Why? Because of my negligence in not seeking out the interpretive possibilities inherent in the phrase. Imagination is required and the desire, the determination not to accept one's first realization, but to search for ways of throwing the phrase into relief, strengthening its profile, rendering it more vividly. In this case, the melody was not an especially inspired one. But all the more reason, all the more obligation on the part of the performer to fulfil the role of obstetrician (in Alfred Bendel's memorable formulation), to bring the work to life and assure its survival.

I don't remember when I began to become aware that I was capable of expressing something in my playing—that it wasn't just a matter of coping with difficulties, struggling with intonation and getting through the piece with as few errors as possible. For me, it was, I believe, quite late in coming. One of the first times perhaps, was when I was about fifteen years old, playing with my mother the major-key trio in the second movement of Mozart's E minor sonata, K. 304. I realized, if crudely, that the simple melody of repeated crotchets (quarter notes) could be expressively heightened by means of dynamic and agogic shaping, involving the use of the bow and vibrato and a simple form of tempo rubato. But I am now not so sure that I was yet aware of the danger of exaggerating such things—of gilding the lily.

Mozart: Sonata for Piano and Violin, K. 304, second movement, bars 102–105.

Mozart: Sonata for Piano and Violin, K. 304, second movement, bars 102–105, violin part with expressive signs added by the present author. A line over a note means a slight lingering on that note; arrows mean slightly urging the three crotchets forward towards the next bar.

As late as my last year at Acadia University, my recollection of learning and performing the first movement of Viotti's Concerto No. 22 is that I was chiefly concerned with overcoming the technical difficulties and memorizing it, hardly at all with projecting an original interpretation. I don't remember asking myself the question, for instance, of how I wanted the opening solo to sound: heroic? Majestic? Melancholy? Smooth and cantabile or forceful and accented? It may have been in 1963, when I performed the Brahms Horn Trio, that I first felt the impulse, specifically in the second theme of the first movement, and sensed that I had the musical means, to convey something of the emotive power of a passage.

This is different from, if related to, the simple desire to produce a pleasing sound, which I remember having had somewhat earlier, almost from the beginning. It was aided and abetted by my development of a vibrato, which at first I had difficulty learning, but which I seemed eventually to acquire almost automatically, almost without conscious effort.

How many times have intelligent, cultured people said to me, smilingly, without the slightest embarrassment, 'I know nothing about music', or 'I'm tone deaf'? In the popular radio programme Desert Island Discs, in which persons who have distinguished themselves one way or another choose their eight favourite pieces of music, I would estimate that roughly 90 per cent of the participants do not choose a single piece of classical music or, if they do, it is as a mere token single piece. Ferdinand Mount, a brilliant, highly sophisticated intellectual, cheerfully admits in his autobiographical *Cold Cream* that he and his mother 'love books, music leaves us cold'.[39] Vladimir Nabokov, in his *Speak, Memory*, tells, with 'regret', of his similar unresponsiveness to music.[40] Charles Ritchie, the distinguished Canadian diplomat and superb diarist-memoirist, in his *Storm Signals*, begins his entry for 2 October 1963 with, 'To a concert of chamber music at Dunbarton Oaks',[41] followed by

---

[39] Ferdinand Mount, *Cold Cream: My Early Life and Other Mistakes* (London: Bloomsbury, 2008), p. 33.

[40] Vladimir Nabokov, *Speak, Memory* (New York: Vintage International, 1989), pp. 35–36.

[41] Charles Ritchie, *Storm Signals: More Undiplomatic Diaries, 1962–1971* (Toronto: Macmillan of Canada, 1983), p. 68.

a long paragraph of musings about former prominent Washington hostesses—not a word about the concert itself, the music, the performers—nothing at all (I wrote peevishly in the margin, 'And the concert?'). Yet this is a man who appreciates the visual arts. He speaks of his 'beloved Phillips Gallery', and the 'exhilarating beauty' of the 'great Renoir of the dancing couples in summer sunshine'.[42] To be fair, in a later entry he writes of the transporting effect of the second act of *Tristan und Isolde* on him and his companion. Ritchie does not reveal his musical preferences, (opera over chamber music?), whereas he often describes what he is reading at the time.

What would all of these people say if I said to them, 'I know nothing about literature. I never read a book. Fiction, non-fiction and poetry all leave me cold'? They would turn away from me in pity and contempt, and rightly so. It depresses me, not just because I am a musician, that classical music is a closed book to most of the population of the Western world, certainly the English-speaking world, including wide swathes of the intelligentsia. The cause in large measure lies in the education of children and young adults, who are taught to read Chaucer, Shakespeare, Austen, Keats, Dickens and Joyce (albeit to a much lesser extent than formerly), but not to listen to Monteverdi, Bach, Mozart, Beethoven, Brahms or Bartók. But then, neither are they taught to appreciate Simone Martini, Piero della Francesca, Velàsquez, Watteau, Turner or Cezanne.

I am aware that these words can be turned against me: 'And what about you? Are popular music, country music, rock, the Beatles, Bob Dylan, etc. a closed book to you?' Well, no, they aren't, though I unreservedly prefer classical music. I will go further: I think classical music is superior to popular music. I think it arouses, is capable of arousing, and certainly arouses in me far deeper emotions than any popular music (I have in mind mature persons, not teenagers or those who have never got beyond their teen-aged tastes). But I listen gladly to some popular music. I was well into my thirties when I first listened voluntarily to a Beatles recording. It was 'When I'm Sixty-Four', a

---

[42] Ritchie, *Storm Signals*, p. 69.

charming song that appealed to my nascent awareness of my own mortality; perhaps it was no coincidence that at around the same time I first read Wyatt's great poem, *Remembrance* ('They flee from me, that sometime did me seek'). I never tire of Serge Reggiani's 'Arthur, où t'as mis le corps?', a minor masterpiece of irony and black humour.[43] My wife Susan is a long-time fan of Leonard Cohen, whom I have come to appreciate, perhaps reluctantly, over time. I console myself with the thought that she has a weakness for elderly Canadian musicians.

I admit freely that I am piqued by the huge audiences attracted to pop music concerts, in comparison with which classical music audiences are pitifully small. Yes, I am envious. But I am also sorry for those thousands of (mostly) young people who go to rock concerts, obviously responsive to music, who are denied the infinitely greater, more profound experience of classical music. Still, I often look over my shoulder gratefully to Don Messer and His Islanders.

Envoi

We all derive a certain pleasure, if that's the right word, from talking about departed ones—remembering the good and the bad. Not a day goes by without my thinking of my parents. I cannot deny that I am disappointed that Susan (who is fourteen years younger than I), because of her dementia, may be unable to remember me—my habits, my turns of speech, my jokes, my foibles, my irritating mannerisms.

So, it will have to be my brother, my cousins and my friends—those who survive me—who remember me. What will they say to each other about me? And then, when they are gone, emptiness. No one, especially one who is childless, as I am, is personally remembered after two or (rarely) three generations. All that is left is the written word, photographs and, for a select few, recordings. Not enough, not nearly enough …

---

[43] Reggiani seems to have recorded this piece several times—the last one (Réenregistrement Polydor), his weathered voice no longer mellifluous, is by far the best.

Susan, June 2016.

Susan, December 2021.

Warwick, Susan, 26 December 2018.

But I have no reason to complain. We have two affectionate sister cats who came to us thanks to a remarkable Italian organization that rescues cats and sends them all over Italy for adoption, subject to rigorous control. These two are natives of Herculaneum. They were sent on the train from Naples, picked up at the Florence station by local members of the organization and delivered to our house. They bring joy

Andromeda in the Boboli Gardens, about 2015.

Paestum, the second Temple of Hera, May 2015. Flickering with a faint gem-like flame. I had read Berenson's lyrical evocation of the view of Paestum from afar in *The Passionate Sightseer* in 1965, of course.

into our lives. I have no doubt that they are descendants of victims (or survivors?) of the eruption of Vesuvius in 79AD.

For years, we have gone walking almost every day in the magnificent Boboli Gardens, just around the corner, especially atmospheric in the winter.

I have travelled much in Italy. But there is more waiting to be seen. And every once in a while, I return to my childhood haunts.

On the Parrsboro golf course, but not to play, about 2018. Remembrance of things past.

I still practise the violin an hour or two a day. Sometimes I think that I play better now than before. I practise more intelligently than I used to. I've been working on the Schubert *Fantasy*, a difficult piece, and brought it to a high enough level to play with a pianist-friend in a house concert the other day.

And when, after an hour of tennis, arriving on my motor scooter at the top of the hill on the winding road up from the Porta San Miniato, I pause—looming directly above me is the basilica of San Miniato al Monte. It has been standing there for more than 800 years. The twelfth-century mosaics on the façade glisten in the setting sun. For a moment,

Minas Basin, flood tide, Cape Blomidon in the distance, about 1998.
Remembrance of things past.

San Miniato al Monte, c.1875. The recently constructed Viale dei Colli (Avenue
of the Hills), landscaping still underway, the trees newly planted, showing the
street joining it, up which I come on my *motorino*. Photo: Alinari Archives.

all my missed backhands are forgotten. I drive home along the Viale dei Colli, one of the great European urban scenic roads, and live to play another day.

INDEX

Mentions of persons in letters are not indexed. For the most part, names of only those musicians whom the author has encountered, heard in person or collaborated with are indexed. The indexing of musical works is similarly selective. Literary works not indexed under authors' names are to be found in pages 216 to 226.

Made in the USA
Columbia, SC
22 February 2025

54160433R00139